Geek House

Geek House
10 Hardware Hacking Projects for Around Home

Barry Press and Marcia Press

WILEY

Wiley Publishing, Inc.

Geek House: 10 Hardware Hacking Projects for Around Home

Published by
Wiley Publishing, Inc.
10475 Crosspoint Boulevard
Indianapolis, IN 46256
www.wiley.com

Published simultaneously in Canada

ISBN-13: 978-0-7645-7956-1
ISBN-10: 0-7645-57956-8

Manufactured in the United States of America

10 9 8 7 6 5 4 3 2 1

1B/SR/QU/QV/IN

For general information on our other products and services or to obtain technical support, please contact our Customer Care Department within the U.S. at (800) 762-2974, outside the U.S. at (317) 572-3993 or fax (317) 572-4002.

Wiley also publishes its books in a variety of electronic formats. Some content that appears in print may not be available in electronic books.

Library of Congress Cataloging-in-Publication Data: 2005004379

About the Authors

Barry and Marcia Press are the authors of several successful computer and networking books, including *PC Toys*, *PC Upgrade and Repair Bible*, and *Teach Yourself PCs*.

They have written weekly columns on hardware and Linux for the Adrenaline Vault gaming Web site (see www.avault.com/hardware/index.asp?reviews=hardgame and www.avault.com/hardware/index.asp?reviews=penguingame).

Barry is an engineer with experience in software and digital design, networking, artificial intelligence, and computer applications. He works as the chief engineer at a large aerospace communications company.

Credits

Executive Editor
Chris Webb

Development Editor
Adaobi Obi Tulton

Technical Editor
William Shaw

Production Editor
William A. Barton

Copy Editor
Luann Rouff

Editorial Manager
Mary Beth Wakefield

Vice President & Executive Group Publisher
Richard Swadley

Vice President and Publisher
Joseph B. Wikert

Project Coordinator
Erin Smith

Graphics and Production Specialists
Karl Brandt
April Farling
Kelly Emkow
Lauren Goddard
Jennifer Heleine
Brent Savage
Rashell Smith

Quality Control Technician
John Greenough
Jessica Kramer

Proofreading and Indexing
TECHBOOKS Production Services

Contents at a Glance

Contents

Part III: In the Kitchen and Dining

Part IV: In the Garage and Out the Door

Acknowledgments

We gratefully acknowledge the assistance of the following people and companies in the development of this book:

George Alfs, Peter Anspach, Al Bilotti, Mike Braun, Melody Chalaban, Annette Clark, Joanna DeKlavon, Karen Franz, Rob Fugina, Ken Gracey, Dan Kardatzke, Bill Kolker, Patti Mikula, Jeff Mucha, PJ Naughter, Nathan Papadopulos, John Paulsen, Jonah Peskin, Joan Peterson, Kris Ponmalai, Jen Press, Kate Press, Will Reeb, Dave Rye, Carolyn Schmidt, Ken Schulz, Will Shaw, Zach Sniezko, John Swinimer, Dave Taue, Lee Thomason, Sam Tingey, Manny Vara, Matt Wagner, and Chris Webb.

Antec, Inc.; ATI Technologies Inc., Belkin Corporation, Davis Instruments, Corp.; DeLorme, Eastman Kodak Company, Ensign Boxers, Great Lakes Industrial Fans and Blower Inc., Homeseer Technologies LLC, InterVideo Inc., Intel Corporation, Logitech Incorporated, MP3Car.com, MPEGBox, OPUS Solutions, Inc.; Parallax Inc., Phidgets Inc., RadioShack Corporation, SageTV, Seagate Technology LLC, Streamzap Incorporated, Wacom Corporation, WeatherRoom.com, Winland Electronics, Incorporated; and X-10 Wireless Technology Incorporated.

Introduction

Finally, to keep my subjects permanently locked in a mindless trance,
I will provide each of them with free unlimited Internet access.

— Peter Anspach, *The Evil Overlord List*

A look at the classified ads for homes for sale typically leads to listings like the following:

> 2 story 2,100 sq. ft. 4 bdrms. 3 ba. Office/den. Family rm. Formal living/dining rm.
> 3-car gar. Excel. view.

Bah. It's probably a lovely house, but your inner geek knows rooms and a view aren't enough.
Add the right electronics, though, and you could have something. Children born in the eighties
and later were born into a world in which computers always existed, and the most adept of
them see computers as indispensable tools, not as small beige packages of evil and confusion.
You and they know that a computer isn't some monolithic entity capable of only the magic
someone else imbues it with; it's an appliance — a minion, really — available to be part of anything you can imagine and create.

What's a Geek House?

You're a geek, and to you a conventional house is boring and inadequate. The commercial market isn't really up to offering you what you want directly, so you're going to have to build and
install it yourself. That's where we come in — we're here to help you imagine and create the
computer-driven electronics you'd like in a house.

In that respect, this book is similar to our previous Extreme Tech book, *PC Toys,* helping you
design and build your own electronic minions. *Geek House* differs from *PC Toys,* however, in
that the projects in *Geek House* demand more from you — more know-how and more time. You
could duplicate many of the projects we built for *PC Toys* by following our instructions, but
we'll be quite surprised if your versions of the *Geek House* projects don't vary considerably from
ours. Not only will you end up using different parts in many cases, you'll end up customizing
the projects to match your own preferences or to do things we didn't envision or didn't choose
to implement.

Geek House includes the projects listed in Table I-1. The common thread is that they all automate something useful (or annoying); nearly all of them have a PC at the core.

Table I-1   Geek House Projects

Chapter	Description
1	X-10 Under the Hood
2	Wireless RS-232 Link
3	Home Television Server
4	Security Monitoring
5	Television Mute on Phone Ring
6	Anything Inventory
7	Kitchen PC
8	Automated BBQ Temperature Control
9	Automated Sprinkler Control
10	Car PC

Some of the projects in this book, such as the automated barbeque controller, have commercial equivalents. The commercial products might be better than your version, might be inferior, or might simply not be available in a pre-assembled form that you can buy. Throughout *Geek House*, the result you get will depend greatly on what you choose to build and on how much work you put into building it. Building the projects to your own design means you're building what you want, not a one-size-fits-all generic solution designed by someone else.

What's Required from You?

We have provided parts lists and directions for the *Geek House* projects in this book, but we expect you will take that information as a baseline and veer off in your own direction. We assume you have some skills with computers, electronics, software, and/or mechanical construction — here's our thinking about you and the components that go into the projects.

Some Skills and Experience

First, we're assuming that you're interested in building *Geek House* devices to begin with, meaning you're not intimidated by computers as monsters from the office automation swamp. We assume not only that you know your computer is just a machine, but also that it's one you can twist to your whim. It won't hurt at all to be a trained engineer or computer scientist. Even if you try to directly replicate what we've described in the book, you'll need some skills:

- **PCs** — You should be comfortable modifying and operating a Windows personal computer using equipment and software you can buy and install, and building or modifying a local area network (LAN). Those are the minimum skills you'll need for the Home Television Server and Anything Inventory projects.

- **Basic to Intermediate Electronics** — If you can build or repair simple electronic devices, you can work with the X-10 Under the Hood, Automated Sprinkler Control, Automated BBQ Temperature Control, Remote Control Finder, Wireless RS-232 Link, and Television Mute on Phone Ring projects.

- **Mechanical Construction** — You'll need to be able to mount some of your projects in cases, including the Wireless RS-232 Link and Television Mute on Phone Ring projects. The Kitchen PC and Car PC projects require you to build far more complex installations, and the Automated BBQ Temperature Control requires that you build both a fan mounting that will withstand hundreds of degrees and an enclosure that will withstand the outdoors.

- **Software** — We've written software for several of the projects in this book (Table I-2). If you're a programmer, you can download the source code from the Internet — we've released it under the GNU Public License (GPL) — and make your own changes. If you're *not* a programmer, executable copies of our versions are on the Internet too, but you'll be limited to what we did.

  The database for the Kitchen PC project is on the Internet, too. See Appendix C, "What's on the Web Site," for information about how to download any of the code.

Table I-2   Geek House Software

Project	Language and Environment
Anything Inventory	C++ under Windows
Automated BBQ Temperature Control	Java on Javelin Stamp
Automated Sprinkler Control	C++ under Windows
Kitchen PC database	Microsoft Access
Security Monitoring	C++ under Windows

Equipment

Only one of the *Geek House* projects, the Home Television Server, requires a sophisticated computer, and even that may only require adding a lot of disk capacity to an older PC. The rest of the projects can use what many people would call obsolete computers, ones in the 350 MHz and faster range. A reasonable amount of memory will help performance — we put at least 512 MB into our machines, with 768 MB or more in ones we use intensively. As cheap as quality memory is now, it's an effective upgrade.

The modest computing demands for the projects give you a lot of choices for what computers to use, which fits in nicely with the fact that many of the projects run constantly on the PC and therefore need the computer to be reliable. The most reliable computer is one that nobody touches, which lets out the computer you use yourself — get one you can stick in a corner and ignore.

Some of the projects assume an Internet connection. Personally, we won't operate an Internet connection without a firewall, and we far prefer separate hardware routers to software firewalls on the individual PCs. A firewall on the PC can complement the hardware router by monitoring and controlling outgoing connections, but for incoming connections a hardware router provides far better security than a Windows PC alone.

Appendix B contains some recommendations for how to work with PC hardware in case you need some guidance or a refresher. If you're after more in-depth information and guidance about PCs, look for our *PC Upgrade and Repair Bible, Desktop Edition* (Wiley, 2004).

Software

We designed all of the projects to run under Windows, and wrote the software specifically to the Windows programming interface. We're aware of the religious wars surrounding the choice of operating system, but as we noted in *PC Toys*, because computers running our personal favorite — the Symbolics Corporation Lisp language and Genera operating system (`kogs-www.informatik.uni-hamburg.de/~moeller/symbolics-info/symbolics.html`) — are in tragically short supply, we chose to use the operating system the largest number of people are familiar with. Like Microsoft or not, that operating system is Windows.

We're not, however, unmitigated fans of Windows. Older versions (Windows 3.1, 95, 98, and Me) have warts, high cholesterol, and an unfortunate tendency towards epileptic seizures. We strongly recommend you use the sturdier, younger versions whenever possible. Windows XP is technically the one to choose, but make sure you're willing to put up with Microsoft's invasions of privacy masquerading under the name Windows Product Activation. If you're not, opt for Windows 2000. Either way, install the service packs and critical security updates from Windows Update (`windowsupdate.microsoft.com`; be *exceedingly* careful configuring the automatic updater if you install it) and stick with the device drivers that come with Windows unless you have no options. You'll also want to ensure that you patch any freshly minted installation of Windows from behind a hardware router, because the average time from connection to attack for a PC on the Internet is now less than the time it takes to download and install the patches. The router will deflect those attacks, giving you time to get your work done.

Appendix A includes more detailed information about these recommendations. Information on the project software can be found in the corresponding chapters of the book.

Internet

We think access to the Internet is essential, as will any respectable geek (there's a phrase for you). The Internet is your best source for the hardware and software you'll need for the projects, and it is a rich source of ideas. Some of those ideas will even be useful. We've included Web links for nearly everything we've used in the projects in the parts lists and accompanying text.

If you have a choice, you're also better off with a broadband connection to the Internet. We assume the "always-on" access most broadband services give you in most everything we do, because that lets us assume direct access to information the projects need. Always-on access also means you don't have to go through the ritual of dialing the modem, waiting for it to connect, waiting for it to authenticate, checking the speed of the connection, and perhaps redialing when you get a lousy connection or are disconnected entirely. Always-on access means that if your computer is on, you're connected to the Internet.

The Home Television Server, Anything Inventory, Kitchen PC, and Automated Sprinkler Control projects specifically assume access to the Internet for things like programming guides, bar code decoding, recipe lookup, and weather forecasts. The Anything Inventory and Automated Sprinkler Control software will work without access, but not as well.

Imagination

We expect you'll start by understanding our versions of the projects, but if you stop there you'll miss the point, which is to get you started down the path of developing your own Geek House and your own projects. The key to taking that step is your imagination and the ability to observe yourself throughout the day, culling out and noting those times when things could be more convenient or when you can't do something the way you want. Learning to think from the point of view that your PC can help solve those problems, learning to see what's possible, can be difficult even with the best imagination.

We've included Chapter 11 to help you see your way, a chapter that sketches concepts and approaches for an entire set of other projects. We haven't provided the details about how to build each one of these suggested projects, just the idea and a short analysis of an approach. Filling in the details is your work for that chapter, using your imagination and what you'll learn building the other projects in the book.

Organization

Every chapter in this book, with the exception of this Introduction and Chapter 11 (Hacking on Your Own), follows the same basic structure — you'll learn what the project is about and how it works, what's on the parts list, how to build the basic project, and ways you might extend the basic project.

How It Works

Every project includes an explanation of what the project is and how it works, including a parts list and description of how to build the project from those parts. We're not going to bore you with the details of hardware or software installation in those sections — we assume you've done your share and there are no big mysteries left — but we do explain the designs we developed so you'll understand the starting point for your own design work.

You'll likely have to get the parts you need from several places, some local and some mail order. We'll tell you what parts we used and where we found them. You're not compelled to build your version our way. Feel free to substitute equivalent parts and fix the rest of the design to make any necessary accommodations. Moreover, differences between your computer or goals and ours may cause our design not to work for you. You'll use our version as a guideline in that case, combining different parts in a different design.

Building Your Own Design

In addition to the instructions that let you replicate the project as we built it, and the descriptions of how our hardware and software designs work, every project includes a section of ideas describing how you could extend or modify the design to improve it or add different capabilities. Some of the suggestions are relatively straightforward applications of the design for other purposes, while others suggest you perform your own software development or hardware modifications to make the implementation more sophisticated. Our build-your-own-design suggestions aren't the only ways to extend the projects—you'll undoubtedly think of your own extensions and modifications, too.

Finding Information and Equipment

Each chapter in *Geek House* describes the equipment we used and provides Web links for the hardware and software you'll need. In many cases, Web sites let you order products or link you to retailers, both online and local. Nevertheless, finding parts (particularly if you're as impatient as we are) can be a challenge, so we've listed some of the ways we did it to get you started.

Searching the Internet

If something you need for your project exists, be it parts or information, you can probably get it on the Internet. There are so many people and companies offering so many things on the Internet that your success is almost guaranteed.

Finding what you want is another matter. You have to ferret out the ones that have what you need, sometimes without knowing what's available; and when you're searching for something particular, the sheer numbers of suppliers can work against you to mask what you need to find.

Searching the Internet effectively is therefore a key skill. We search in several ways—ranging from very direct to general based on how well what we want is defined:

- **Go directly to the manufacturer's Web site and search there.** If you know the company that makes what you need, it's most efficient to find their Web site and look up the product. Company Web sites are often of the form `www.company.com`; if that doesn't work, you can typically use a search engine to find the site. Surprisingly few companies we've looked for don't have a Web site.

- **Search on a specialized Web site.** More general searches will frequently turn up Web sites that focus on specific ideas, technologies, or types of products. Good sites like that are worth bookmarking, because they're good places to search for future needs. You'll find a variety of them, ranging from pure information sites such as `gpsinformation.net` to specialized retailers like `www.smarthome.com`.

■ **Search by make and model, or with keywords.** Internet search engines wade through billions of pages for you, and will turn up pure gold if you can invent the right set of search terms. We've used many of them, but Google (`www.google.com`) is the one we prefer and the one that was the most useful while writing this book. You'll be doing a lot of searching, which you can make much more convenient by loading the Google toolbar and/or making Google the default search engine in your Web browser. Instructions for doing that are on the Google Web site on their tools page.

A particularly effective way to find retailers once you know the make and model of what you need is to search for the make and model using Google. The Web pages that turn up will be either users of the product (useful in their own right) or sites listing the product for sale.

Take the time to learn how to use the features the search engine offers. Google normally treats words you type as independent search entities, but looks for a phrase if you enclose it in quotes. You can require that a word or phrase *not* appear by prefixing it with a minus sign, and you can refer to specific Web hosts using modifiers listed on the Google site.

Google isn't limited to searching the entire Web. If you install the Google toolbar, you'll have buttons available to search just the site containing the page you're looking at, which makes up for sites that lack their own search engines. Sites whose listings are driven from a database may not index well under Google, but it's worth a try if there's no site-specific alternative.

■ **Ask a question.** You don't always know a good set of keywords, causing search engines to return either nothing or too many irrelevant results. Ask Jeeves (`www.ask.com`) is useful in those circumstances — you can ask a question, such as "What is the average annual temperature in Atlanta?" and get back a selection of relevant places to look. The technology underlying Ask Jeeves is different than keyword-based search engines, something that becomes evident if you enter the same question as keywords into Google.

There are yet other places to look for what you need on the Internet. You can often find equipment on eBay, sometimes at a discount and sometimes not. Information and opinions are nearly always available in the Internet newsgroups (also searchable with Google — pick the newsgroups tab on the Google main page). Good newsgroups can be rich in important information, and often offer you the capability to ask your own question and get answers back from well-informed contributors, but use them with caution: They can also be homes for idiots with no idea what they're talking about. Differentiating one from the other can be hard if you're not reasonably well informed yourself.

Local and National Sources

We buy parts for projects at both local stores and national chains. Radio Shack, Best Buy, CompUSA, Costco, and Home Depot all have stores near us and have been sources of equipment, but so have local merchants with only one or a few locations. The local stores sometimes have better-informed staff than what we find in the chains. Specialized electronic parts may only be available in small quantities through local distributors.

We've also found Web sites for what looked to be good sources in England and Canada. There will be good sources in medium to large cities worldwide, but unfortunately we can't read many of their sites.

Computer Upgrades

Where we buy computer parts depends a lot on what we're looking for and how much of a hurry we're in. We rarely buy memory anywhere but Crucial (www.crucial.com). We've done well buying parts several times at www.allstarshop.com, and inevitably buy cables from Cables N Mor (www.cablesnmor.com).

The downside to all of the Internet-only stores is that you'll wait several days for shipping, longer if you need to order on a weekend. The big chains, such as Best Buy, CompUSA, and Circuit City, have coordinated their Web sites with their stores, so you can find what you need on the site and check if the store near you has it in stock. They don't always get it right, but it's every bit as good as waiting on hold for someone who doesn't check for the right item anyhow, and it's nice to get the wrong answer faster.

We also watch for the ads that the big stores put in the newspaper. Sales on disk drives are common, and sometimes offer huge 7200 RPM drives for a dollar per gigabyte or less. (We like Seagate and Maxtor.)

Sensors

A Google search for *sensors* returns over 1,850,000 pages, a result that indicates that a lot of people are involved in building and using sensors but is otherwise useless. We've found sensors we needed at times using direct searches, such as *temperature sensors*, but typically go looking for sites that catalog and list sensors. A search on *sensors catalog* returns about 250,000 pages, a far smaller number, but one that still needs some pruning. You could keep adding keywords to narrow the search, or you could bookmark sites that seem to have collections of what you're looking for. Scrolling through the hits on *sensors catalog*, we found a number of those, including:

- www.measureanything.com
- www.temperatures.com
- www.thomasregister.com (search for sensor)
- www.findasensor.com
- www.sensorsportal.com

We list sources for the sensors we use in the individual chapters; most of them are from Davis Instruments (www.davisnet.com), Parallax (www.parallax.com), Phidgets (www.phidgets.com), SmartHome (www.smarthome.com), or X-10 (www.x10.com).

Home Automation

The home automation equipment we use in the book is based on the X-10 power line signaling and control technology. The equipment is no longer available at retail as extensively as it once was, but some simple modules can be found at Radio Shack stores (a wider selection is offered at their Web site) and Lowes. Your best sources will be online, including www.x10.com and www.smarthome.com. Don't ignore these projects if you happen to live in an area with 220-volt power — versions of some of the X-10 equipment adapted for 220 volts are available.

Subsystems

You'll need some independent subsystems (radio modules, for example) building the projects. The individual chapters include Web links to where we obtained the equipment, but you'll want to search the Web before you buy anything to look for the best prices and for alternative equipment that might better suit your interests.

You'll need some miscellaneous hardware, too, including computer cables and networking equipment. Try the same places previously listed for computer upgrades.

Software

Most of the software we used in the book is available on the Web — there are links in the individual chapters — or comes with products you'll use building the projects. We built the software we wrote for *Geek House* using Microsoft Visual C++ version 6. If you don't have Visual C++, you could investigate the Visual C++ Toolkit 2003 (msdn.microsoft.com/visualc/vctoolkit2003), where you can find a free download of the compiler, linker, and more.

Enjoy the book!

In the Basement

part

in this part

X-10 Under the Hood

Home automation has much in common with car modification and repair — anyone can plug in parts or bolt on wheels, but you need to look under the hood and understand what's going on in there before you take on anything significant. This chapter will teach you the internals of how X-10 home automation works and give you the know-how to design and build your own systems that work reliably and do what you want.

Before you read on, please read this caution: *Power line control devices, such as the ones we cover in this chapter, operate on hazardous power line voltages. Touching the wrong wire at the wrong time can kill you. If you don't know how to work on home power wiring safely, stick to the modules that plug in and don't attempt anything more adventurous without trained help.*

One of my advisors will be an average five-year-old child. Any flaws in my plan that he is able to spot will be corrected before implementation.

Peter Anspach,
The Evil Overlord List

Project Description

X-10 home automation systems transmit signals over your house wiring, a difficult challenge because of noise and transmission problems inherent in using the wiring for an application it's not designed to handle. Building successful X-10 systems requires that you

➤ Understand how the technology works so you know what's possible within the framework and constraints of the technology

➤ Know what components you have to work with so you design low-cost systems you can readily implement

➤ Anticipate the problems your system will encounter and take steps to avoid or cure them

We'll start by looking at the technology as a network, covering how signals operate on the wires and how the system transports messages using those signals. We'll then look at what can go wrong and what those problems do in your system. Along the way, you'll learn about protocols, and software, noise, and signal measurements.

in this chapter

☑ Power line control
☑ Layered communications model
☑ X-10 power line protocols
☑ Standard modules
☑ Troubleshooting and noise
☑ Installation and wiring
☑ Custom modules

System Diagram

Figure 1-1 diagrams the overall system for the simplest X-10 application, remote control of a device. Instead of the typical circuit in which the switch controls the power flowing to the lamp, the switch signals an X-10 transmitter. That transmitter sends a message to the X-10 receiver using signals over the power lines. The receiver detects the signals, decodes the message, and controls the power flow to the lamp according to the content of the message. Messages can command the lamp to be on, off, or dimmed to a specified level.

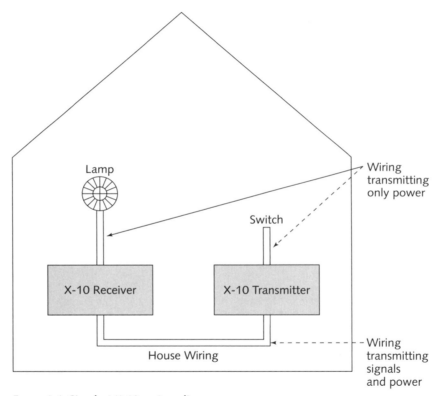

FIGURE 1-1: Simplest X-10 system diagram

The standard ISO seven-layer communications model (Figure 1-2) describes any communication system, and so applies to X-10 systems. We'll start with the physical layer and work upwards. X-10 systems don't implement layers three (networking) through five (session), so we'll skip directly from the link layer to the presentation layer.

7: Application	Specifies interactions among applications
6: Presentation	Controls information formatting for display or print, and data encryption
5: Session	Monitors and brokers communication between systems, including security, logging, and administrative functions
4: Transport	Supports end-to-end movement of data between systems, and ensures error-free transmissions through error checking and correction or retransmission
3: Network	Routes data between systems across the network to ensure data arrives at the correct destination
2: Data Link	Defines the rules for sending and receiving information from one computer to another
1: Physical	Implements the physical transfer of information between computers

FIGURE 1-2: ISO seven-layer model

Our discussion starts with the physical layer, showing how information physically moves from one device to another.

Physical layer

The physical layer in an X-10 system transmits data over the power lines. The challenge is to send the signal reliably, with relatively low-power, inexpensive electronics. X-10 chose a simple scheme using a tone or its absence to convey a one or zero data bit, respectively, and uses redundant signaling to help improve reliability.

Figure 1-3 shows the fundamental approach. An X-10 transmitter will output a 120 kHz tone in a 1 ms burst starting when a rising line voltage crosses the zero point. The presence of the tone signals a one bit; the absence of a tone signals a zero. The burst is further transmitted two more times, at 1.047 radian intervals (2π / 6 radians, dividing the half cycle in thirds), to provide signals that will have appropriate zero crossing timing when bridged to the alternate phases in a three-phase circuit.

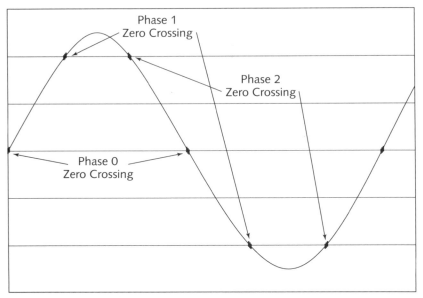

FIGURE 1-3: X-10 signal transmission

Figure 1-3 shows bursts at the rising voltage zero crossing points, along with bursts starting at the zero crossing for the negative-going power line voltage. The X-10 signal protocol sends the complement of the bit being transmitted at that time (and in the following bursts for the other line phases) to provide error checking at the receiver on the received signal. For example, if there is a tone at the rising voltage zero crossing, representing a one bit, there will not be any tone at the falling voltage zero crossing, and vice versa. This approach provides no error correction, but helps the receiver detect when a bit has been corrupted.

Timing the signal at the zero crossings simplifies the receivers, reducing cost, because the underlying 60 Hz carrier provides precise timing for the window in which the 120 kHz tone will arrive. The physical layer protocol requires that the tone burst start no more than 200 μ (microseconds) after the zero crossing, defining the limits within which a tone detector must operate.

Because the system only transmits one bit per cycle of the underlying carrier, the raw signaling bit rate of the X-10 system is 60 bits per second (bps). The actual payload data rate is less, as shown in the next section. Because of the very low data rate, and because the physical layer has no provision to detect or avoid collisions, it's important that X-10 messages be short and infrequent.

Link layer

All the physical layer does is convey bits over the power line. The link layer is responsible for conveying information from one device to another, including providing mechanisms for framing messages and rules for sending and receiving messages.

The first task the link layer must accomplish is to mark the start of each message so the receiver can reliably know where in a bit stream the actual message starts. X-10 does this with a unique start code (Figure 1-4), a signal pattern that cannot occur within a message. That start code is the sequence tone-tone-tone-no tone (1110) transmitted on sequential half cycles, starting at a rising voltage zero crossing. The first two zero crossings — the first full waveform cycle — are an invalid sequence, violating the requirement that the complement of a rising voltage zero crossing be transmitted on the following zero crossing. The second full cycle is a valid sequence, representing a one bit. Including an invalid sequence in the start code, an instance of what is more generally called *out-of-band signaling*, ensures that no error-free message can be mistaken for a start code.

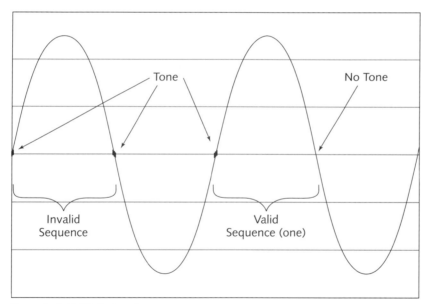

FIGURE **1-4**: X-10 start code

Nine bits of data immediately follow the start code in the subsequent nine cycles, as shown in Figure 1-5. The information in the message is comprised of four bits of *house code*, followed by five bits of *key number* or *function code*. The house code is simply a group address, while the key number identifies the specific device within the group. Function codes are operations such as *on* or *off*.

Start Code	Cycle	Tone Tone
	Cycle	Tone No Tone
House Code	Cycle	Bit Bit Inverse
	Cycle	Bit Bit Inverse
	Cycle	Bit Bit Inverse
	Cycle	Bit Bit Inverse
Key Code	Cycle	Bit Bit Inverse
	Cycle	Bit Bit Inverse
	Cycle	Bit Bit Inverse
	Cycle	Bit Bit Inverse
	Cycle	Bit Bit Inverse

FIGURE 1-5: X-10 standard message format

In another layer of error detection, every message gets transmitted twice. Ordinary messages should have three full empty cycles between messages, but bright/dim commands should be sequential, with no intervening empty cycles.

Presentation and application layers

The presentation and application layers define the content of the messages and how they're interpreted. House codes are represented by specific sequential four-bit patterns, as shown in Table 1-1. Bit 0 is transmitted first, followed by the rest in order. The bit patterns for the codes do not correspond to ASCII codes, which would represent "A" as 1000001, but are unique to the X-10 system.

Table 1-1 X-10 House Code Bit Patterns

Code	Bit 0	Bit 1	Bit 2	Bit 3
A	0	1	1	0
B	1	1	1	0
C	0	0	1	0
D	1	0	1	0
E	0	0	0	1
F	1	0	0	1
G	0	1	0	1
H	1	1	0	1
I	0	1	1	1
J	1	1	1	1
K	0	0	1	1
L	1	0	1	1
M	0	0	0	0
N	1	0	0	0
O	0	1	0	0
P	1	1	0	0

X-10 key and function codes are represented by the sequential five-bit patterns shown in Table 1-2. You can distinguish key codes from function codes using the last bit, which is zero for key codes and one for function codes. The key codes correspond to what X-10 calls *unit codes* in most retail documentation.

Table 1-2 X-10 Key and Function Code Bit Patterns

Code	Bit 0	Bit 1	Bit 2	Bit 3	Bit 4
1	0	1	1	0	0
2	1	1	1	0	0
3	0	0	1	0	0
4	1	0	1	0	0

Continued

Table 1-2 *(continued)*

Code	Bit 0	Bit 1	Bit 2	Bit 3	Bit 4
5	0	0	0	1	0
6	1	0	0	1	0
7	0	1	0	1	0
8	1	1	0	1	0
9	0	1	1	1	0
10	1	1	1	1	0
11	0	0	1	1	0
12	1	0	1	1	0
13	0	0	0	0	0
14	1	0	0	0	0
15	0	1	0	0	0
16	1	1	0	0	0
All Units Off	0	0	0	0	1
All Lights On	0	0	0	1	1
On	0	0	1	0	1
Off	0	0	1	1	1
Dim	0	1	0	0	1
Bright	0	1	0	1	1
All Lights Off	0	1	1	0	1
Extended Code	0	1	1	1	1
Hail Request	1	0	0	0	1
Hail Acknowledge	1	0	0	1	1
Pre-Set Dim	1	0	1	X	1
Extended Data (Analog)	1	1	0	0	1
Status = on	1	1	0	1	1
Status = off	1	1	1	0	1
Status Request	1	1	1	1	1

If you've been planning how you'd use these codes as you read, you've noticed that you can't form a complete command in one transmission — that is, you can say things like B12 or B On, but you can't write a message that says B12 On. What you have to do is send message sequences, such as B12 followed by B On. The requirement to send each message twice with a three-cycle gap between messages results in the final message sequence:

B12 - B12 - B On - B On

This example shows that it takes at least four messages to complete a command, and of course transmission errors can corrupt any of the four. The specific behavior you'll see if one or more of the messages are corrupted depends on the devices involved, but all the effects are likely to appear as unreliable or erratic operation.

Because the addresses and commands are separate in the protocol, you can combine messages to give more complicated commands. For example, if you wanted to turn on both B3 and B12, you could use the command sequence:

B3 - B3 - B12 - B12 - B On - B On

Many command codes have straightforward meanings; On, Off, and All Lights Off, for example, do just what you'd expect. Status Request commands the addressed unit to respond with Status = on or Status = off if it supports status responses.

Less straightforward are Dim, Bright, Extended Code, Hail Request / Acknowledge, Pre-Set Dim, and Extended Data. Here's what they do:

- **Dim, Bright, and Pre-Set Dim** — Standard X-10 incandescent lamp dimmers have 16 dimming steps. The standard protocol for dimming to a specific level is to turn the lamp on, then send a dim command pair (which would be two Start code-house code-dim sequences back-to-back with no intervening empty cycles) for each dim step. A sequence of 16 pairs should turn the lamp off completely. You can similarly send Off followed by a series of Bright commands to get the same effect.

  The requirement to start at full on or full off, then ramp the intensity to reach a known level produces awkward results. The Pre-Set Dim command was intended to address that problem by directing the dimmer to go to a specific level directly. A typical message sequence, one to set unit A1 to a level, was

  A1 - A1 - <value>Pre-Set Dim - <value>Pre-Set Dim

  where <value> was a house code from A to P. If you look back at the encodings for the house codes, you'll see that used in the sequence M, N, O, C, D, A, B, E, F, G, H, K, L, I, J they correspond to the binary sequence 0, 1, 2, ... 14, 15. The sequence

  A1 - A1 - BPre-Set Dim - BPre-Set Dim

  would, therefore, set the dimmer to level six. X-10 apparently never made any products that implemented the Pre-Set Dim command, although some others did, so it's no longer defined in the protocol. (The sequence also violates the requirement that commands have the same house code as the prior address packets, potentially lowering the reliability of the system.) In the most recent documentation, X-10 has re-designated the Pre-Set Dim command code as being "for security messages." Products using Pre-Set

Dim will continue to work, of course, but as products come to market using that command code for security functions, your chances of conflicts go up should you use both categories of device.

- **Extended Code/Data** — You can do a lot more with the X-10 protocol than the basic function code commands in Table 1-2 permit, because the Extended Code and Extended Data function codes let devices send arbitrary information. Standard X-10 devices ignore everything in the message following those function codes up to the next gap (i.e., power line cycles with no tones in either zero crossing), so in theory extended messages can be any length.

  In practice, X-10 has defined specific extended message formats (see `ftp://ftp.X10.com/pub/manuals/xtc798.doc`). Extended message format 1 follows an Extended Code function, and consists of 4 bits of unit code, 8 bits of data, and 8 bits of command. Five types of interpretation are defined for the data and command bytes:

  - **Type 0:** Shutters and Sunshades
  - **Type 1:** Sensors
  - **Type 2:** Security
  - **Type 3:** Control Modules (Dimmers and Appliances)
  - **Type 4:** Extended Secure Addressing
  - **Type 5:** Extended Secure Addressing for Groups

  Nothing prevents you from using your own message formats with Extended Code or Data functions, except that repeaters may not properly echo your messages onto the other power line phases.

  The longer messages increase the probability that one X-10 transmission will collide with another, so the `xtc798.doc` specification adds some access requirements to the protocol. Specifically, it says Extended Code systems must follow specific steps to ensure the power line is not being used by another device, must check for collisions during transmission, and must respond to collisions by terminating the operation and starting over from the state in which it's verifying the power line is idle.

- **Hail Request/Acknowledge** — A device can send Hail Request to locate X-10 transmitters on the system. Those transmitters are to respond with Hail Acknowledge. The commands are used for other purposes by some equipment, and not implemented by all transmitters.

Implementation factors

The wiring in a house isn't a perfect transmission system. Worst of the transmission impairments the signal sees is the power transformer that feeds your house, as shown in Figure 1-6, because it splits the single-phase power into two sides, with a neutral tap between the two. Appliances see 120 V between a power rail and neutral, or 240 V, between the two power rails.

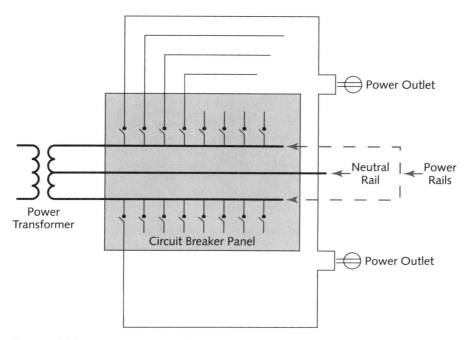

FIGURE 1-6: Home power system schematic

Suppose there's an X-10 transmitter connected to the upper power outlet in the figure and an X-10 receiver on the lower outlet. Signals output from the upper power outlet transmitter are referenced between the one power rail and the neutral, and are carried directly on those two wires to any receiver on the same circuit or with some loss to any circuit connected to the upper power rail. To get to the lower rail, however, the signal has to be coupled through the power transformer (or some 240-volt appliance) onto the lower rail. Power transformers are tuned to be efficient at 60 or 50 Hz, however, and their relatively high impedance at the 120 kHz signal frequency does not couple energy well — it's entirely possible that only a tenth of the original signal passes to the other side of the breaker panel. Even ignoring noise and other problems, should the coupled signal drop below the 100 mV (millivolt) reception threshold, receivers on the other side of the transformer won't work reliably, or won't work at all. You fix this problem using a *coupler*, a device that provides a low impedance path for the 120 kHz signal from one side of the breaker panel to the other to reduce the loss, or a *repeater*, a device that actually amplifies the signal before retransmitting it onto the other side.

Signal attenuation comes from other sources, too, because many types of devices on the power line will themselves attenuate the X-10 signal. Relatively small capacitances in power supplies and other electronic circuits look like high impedances to the normal 60 Hz power waveform, but may look like a low impedance to the 120 kHz signal and therefore reduce its strength considerably. The effects of each such small loss add together, too, so while no one computer, television, or other device may be enough to make your system unreliable, a large enough number of them may. You need a *filter* to fix this problem. Filters work as shown in Figure 1-7. Coils are the dual of capacitors, in that their impedance goes up with higher frequency, while a capacitor's impedance goes down. Putting a small inductance coil in series with each wire in the power line lets the power flow without hindrance, but blocks noise and the 120 kHz signal. The filter blocks any X-10 signal present on the power line on the left in Figure 1-7, keeping that signal from being attenuated by the low impedance capacitance in the device on the right.

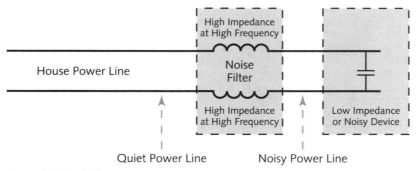

FIGURE 1-7: X-10 filtering

Noise also corrupts X-10 signals. The theoretical waveform of Figure 1-3 is what you think about, but what you get may be the mess in Figure 1-8 that results from even a moderate amount of noise on the power line. We've left the tones in, but no X-10 receiver is likely to figure out where they are and whether a zero or one is being sent. The figure is the same one as Figure 1-3, with random 10-volt peak-to-peak noise added on to the 120 volt power line signal.

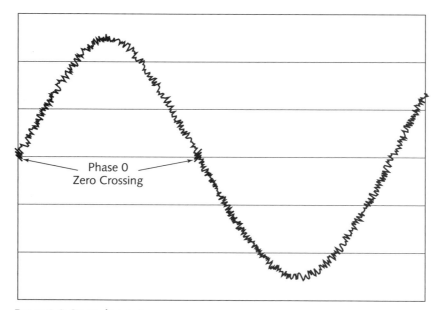

FIGURE 1-8: Power line noise

Devices that switch the power line on and off generate noise. Devices that generate noise that can affect your X-10 system include:

- **Power supplies** — Decades ago, power supplies used transformers to change voltage levels, then rectified and filtered the output to produce direct current. Such *linear power supplies* aren't very efficient, though, so the newer *switching power supply* design has almost completely replaced the older design. A switching power supply turns the power feed to a filter on and off very quickly, keeping just the right amount of charge in the input capacitor of the filter to maintain the precise output voltage. The switching operation generates noise back into the power line, however, noise that can affect X-10 systems if the power supply or an external filter doesn't block it. Everything electronic that doesn't run on batteries has a power supply.

- **Fluorescent lamps** — A fluorescent lamp contains an arc between two electrodes that dies and re-strikes at every voltage zero crossing of the power line. Each time the arc re-strikes, it generates wideband, high-frequency noise. Compact fluorescent lights are worse, because they contain switching power supplies, too.

- **Motors** — Many motors include a *commutator* and *brushes* to rapidly switch the incoming power among the different coils in the armature. Every time the commutator and brushes disconnect one coil and connect another, there's a surge of current that generates power line noise.

- **Your neighbor's X-10 system** — What's signal to your neighbor is noise to you, and if X-10 signals from adjacent houses couple in to your system, you'll see strange results as your equipment interprets and acts on commands leaking in from next door. The coupling is through the main power transformer and power lines feeding your house, so a filter on the mains is all you need to solve the problem should it occur.

Parts

There's a wide variety of X-10 components available as pre-built devices you can use to build systems. You can also build your own components using readily available building blocks. This section covers pre-built modules; the later section "Building Your Own Modules" shows how to use the building blocks.

Switches and dimmers

The simplest X-10 receiver is a plug-in appliance module, such as the Radio Shack module shown in Figure 1-9. It requires no special wiring concerns, and because it is either on or off, with no dimming capability, it can control any type of load up to its rated capacity.

The type of load you connect to a module is important for all other kinds of receivers. Resistive loads, such as heaters and lamps, do not respond to variations in the AC waveform. Reactive loads have capacitive and/or inductive components, in addition to the resistive load, that make the loads unsuitable for control by *triac* semiconductor devices that modify the AC waveform.

FIGURE 1-9: Appliance module

A triac is a three-terminal semiconductor device used by all modern dimmers to control an AC line. Two of the terminals form a path for the load current, while the third terminal turns the device on (the triac turns off at every zero crossing of the AC waveform). If the control terminal is always on, you get a standard AC sine wave. If there is a delay after the zero crossing before the control terminal turns on, you get a truncated AC waveform such as in Figure 1-10. Triacs replaced rheostats in dimmers because they're smaller and generate far less heat.

The frequency analysis in Figure 1-11 (derived from Figure 1-10) shows the problem the triac output waveform creates for reactive loads. The solid line is the fundamental frequency, while the dashed lines show the additional frequency components introduced by the waveform truncation. Reactive loads respond to those additional frequency components, and not necessarily in a good way.

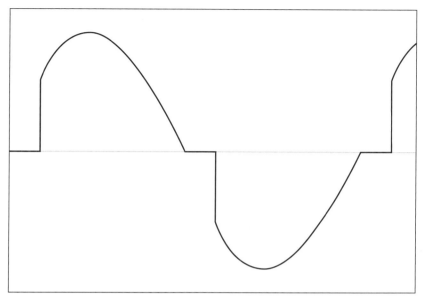

FIGURE 1-10: Dimmer waveform output

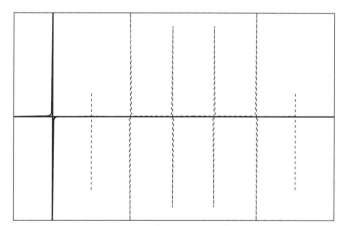

FIGURE 1-11: Dimmer output frequency analysis

The net result you need to remember from Figure 1-11 is that you must only use a dimming-capable X-10 module with a resistive load. Reactive loads — essentially anything but an incandescent lamp — require appliance modules rated for the more complex load. Even halogen lamps may have transformers in their circuitry, making them a reactive load and unsuitable for dimming.

Most X-10 light switches can dim, although the dimming function may only be accessible from a remote controller and not from the switch itself. Some, but definitely not all, can report their on/off status back to the controller.

Modules capable of replacing a single, standard light switch are not suitable for use in three-way or one-way configurations. Special module sets (Figure 1-12) are available for that purpose, and must be paired in a master/slave configuration.

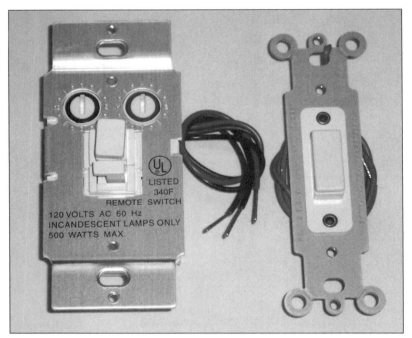

FIGURE **1-12:** X-10 three-way light switch set

Controllers

There's a wide variety of controllers available to transmit X-10 commands over the power line, varying from simple table-top models to computer-controlled units. We've used the X-10 model CM11A PC controller, although many others exist. Table 1-3 lists a representative selection, all of which are controllable using the HomeSeer software. The Smarthome unit is particularly attractive because of its USB interface, helping you migrate away from serial ports.

Table 1-3   X-10 Compatible Computer Interface Controllers

Controller	Source
X-10 CM11A	X-10 www.X10.com/automation/X10_ck11a.htm
Smarthome PowerLinc USB	Smarthome www.smarthome.com/1132U.html
ACT TI103-RS232	Advanced Control Technologies, Inc. www.act-solutions.com/pdfs/PCCSpecs/ ti103_spec.pdf

Although you'll typically use one of these controllers as the main transmitter in your system, controlling all your other devices through it, you don't have to restrict them to that role. You can have more than one in your system, and you can use them with a serial interface to devices like the Basic Stamp in the section "Building Your Own Modules" below or the Java Stamp we use in the Automated BBQ Temperature Control project (Chapter 6). That's a particularly attractive option with the Java Stamp, because (unlike the Basic Stamp) the Java Stamp does not have built-in routines to handle the low-level interface of the TW-523 Two-way Powerline Interface and related devices.

The protocol your PC uses to talk to a CM11A is defined in an X-10 document (ftp://ftp.X10.com/pub/manuals/cm11a_protocol.txt), including the information you'd need to use the interface with a Java Stamp.

The electrical connection to a CM11A is a standard RS-232 serial port, operating at 4.8 Kbps with 8 data bits, 1 stop bit, and no parity. The CM11A presents an RJ-11 connector; using the supplied serial cable, the signals are on the standard pins for a 9-pin connector (Signal In = pin 2, Signal Out = pin 3, Signal Ground = pin 5) plus one addition: the Ring In signal is used, and is on pin 9. The interface asserts Ring In when it needs service from the PC, such as when it hears a command or status message on the power line from another device. The interface can operate on any house or unit code.

Here's an example (Figure 1-13) of what you can do with just a CM11A and some switch modules. The HomeSeer software (www.homeseer.com; see Chapter 9) lets you enter your location, and from it calculates times for sunrise and sunset. Rules in HomeSeer then turn the lights in front of your house on at sunset and off at sunrise, with small random changes backwards or forwards each day to avoid making it look like the lights are on a timer.

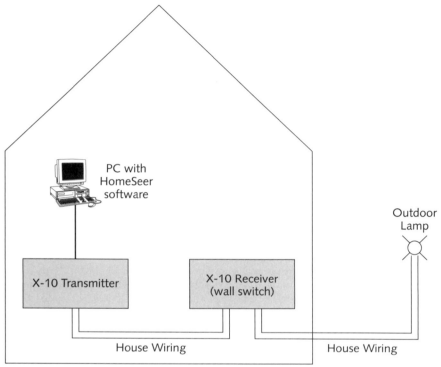

FIGURE 1-13: Outdoor lighting control

Wireless controllers and switches

Power line communications requires a power line connection, of course. It's inconvenient to walk around trailing an extension cord, which led to the creation of modules that let wireless devices interact with X-10 networks. The X-10 model TM751 Wireless Transceiver Module provides the interface between wireless units and the power line network, receiving wireless signals and generating the appropriate messages onto the power line.

One restriction you need to keep in mind using the TM751 is that, although you can select the specific one, the device only responds on a single house code. That's an advantage in applications where you have a large area to cover wirelessly. At most, you're only going to get approximately a 100-foot range between a wireless transmitter and the transceiver, and the range can be severely reduced by intervening metallic surfaces. You can usually solve the range problem by adding more transceivers, but you'll want them on different house codes to ensure they don't both receive a transmission and output to the power line.

Two alternatives to the TM751, shown in Table 1-4, give you some other options. The Smarthome All Housecode X-10 RF Receiver works at longer ranges, and can be programmed through your PC to operate on multiple house codes. The Smarthome X-10 RF Receiver to RS-232 Adapter gives you a direct wireless interface to your PC, giving you more options for wireless control of software such as HomeSeer.

Table 1-4   Wireless Transceivers

Transceiver	Source
X-10 TW751	X-10 www.x10.com/automation/x10_tm751.htm
Smarthome All Housecode X-10 RF Receiver (also requires X-10 TW523 or Smarthome PowerLinc)	Smarthome www.smarthome.com/4831.html
Smarthome X-10 RF Receiver to RS-232 Adapter	Smarthome www.smarthome.com/4832.html

An interesting problem you can solve wirelessly with X-10 control is putting a switch where there presently are no wires. The Smarthome X-10 Wireless Wall Switch enables you to do that — it looks like a four-element wall switch, but instead of wiring into a switch box in the wall, it transmits wireless codes to a nearby transceiver. You can let the transmitted codes control X-10 lamp or switch modules directly, or you can receive the transmission at your PC through a controller and execute any actions you desire.

Motion and light sensors

You don't always want to have to push buttons — wireless or not — to make something happen. Instead, as with outdoor security lights, you may want to trigger actions based on light (or its absence) or motion. Motion sensors (Table 1-5) solve that problem, sending messages for both motion and light. The X-10 MS14A is a wireless motion and light sensor you combine with a wireless transceiver, while the wired PR511 combines outdoor lamps with a motion and light sensor.

Table 1-5   Wireless Transceivers

Sensor	Source
X-10 Eagle Eye Motion Sensor	X-10 www.x10.com/automation/x10_ms14a.htm
X-10 Dual Motion Monitor (outdoor lamps with motion sensor)	X-10 www.x10.com/automation/x10_pr511.htm

Figure 1-14 shows a sample motion sensor application — controlling overhead lights in a garage. We placed three motion sensors, to make sure people were seen when they entered the space, and located the transceiver so there would be direct line of sight from the wireless motion sensors (we used X-10 MS14A sensors) to the transceiver. If you were to move the transceiver to an outlet directly above the metal shelves, for example, the path from the sensor on the bottom wall would be blocked and the sensor would operate only erratically, confusing the system when Off messages were dropped.

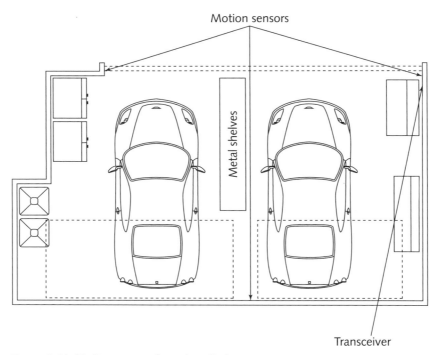

FIGURE 1-14: Motion sensors for automatic lamps

Low-voltage sensors and relays

Some X-10 applications require that you sense the status of a remote circuit, or control a device, but are strictly on/off in nature, and only involve relatively low voltages. Specific modules are available to meet those requirements, as listed in Table 1-6. The Universal Module lets you control devices needing a low power, low-voltage contact closure. You'll see an application of a Universal Module in the chapter on Automated Sprinkler Control (Chapter 5), where we've used one to enable or disable the 24-volt drive to the valves by a sprinkler controller.

Table 1-6   Low-Voltage Modules

Sensor	Source
X-10 Universal Module	X-10 www.x10.com/automation/x10_um506.htm
X-10 Powerflash (also Burglar Alarm Interface)	X-10 www.x10.com/security/x10_pf284.htm

The Powerflash does the inverse of the Universal Module, sending an X-10 message out on the power line when a contact closes or opens. You could use it to detect a switch closing and tell your PC when the garage door is open or closed; we used one in *PC Toys* (Wiley, 2003) as part of a system that warns you when a freezer gets too warm.

Filters, couplers, and repeaters

As Table 1-7 demonstrates, there's a wide variety of signal improvement and noise suppression equipment available. The devices in the table, many of which have both wired and plug-in versions, have these functions:

- **Noise Filter** — A simple noise filter works along the lines of Figure 1-7, keeping power line noise from crossing the filter in either direction. You can use one to isolate a noise source from the rest of your system, or to isolate a malfunctioning device from high levels of noise on your overall system. Some noise filters allow signals at the X-10 120 kHz frequency through, but block nearby frequencies, while full-spectrum filters block frequencies above the power line 60 Hz.

- **Noise Block** — A noise block is no different from a full-spectrum noise filter in principle, but it is packaged to make it convenient to install it right at the noisy equipment.

- **Signal Bridge** — Also known as a *passive phase coupler*, a signal bridge transfers signals from one side of the electrical panel to the other. A passive coupler divides the available signal energy, lowering the signal on the sending side and increasing it on the receiving side.

- **Blocking Coupler** — A blocking coupler, which is also a passive coupler, blocks entering X-10 signals as well as coupling signals between sides.

- **Phase Coupler / Repeater** — You can boost the signal strength of the receiving side of your system with a phase coupler/repeater. The device actually receives and re-transmits the received signal, outputting it with far more strength than was received.

Table 1-7   Filters, Couplers, and Repeaters

Sensor	Source
FilterLinc Plug-In Noise Filter	Smarthome www.smarthome.com/1626.html
Leviton Noise Block	Smarthome www.smarthome.com/4835.html
Leviton Signal Bridge	Smarthome www.smarthome.com/4815.html
Leviton and X-10 Whole-House Blocking Couplers	Smarthome www.smarthome.com/4850.html
SignaLinc Plug-in Coupler-Repeater	Smarthome www.smarthome.com/4826.html
X-10 Phase Coupler / Repeater	X-10 www.x10pro.com/pro/catalog/ xpcp.xpcr.page5.html
X-10 XPF 3-Wire Noise Filter	X-10 www.x10pro.com/pro/catalog/ xpf.xppf.page5.html

You have to be careful when installing filters to ensure that you don't isolate X-10 transmitters or receivers from the network by blocking their signals. Noise blocks, for example, must be installed between the controlling receiver and the load, not on the power line side of the receiver.

It's also important to avoid using multiple couplers or repeaters, because they're not designed to work as multiples, and can either interfere with each other or (worse) echo signals endlessly until you disconnect one of them.

Troubleshooting

We like to start troubleshooting problems by thinking about what might plausibly go wrong. X-10 networks are simple enough in operation that there are only a few options:

- **No signal reached the power line** — The transmitter might be defective, or the transmitter might be disconnected from the power line.

- **Unreliable wireless operation** — The X-10 motion detectors are the most common wireless transmitters; if their signal isn't received, the system will behave as if the sensor isn't working. Poor wireless signal reception can be caused by weak batteries, competing radio signals acting as noise and jamming the signal, blockage between transmitter and receiver, or excessive range between transmitter and receiver.

- **No signal, a weak signal, or a noisy signal reached the receiver** — There might be filters or other losses on the power line, the signal might not be coupling into the other side of the power panel adequately, or noise signals might be corrupting the incoming signal. Noise sources include contention between multiple X-10 transmitters operating at the same time.

- **The receiver isn't responding** — The receiver might be broken, might not be properly connected to the power line, might be receiving on an address different than the transmitter is sending, might not respond to an unusual command sequence being sent, or might be connected to a load that doesn't work.

Figure 1-15 shows that problems can afflict every part of the network, but because of the serial nature of the connections, shows that you can troubleshoot by starting at one end and following the signal (or its absence). You can start at either the controller or the load.

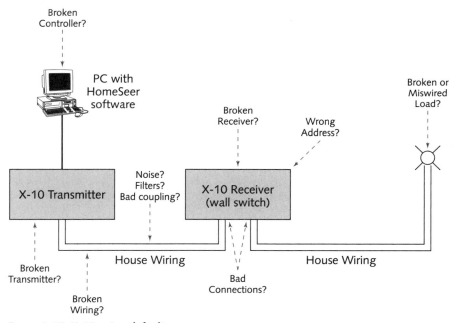

FIGURE 1-15: X-10 network faults

If you start at the load, your sequence might follow this sequence:

1. If there's a manual switch at the receiver, see whether it will turn the load on or off. If not, substitute another receiver temporarily and see whether it controls the load where the proper one will not.

2. Assuming the receiver can control the load, try isolating the receiver and a known good test transmitter on a power line isolated by a filter from the rest of the house, and see whether the transmitter will control the receiver. If not, check the addressing and connections, and perhaps replace the receiver.

3. The receiver working in isolation suggests that either the problem is external to the isolated segment or the receiver is not as sensitive as it needs to be. Use a signal strength meter, such as the combination of the X-10 Pro XPTT transmitter and XPTR receiver, respectively. The XPTT sends a continuous signal turning address P1 on and off; the XPTR measures the strength of the received signal for P1. If you connect the XPTT at the location of your transmitter and the XPTR at the receiver, you can measure the signal transported by the power line between the two sites. You need 200 mV (millivolts) by specification, but if the signal is that low you'll need a very clean, noise-free system.

   If the problem *is* noise, you'll need to try to identify the source. Don't just turn units off, unplug them — many electronic designs don't really turn off even when they look off, and noise or loading from the power supply won't vanish unless you disconnect the power supply from the power line. Should you find a significant noise source, use a filter or noise blocker to clean up the pollution.

4. Use a known good receiver in an isolated segment against the transmitter, and try a test transmitter instead of the real transmitter.

5. Finally, although unlikely, erratic operation could be caused by signals fed in through the power transformer from a neighboring house. Use the XPTR to look for signals on the line when nothing should be happening.

It's not too likely you'd see unreliable operation from network collisions unless you're operating specialized equipment such as drapery or blind controls, but you can use the XPTR to see traffic loads. Figure 1-16 shows the X-10 Pro XPTT and XPTR units (www.x10pro.com/pro/catalog/x10tools.html). There are no controls on the XPTT; the single LED on the faceplate flashes when the device is in operation.

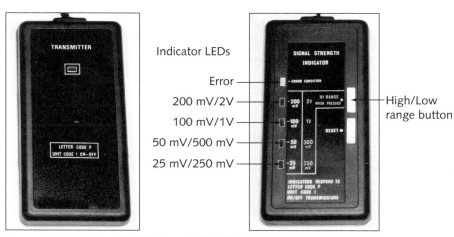

FIGURE 1-16: X-10 Pro XPTT (left) and XPTR (right)

The XPTR faceplate is organized into columns. The left column has LEDs to indicate a reception error or one of four signal levels; the right column has the Hi/Low Range button and the Reset button. Pushing Hi/Low Range sets the LEDs to indicate 250 mV to 2 V; releasing it selects the 25 to 200 mV range. There are no other controls — you just plug them into the outlets you want to test.

Home Automation with Standard Modules

The key requirement for wiring X-10 modules into your home is that they always have a connection between the hot and neutral power lines. Figure 1-17, for example, shows how you connect a basic dimming receiver to a light. The receiver connects in *series* with the light, not across the power line in *parallel*, and should be in the hot line, not the neutral. If you connect it in parallel, you'll blow the receiver the first time you turn it on.

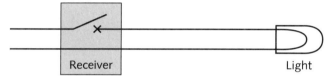

FIGURE 1-17: Basic receiver/lamp circuit

The receiver draws operating power from the circuit through the lamp. The light has a much lower resistance when it's off than when it's on, typically by a factor of 10 or more, so as the equivalent circuit of Figure 1-18 shows, there's less voltage drop across the receiver when on. The X-10 signal drops proportionally, so there's a smaller X-10 signal available to the receiver when the light is on. The effect is worse for small-wattage lamps — night-light bulbs have such a high on resistance that reliable X-10 control with a two-wire dimmer is unlikely. This effect causes Off commands to be less reliable when the X-10 signal strength is marginal, a condition you may be able to correct with an amplified repeater.

When you must control a small-wattage lamp, or if the system delivers marginal signal strength, the reduction of the X-10 signal to receivers in the on state can account for units you can turn on but not turn off reliably. You have to boost the received signal to solve that problem, or convert the installation to use a three-wire dimmer (Figure 1-19; don't confuse a three-wire dimmer with a three-way dimmer). Connecting the three-wire receiver directly across the hot and neutral wires lets it receive the X-10 signal unaffected by the on or off state of the lamp.

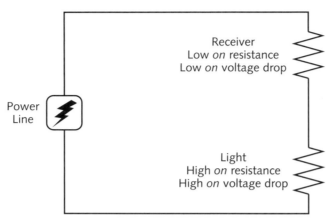

FIGURE 1-18: Equivalent circuit—light on

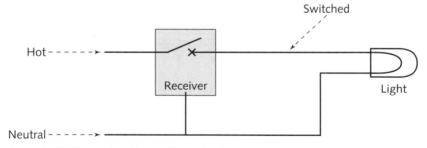

FIGURE 1-19: Three-wire dimmer/lamp circuit

Perhaps the most confusing X-10 installation topic is the requirements for wiring X-10 dimmers into a three-way circuit — that is, a circuit with two switches controlling a single light. Figure 1-20 shows the one way to wire conventional switches into a three-way circuit. The light will be on if both switches are up or are down, and off otherwise.

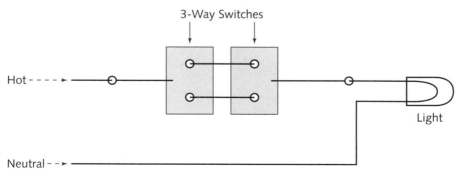

FIGURE 1-20: Simple three-way circuit

Unfortunately, the circuit in Figure 1-20 will not work if you simply replace one of the three-way switches with an X-10 dimmer, because for the wrong setting of the second three-way switch, there's no complete circuit through the light, and the dimmer gets no power. Because it gets no power, it never sees the signal to turn on. For that reason, X-10 three-way circuits are *entirely different* than the mechanical equivalent of Figure 1-20. An X-10 dimmer must connect directly to the light at all times, so the fundamental circuit has to be the same as the standard dimmer circuit of Figure 1-17. The second switch no longer controls the primary circuit; instead, it signals the dimmer. Figure 1-21 shows the idea — the second switch drives a control input to the dimmer, telling it to turn on or off by a pulse on the input. The light is always under control of the dimmer, and never directly under control of the slave.

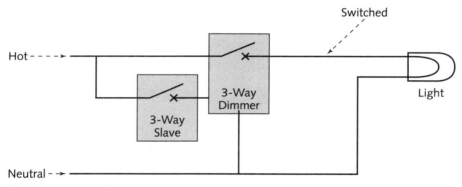

FIGURE 1-21: Basic three-way X-10 circuit

If you imagine the two wires between the switches in Figure 1-20 as corresponding to the two wires in the gap between the slave and the dimmer in Figure 1-21, you can see how you might wire the dimmer/slave pair in practice. There are a lot of different ways to wire three-way circuits, however; for more detail and explanation, and for how to extend the idea to one-way circuits, see the Advanced Control Technologies Web pages at www.act-solutions.com/kingery06.htm and www.act-solutions.com/kingery07.htm.

Of course, all of that is the hard way. If you simply install X-10 switches that output signals to the power line, you can then use your PC to signal any number of devices to turn on, off, or dim, regardless of the actual connections (or lack thereof) between the switches and anything else. No X-10 design problem has only one answer.

Building Your Own Modules

The X-10 TW523 is a two-way power line interface you can drive with your own circuits. It operates at a much more primitive level than PC interfaces such as the CM11A, which has a serial port interface, so you'll need both good electronics skills and experience with real-time embedded software. The interface gives you the following opto-isolated signals (Figure 1-22):

■ **Zero Crossing** — Output from the TW523, the Zero Crossing signal goes high at the start of each zero crossing interval. The signal is not a conventional data valid signal; see the transmit and receive signal descriptions. Use a pull-up resistor on the signal.

■ **Signal Ground** — Pin 2 is the common reference for the other three pins.

■ **Receive from Power Line** — This signal is high if the received signal from the power line is a one, and low if it's a zero. The signal is not valid until 200 >s after Zero Crossing goes high, and is only required to stay valid for 1 ms after Zero Crossing goes high even if Zero Crossing remains high. Use a pull-up resistor on the signal.

■ **Transmit to Power Line** — Output a high on this line within 200 μ of Zero Crossing going high, and hold the line high, to output a one on the power line — that is, to turn on the 120 kHz oscillator. Use the same timing with a low output to output a zero. The line should be low if the interface is not to transmit data, since that keeps the oscillator off.

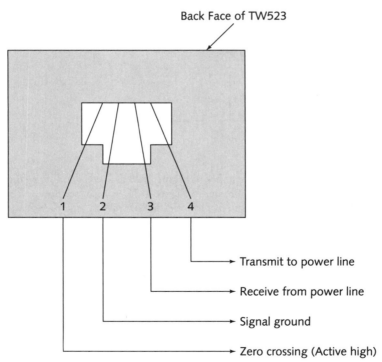

FIGURE 1-22: X-10 TW523 interface signals

Using the TW523 is somewhat difficult, because it provides only the physical layer interface, and requires compliance with relatively precise and demanding timing to ensure meeting the physical layer specification. The requirement to handle the physical layer timing plus all link layer requirements in your electronics implies you'll need some intelligence in devices you build using the TW523, not just sensors or switches. The Smarthome and Advanced Control Technologies interfaces in Table 1-8 relieve the requirement to handle critical timing in your implementation, substituting an RS-232 interface and more intelligence in the interface device, but you'll still need enough intelligence to handle the link layer. Those devices also add the capability to handle X-10 extended codes and data, whereas you can't receive the extended formats with the TW523.

Table 1-8   Two-Way X-10 Interfaces

Interface	Source
X-10 TW523	X-10 www.x10.com/automation/x10_tw523.htm
X-10 Pro PSC05	X-10 Pro www.x10pro.com/pro/catalog/ psc04.psc05.page12.html
Smarthome PowerLinc II Serial/TW523 X-10 Interface with 12VDC Output	Smarthome www.smarthome.com/1132.html
Advanced Control Technologies TI103-RS232	Advanced Control Technologies www.act-solutions.com/pdfs/PCCSpecs/ ti103_spec.pdf

A PC is far more elaborate than you want for a remote X-10 device; instead, you'll want to include an embedded microcontroller. We've used two different ones from Parallax in this book, as shown in Table 1-9. You can find many others available by searching the Internet; we chose the Parallax units because of their combination of capability, availability with boards supporting a circuit prototyping area, and integration with support software. The Basic Stamp runs a variant of the Basic programming language, while the Javelin Stamp runs an embedded subset of Sun Microsystems' Java.

Table 1-9 Embedded Microcontrollers

Embedded Microcontroller	Source
Parallax Basic Stamp Starter Kit with Board of Education	Parallax www.parallax.com/detail.asp? product_id=27203
Parallax Javelin Stamp Starter Kit	Parallax www.parallax.com/detail.asp? product_id=27237

Basic Stamp overview

The Basic Stamp (shown wired for the X-10 TW523 in Figure 1-23) is a small microcontroller programmed with firmware to interpret the Basic programming language. The Basic Stamp 2 (BS2) module we used includes 32 bytes of RAM, of which 6 are used for I/O and 26 for variables, and 2KB of EEPROM, enough to hold around 500 instructions. There's a comparison of all the Basic Stamp versions at www.parallax.com/html_pages/tech/faqs/stamp_specs.asp; other versions support more I/O pins, provide a scratch pad RAM, add more built-in commands, and hold much larger programs. They all consume more power, too.

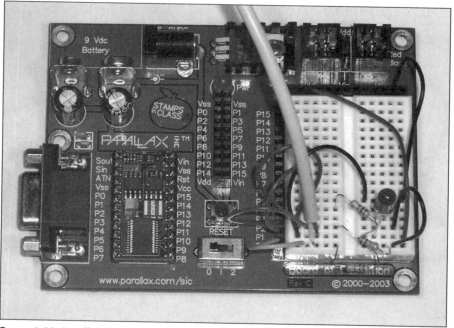

FIGURE 1-23: Parallax Basic Stamp

Performance of the Basic Stamps ranges from about 4K to 12K instructions per second, a range of about 3:1. We used the following program to make the performance measurements in Table 1-10, commenting out different parts of the program and changing variable types for the different tests. The version in the listing is the one used for the GOSUB benchmark.

```
'{$STAMP BS2}
'{$PBASIC 2.5}

Foo   VAR Byte
ix_1  VAR Word

DEBUG "Start", CR
FOR ix_1 = 0 TO 30000
  'Foo = 1
  GOSUB Sub
NEXT
DEBUG "Done", CR
END

Sub:
  RETURN
```

Table 1-10   Basic Stamp Performance (Stopwatch Timing)

Statement	Time for 30K Iterations (s)	Time per Iteration (>s)
Assignment (bit)	8	267
Assignment (nibble)	7	233
Assignment (word, byte)	6	200
FOR – NEXT (word variable)	22	730
GOSUB – RETURN	23	767

The Basic Stamp doesn't have a built-in real-time clock, so we timed execution with a stopwatch, adjusting the loop count to require 20–30 seconds total except for the GOSUB, which required about twice as long. Times shown in the table for the assignments and GOSUB tests are after subtracting off the 22 seconds required for the FOR-NEXT loop using a word variable. Depending on the actual program you run, the table results are reasonably consistent with the performance Parallax states for the BS2, which is about 4K instructions per second. In comparison, the Javelin Stamp Java processor runs far faster, at about 1 μ per FOR loop iteration—over 700 times faster than the Basic Stamp.

The BS2 performance is acceptable for relatively slowly changing work, such as user interfaces, weather readings, or process control calculations, but won't handle the faster demands of interfaces to A/D or D/A converters, or to many I/O devices. The TW523 is a good example — zero crossings occur a little more than 8 ms apart, leaving time for very few instructions, and fewer yet if you tried to organize your program with a modular structure involving loops and subroutines. The need for an interpreter running on the small embedded microcontroller to execute the Basic Stamp language accounts for the relative slowness when compared to the processor's 20 MHz clock. The Basic Stamp language compensates for the overhead of the interpreter by including several built-in commands to execute common embedded functions at much higher speed. Those built-in commands include ones to do A/D and D/A conversions, interface to serial communication ports and synchronous serial devices, generate DTMF tones used on telephone lines, and support raw interfaces to LCDs.

Build an X-10 test transmitter

One of the built-in commands in the Basic Stamp language, XOUT, supports X-10 physical layer output to a TW523 interface. The command synchronizes with the Zero Crossing signal input on one pin, and drives the Transmit to Power Line signal on a second pin. The following program drives a sequence of P1 On and P1 Off commands onto the power line, somewhat similar to the constant stream of P1 On commands output by the X-10 Pro XPTT. (Indeed, if you modified the program to have no PAUSE delays, the output would be essentially equivalent.)

```
'{$STAMP BS2}
'{$PBASIC 2.5}

Zpin     CON 0     'Zero Crossing on Pin P0
Mpin     CON 1     'Modulation output on Pin P1
HouseA   CON 0     'House code base
Unit1    CON 0     'Unit code base

TheHouse CON HouseA+15       '+15 is P, for XPTR (wants P1)
TheUnit  CON Unit1          'e.g., +4 is Unit5

reps  VAR Word

  DEBUG  DEC ? TheHouse, DEC ? TheUnit

  FOR reps = 1 TO 100
    DEBUG DEC ? reps

    DEBUG "On", CR
    XOUT  Mpin, Zpin, [TheHouse\TheUnit]
    XOUT  Mpin, Zpin, [TheHouse\UNITON]              'Turn it on
    PAUSE 1000
    DEBUG "Off", CR
    XOUT  Mpin, Zpin, [TheHouse\TheUnit]
    XOUT  Mpin, Zpin, [TheHouse\UNITOFF]             'Turn it off
    PAUSE 1000
  NEXT

  DEBUG CR, "Done"

  END
```

We investigated writing software to read and report X-10 commands with the Basic Stamp, but ultimately the device is too slow. The SHIFTIN command looked promising for a time, offering the capability to clock in data from a serial line, but because the Basic Stamp can only generate the clock pulse for SHIFTIN and not accept a clock from the external device, it's not usable with the TW523. So you'll understand our approach, the following program was intended to test X-10 input using direct pin I/O, but it does not work because it can't cycle fast enough to read the pins at the 120 Hz half-cycle rate. If you rewrote it in Java, the Javelin Stamp is likely to be fast enough.

```
'{$STAMP BS2}
'{$PBASIC 2.5}


' X-10 input example
' Geek House
' Software copyright (C) 2004 by Barry and Marcia Press


'  ================================================================
' Data Declarations
'  ================================================================
Dpin   PIN 2          ' X10 data input = P2
Opin   PIN 3          ' LED output = P3
X10Out PIN 1          ' X10 command pulse output = P1
Cpin   PIN 0          ' X10 zero crossing input pin = P0

DataIn  VAR Bit       ' Sampled X-10 input data
ClockIn VAR Bit       ' Clock state when DataIn sampled
Error   VAR Bit       ' Non-zero if error found
Xbit    VAR Bit       ' X-10 sampled bit (not just data)
Xerror  VAR Bit       ' Aggregate address / command error

IXBits   VAR Byte     ' Loop counter for accumulating X-10 bits
Nbits    VAR Byte     ' Input parameter, GetBits bit cound
Xbits    VAR Word     ' Output result, GetBits
Xaddress VAR Word     ' X10 address result
Xcommand VAR Word     ' X10 command result
Ncmds    VAR Word     ' How many commands received


'  ================================================================
' Main Program - X-10 input example
'  ================================================================

  ' Ensure X-10 output pin inactive
  OUTPUT X10Out
  LOW X10Out

  ' Initialize output pins
  OUTPUT Opin
  HIGH Opin

  ' Initialize input pins
  INPUT Cpin
  INPUT Dpin
```

```
    DEBUG "Ready", CR

    ' Input and print 9-bit X-10 commands
    Ncmds = 0
    DO
      ' Read in the address and command packets
      Nbits = 9
      GOSUB WaitNoZC
      GOSUB GetBits          ' Address
      Xaddress = Xbits
      Xerror = Error

      GOSUB GetBits          ' Command
      Xcommand = Xbits
      Xerror = Xerror | Error

      DEBUG DEC Ncmds, " = "
      TOGGLE Opin
      DEBUG BIN Xaddress, " | ", BIN Xcommand

      IF (Error) THEN
        DEBUG " Error"
      ENDIF
      DEBUG CR
      Ncmds = Ncmds + 1

    LOOP

END

' =================================================================
' Make sure not in zero crossing
' =================================================================
WaitNoZC:
  DO WHILE (Cpin = 1)
  LOOP
  RETURN

' =================================================================
' Read a sample from the next synchronous X-10 input zero crossing
' Returns data value in DataIn, clock for sample in ClockIn
' Sets Error non-zero if clock problem
' =================================================================
GetSample:
  ' Wait for zero crossing interval to start
  DO WHILE (Cpin = 0)
  LOOP

  ' Get data line and sample clock for verification
  DataIn = Dpin
  ClockIn = Cpin
  Error = ClockIn ^ 1
  IF Error THEN
```

```
      DEBUG "."
  ENDIF

  ' Spin loop wait until not in zero crossing
  'DO WHILE Cpin = 1
  'LOOP

  RETURN


' =================================================================
' Wait until start code (1110) found on X-10 data line
' =================================================================
WaitStart:
  ' Wait for sequence of three ones. First one just hangs waiting for
  ' a one. Subsequent ones do not wait, but decode.
SequenceStart:
  DO
    GOSUB GetSample                    ' First sample
  LOOP WHILE (Error = 1 OR DataIn = 0)

  GOSUB GetSample                      ' Second sample
  IF (Error = 1 OR DataIn = 0) THEN SequenceStart

SequenceOnes:
  GOSUB GetSample                      ' Third sample
  IF (Error = 1 OR DataIn = 0) THEN SequenceStart

  GOSUB GetSample                      ' Fourth sample
  IF (Error = 1) THEN SequenceStart
  IF (DataIn = 1) THEN SequenceOnes

  'Found it, exit the subroutine
  RETURN


' =================================================================
' Get one bit from X-10 input.
'    Xbit is returned bit
'    Error is non-zero if receive error or the bit fails parity test
' =================================================================
GetBit:
  ' Get actual bit, exit if error receiving it
  GOSUB GetSample
  Xbit = DataIn
  IF (Error <> 0) THEN
    RETURN
  ENDIF

  ' Get complemented bit, error if receive error or not complement
  GOSUB GetSample
  Error = Error | (DataIn ^ Xbit ^ 1)
  RETURN
```

```
' ==================================================================
' Get bits from X-10 input.
'   Nbits is number of bits to read
'   Xbits is returned bit sequence shifted in from low end
' ==================================================================
GetBits:
  Xbits = 0
  GOSUB WaitStart
  FOR IXBits = 0 TO Nbits
    GOSUB GetBit
    IF (Error) THEN
      RETURN
    ENDIF
    Xbits = (Xbits << 1) | Xbit
  NEXT
  RETURN
```

Summary

The ability to send and receive signals across the power line, albeit at low rate, and to add both PCs and embedded microprocessors to the control system, gives you complete control over any powered device in your home. This chapter showed you the basic components you have to work with, and how to build systems using them. What you do with those elements is up to you and your imagination.

In Chapter 9 we'll show you how X-10 controls let you keep your yard watered just the way it should be, regardless of extraordinary heat or precipitation.

Wireless RS-232 Link

It's almost inevitable that a PC in a geek's house will be connected to sensors and actuators. Serial (RS-232) ports are still the most common way to do that, although USB is finally very common, and building your own USB devices is, with some constraints, within reach. Either way, it's really inconvenient to have to run wires from the PC to all over the house.

Project Description

You don't have to accept random wires strewn everywhere, and don't have to plumb the attic with a rat's nest of cables. Instead, you can use small wireless transmitters and receivers to extend a wireless link between a PC and a connected remote device. This project does exactly that, showing you how serial links work and how to integrate the radios.

The most common serial port transmissions send characters asynchronously over the wire, meaning there's no necessary timing relationship between the signaling for one character and the signaling for the next. Figure 2-1 shows an oscilloscope photograph of the signal waveform for an ASCII A (hex 0x41) sent at 2400 bits per second (bps). You can see the overshoot in the signal on the transitions between states, settling to the signaling voltage after a while.

If my advisors ask "Why are you risking everything on such a mad scheme?" I will not proceed until I have a response that satisfies them.

Peter Anspach,
The Evil Overlord List

in this chapter

☑ Connections without the wires

☑ RS-232 signals

☑ Radio signals

☑ Multiple channels

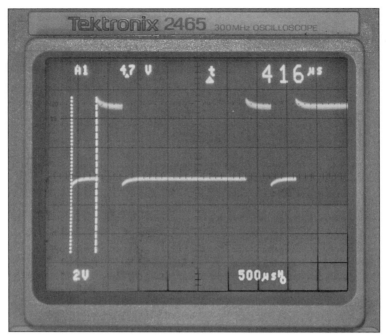

FIGURE 2-1: Scope trace for ASCII A

We generated the trace by monitoring the output pin from a Javelin Stamp
(www.javelinstamp.com) driven with this program:

```
public class SerialDataOutGenerator {

  public static void main() {
    Uart OutPort = new Uart( Uart.dirTransmit, CPU.pin15, Uart.dontInvert,
                             Uart.speed2400, Uart.stop1 );
    char c;

    // The A character is 01000001
    c = 'A';
    while (true) {                          // Never stop
      if (OutPort.sendBufferEmpty()) {      // One character, then pause
        OutPort.sendByte( c );              // A = 0x41
        CPU.delay( 628 );                   // ~60 ms
      }
    }
  }
};
```

We send one character with a large delay before the next to make isolating the signal on the scope easy. One bit time is shown between the two vertical dashed lines. If you calculate that bit time as 1 second/2400 bits per second, you get 416 microseconds, the same as the duration between the two lines, as shown in the upper-right corner of the scope.

An asynchronous character, assuming we're not sending a parity bit, consists of a *start bit* (a low signal), the eight data bits, sent least significant bit first, and a *stop bit* (a high signal). You'll see 1.5 or 2 stop bits sent at very low data rates, but sending data that slow is very uncommon. Figure 2-2 decomposes those parts of the waveform.

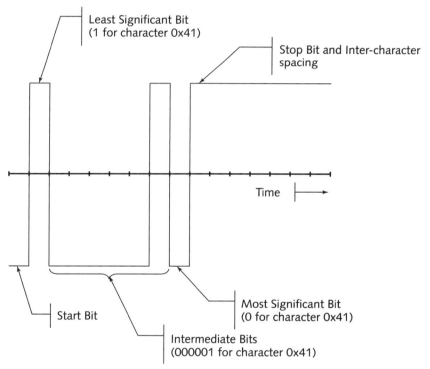

FIGURE 2-2: Serial character waveform parts

These waveforms can be represented many ways. Over an RS-232 interface, a one (high in the waveform) is represented by +12 V, and a zero (low in the waveform) by -12 V. Over a 5 V digital interface, one will be +5 V and zero will be 0 V. Over a wireless link, the radio waveform will depend on the transmitter and receiver used (for more information about that, see the next section). All those representations are the same waveform, but with a different physical representation.

The serial ports on a PC use RS-232 signaling, and implement both transmit and receive paths to support full duplex operation. The wired connection uses separate wires separated by insulators. Radio signals have no direct equivalent to insulation, so they have to use one of these approaches to send two signals at the same time:

- **Time Division Multiple Access (TDMA)** — It's not necessary to actually send characters simultaneously in opposite directions. Instead, if you sent characters at twice the data rate of a single direction, you could alternate sending from one end with sending from the other end. That approach, an example of TDMA, lets both signal directions share the same frequency and give the appearance of simultaneous full duplex transmission.

- **Code Division Multiple Access (CDMA)** — Pseudo random numbers give radios another way to communicate simultaneously. By shifting the radio frequency over a wider span according to a high-speed random sequence, or by mixing the data stream with the higher-rate random sequence, two independent channels can share the same spectrum without interfering with each other.

- **Frequency Division Multiple Access (FDMA)** — Two radio links on frequencies sufficiently separated won't interfere with each other, much as TV channels 2 and 4 transmit independently and simultaneously.

Each approach has its advantages and disadvantages. TDMA uses the least spectrum, but requires synchronization among all transmitters so only one is on at a time. CDMA requires relatively complex transmitters and receivers, but has much better immunity to noise. FDMA is very simple to implement, requiring only tuning the channels to different frequencies, but makes it more complex to implement many simultaneous transmissions. We were only interested in making one wireless RS-232 link work at a time, so we chose FDMA, operating the two directions at separate frequencies.

You can't choose frequencies at random — nations allocate frequency usage and regulate what equipment is allowed to radiate. Most frequencies are allocated for specific purposes, and many require licensed operators. Bands of spectrum are allocated for *Industrial, Scientific, and Medical (ISM)* applications in most countries (although not the same bands in all countries); under ISM rules, the design of the equipment is certified, after which anyone can operate the equipment in its approved configuration. In the United States, for example, there are ISM bands at 916 MHz, 2.4 GHz, and several other frequencies. Small, inexpensive radio modules are widely available for use in the ISM bands, making it easy to build radio links operating legally in the ISM bands.

System Diagram

The diagram shown in Figure 2-3 shows the elements of the system, including the radios and the interfaces to the processor and sensor. The processor would typically be a PC, but the idea is just as useful with an embedded processor such as the Javelin Stamp. The Javelin Stamp also simplifies integrating and testing the wireless link, because it's far simpler than a PC running a large operating system and therefore easier to peel apart and discover what's going wrong.

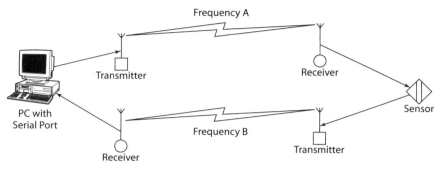

FIGURE 2-3: Wireless link block diagram

The two directions of transmission use completely identical equipment with the exception that they use different frequencies. The transmitters and receivers typically have digital interfaces expecting a 0 to 5 V signaling, while PCs use RS-232 ports with ±12 V signaling. Fortunately, converting between the two signaling levels is trivial, requiring only one transceiver chip (such as a Texas Instruments MAX232 or Intersil HIN232) at either end. Hosted on the Javelin Stamp Demo Board, the Javelin Stamp has both direct and shifted levels available, and so can interface to either signaling approach.

Figure 2-4 shows how a radio module connects. The modules we chose have asynchronous interfaces, meaning signal edge transitions may occur at any time so long as the data rate is within the capabilities of the module. There's no clock signal coming from the module as a result — the only connections are data, power, and the antenna.

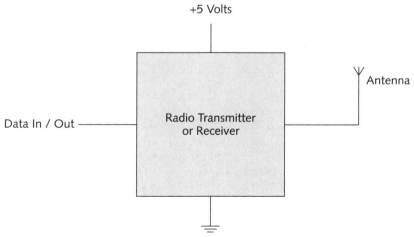

FIGURE 2-4: Radio module interfaces

Figure 2-5 shows how you could connect a Javelin Stamp to loop a data stream from a transmit pin out to the transmitter, onto a radio wave, through the receiver, and back into the Javelin Stamp. That complete loop forms one half of the project; a second loop on a different frequency provides the other half. If your application only needs to transmit data in one direction, such as to a PC from a sensor that accepts no commands, you only need one transmitter and one receiver.

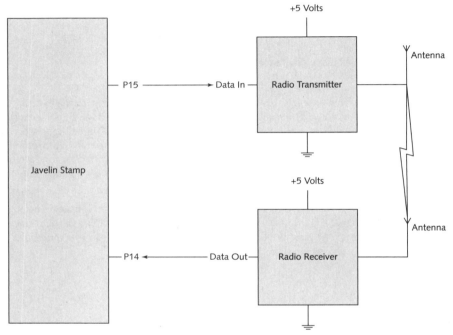

FIGURE 2-5: Half duplex loop back

Parts and Designs

Our design uses four pre-built ISM band radio modules, two (transmitter and receiver) at either end to form a wireless terminal. The terminals are not identical, as they must transmit at different frequencies. Figure 2-6 diagrams a single terminal of the pair. The transmit and receive antennas are separate. If the frequencies you use are too close together, you may have to isolate the transmitter and receiver from each other with grounded metal shield cans; and you may need to create some separation between the two antennas. Some experimentation with separation before you finalize your packaging should show you what's necessary.

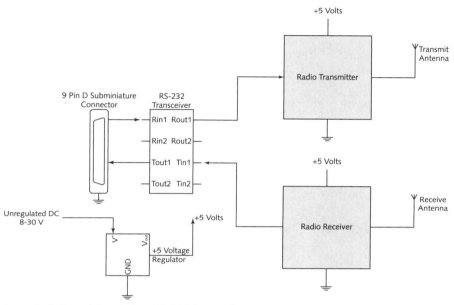

FIGURE 2-6: Complete wireless RS-232 terminal

Table 2-1 lists the basic components for the project.

Table 2-1   Wireless RS-232 Parts List

Component	Source
Radio Receivers	Ramsey Electronics 433 MHz: www.ramseyelectronics.com/cgi-bin/ commerce.exe?preadd=action&key=RX433 916 MHz: www.ramseyelectronics.com/cgi-bin/ commerce.exe?preadd=action&key=RX916
Radio Transmitters	Ramsey Electronics 433 MHz: www.ramseyelectronics.com/cgi-bin/ commerce.exe?preadd=action&key=TX433 916 MHz: www.ramseyelectronics.com/cgi-bin/ commerce.exe?preadd=action&key=TX916
Voltage Regulator LM3405-5.0 or LM7805CT	Hobby Engineering www.hobbyengineering.com/SectionSM.html #CatSMVREG

Continued

Table 2-1 (continued)

Component	Source
RS-232 Transceiver TI MAX232 or Intersil HIN232	Hobby Engineering www.hobbyengineering.com/SectionSM.html
Prototyping Printed Wiring Boards	Hobby Engineering www.hobbyengineering.com/SectionCP.html
Power Adapter	Radio Shack www.radioshack.com/category.asp?catalog% 5Fname=CTLG&category%5Fname=CTLG%5F009% 5F001%5F001%5F001&Page=1
Enclosure	Radio Shack www.radioshack.com/category.asp?catalog% 5Fname=CTLG&category%5Fname=CTLG%5F011% 5F002%5F012%5F000&Page=1
D Subminiature Connectors	Radio Shack www.radioshack.com/category.asp?catalog% 5Fname=CTLG&category%5Fname=CTLG%5F011% 5F003%5F006%5F000&Page=1

Figure 2-7 shows the Ramsey Electronics modules. The larger boards are the receivers; the 916 MHz modules are on the left. The four pads you connect to are on the undersides of the boards. Ramsey rates them for operation up to 2.4 Kbps.

You'll want to package the terminals well enough to make sure that they can take the casual abuse PC equipment gets, and you'll need to make connections between the printed wiring board (PWB) components, such as the voltage regulator and transceiver, and modules such as the radios, connectors, and power adapter. The *ONE PASSircuit* prototyping boards help solve this problem, having the layout of a solderless prototyping boards, but being PWBs you solder to. They also have shapes that fit the Radio Shack enclosures. You'll want to mount the radio modules to the PWB; we suggest insulated standoffs.

Insulated wire of the lengths suggested for the modules you use should do for the antennas.

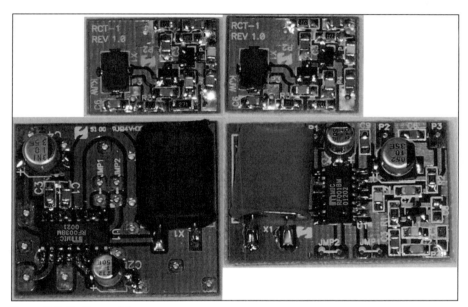

FIGURE 2-7: Radio modules

Software

Strictly speaking, there's no software required to run the project. You simply take a working serial link running at 2.4 Kbps or less and insert the radios into the link. Nevertheless, software is essential for integration and test of the project so you can incrementally build and test under known conditions. We integrated the transmitter and receiver for one frequency at a time, verifying first at low rate and range and then extending to maximum frequency and testing for range.

We used a Javelin Stamp to support those tests, verifying initial link operation with the loop-back circuit of Figure 2-5. Here's the software we used to test the loopback function:

```
public class SingleChannelLoopback {

  public static void main() {
    Uart OutPort = new Uart( Uart.dirTransmit, CPU.pin15, Uart.dontInvert,
                             Uart.speed2400, Uart.stop1 );
    Uart InPort  = new Uart( Uart.dirReceive, CPU.pin14, Uart.dontInvert,
                             Uart.speed2400, Uart.stop1 );
    char c, x;
```

```
    c = (char)0x01;
    while (true) {
      if (OutPort.sendBufferEmpty()) {          // One character, then pause
        OutPort.sendByte( c );
        CPU.delay( 700 );                        // >60 ms, time to send
        if (!InPort.byteAvailable()) {
          System.out.print( "X" );
        }
        else {
          x = (char)InPort.receiveByte();
          if (c != x) {
            System.out.print( "|" );
          }
          else {
            System.out.print( "-" );
          }
        }
        ++c;
      }
    }
  }

};
```

The code outputs a stream of '-' characters to the console if loopback works, '|' characters if an incorrect character is received, and 'X' characters if no character is received after a sufficient delay. We increment the character being sent and received to ensure that only live data is accepted, not any stale data that might be in the buffer if an error occurs, and only output when the transmit buffer is empty.

Once you prove out basic half duplex operation, try strings of characters at full speed, with buffering, and then advance to a full duplex pair of paths. If everything's working properly, you should be able to transmit virtually limitless numbers of characters at close range with no errors. (You could put error counters in the code to monitor performance, because you don't want to sit there watching for an error indication that should never come.)

Extending the Project

The biggest limitations of this project are that it doesn't handle very high data rates — if you were going to remote a modem, for example, you'd want it to run at 56 Kbps, not 2.4 Kbps — and it only supports one active full duplex link.

Different radio modules are the key to addressing these issues. We found a variety of other possibilities, some suited to building a few prototypes, and others targeted at production runs.

- **Radiotronix** — Their business is building radio modules, including products for rates as high as 152.34 Kbps (www.radiotronix.com/prodsel.asp). Their Wi.232DTS module runs in a low-power mode up to 38.4 Kbps, or in a high-power mode at up to

152.34 Kbps. Either way, the modules handle multiple links in the same spectrum and are suitable for battery-driven applications. The Wi.232DTS-EVM evaluation module — $80 in relatively small quantities — would simplify building a few prototypes, as would the rapid development kit (`www.radiotronix.com/products/ prodevalrnnm.asp`).

■ **Microhard Systems** — This company is in the business of complete serial wireless modules, too. Their MHX-910 OEM Wireless Modem Development Kit (`www.microhardcorp .com/products_oem_910_dev.htm`) is intended to support product development prior to production runs using their MHX-910 modules, but everything's there you'd need to build a link for your own use. The module itself runs in the 900 MHz band (there's an equivalent one for the 2.4 GHz band), uses a single 5-volt supply, and supports rates to 115.2 Kbps. The kit adds RS-232 transceivers, connectors, power supplies, and status indicators. Cost could be a factor, as the kit is $200 in quantity.

■ **Pegasus Technologies** — Addressing much the same market as the units from Radiotronix and Microhard, the PTSS-2003 Developer's Kit (`www.sss-mag.com/ ptss2003dk.html`) includes transceiver modules, demo boards (including RS-232 interfaces, connectors, and batteries), antennas, cables, software, and other bits and pieces. The Developer's Kit (including enough for a full wireless link) is about $400. The modules themselves run at rates up to 115.2 Kbps.

■ **Texas Instruments** — The TI evaluation board (`focus.ti.com/docs/toolsw/ folders/print/msp-us-trf6900.html`) is as expensive as the one from Pegasus Technologies, at $200 apiece, but only supports rates to 38.4 Kbps. The radio hardware is more capable than that; the data rate limitation is elsewhere on the board. The key advantage of the TI product is that it's highly configurable for a variety of error codes, frequencies, and other characteristics, giving you a platform for more advanced experimentation.

■ **RF Monolithics** — This is a high-volume manufacturer of radio modules (`www.rfm.com/products/vwire.htm`); they expect you to work out the details of a complete system. They do offer development kits, such as the DR1200-DK (`www.rfm.com/products/dr12.pdf`), able to run at up to 19.2 Kbps using firmware in an associated 8051 microprocessor. The development kit runs about $350, and includes both ends of the link.

Somewhat harder is to build a wireless USB data link. Inserting a radio link transparently into a USB connection means you'll need to run at data rates of at least 1.5 Mbps for low speed USB or 12 Mbps for full speed. You *must* supply power at the remote (non-PC) end too, because USB devices expect to get power from the USB connection. We found development kits from Eleven Engineering (`www.elevenengineering.com/kits/catalog.php?s=DK`) good for 1.5 and 3.0 Mbps, and Micro Linear (`www.microlinear.com/products/index.asp`).

The truth be told, we did find a complete USB RF modem (`www.maxstream.net/ products/xstream/pkg/9xstream-usb.php`) by MaxStream (`www.maxstream.net`). It's available from Sealevel Systems for $250 each (`www.sealevel.com/product_ detail.asp?product_id=813&Wireless_USB_900_MHz_RF_Modem`). Of course, where's the fun in just plugging it in?

Summary

Wires are just one way to get signals from one place to another; and cheap as they are, they can be wildly inconvenient. Wireless links transport signals too, and the widespread availability of certified radio modules means you can break the wire yourself, requiring only that you understand the signal well enough to do the underlying engineering necessary to choose the right radio modules.

In the Den or Family Room

part

Home Television Server

In stark contrast to the pre-rural electrification farmhouse of yore, the geek's house is a thicket of networks. Considering anything that passes a signal (and hence information) from one point to another as a network, here are the ones we identified in our own home:

➤ **Wired and wireless telephone** — Plain old telephone service (POTS) voice over paired telephone wires or radio signals. Wireless telephone includes both radio connections from wired telephone jacks to handsets and ones from remote sites to cellular handsets.

➤ **Wireless PDA** — Radio connections from remote sites to handsets, supporting e-mail and POTS voice.

➤ **Broadcast television** — Radio connections from remote sites to local antennas and coaxial cable distribution, supporting 6 MHz standard definition (SDTV) analog signals.

➤ **Cable television** — Coaxial cable from the cable company's external demarcation point to a modem supporting broadband Internet. Other people also use the cable television feed distributed throughout the house for both SDTV and HDTV reception.

➤ **Satellite television** — Coaxial cable from an external parabolic dish and low noise amplifier through amplifiers and switches supporting reception of digital MPEG-2 encoded television signals.

➤ **Wired and Wireless LAN** — Ethernet over Cat 5 or Cat 6 cable, or IEEE 802.11 radio, interconnecting the broadband modem, switches, routers, servers, and client computers supporting IP networking and Internet access.

➤ **Others** — There's a wide variety of other information connections you might have, including weather and rain sensors, X-10 power line communications, wireless garage door openers, the doorbell/intercom combination, atomic clocks, and wireless cooking thermometers.

More than anything, this list shows that up to now the cost of electronics has been high enough to force connections to be tailored to the specific information being sent — no one network technology carried all the different signals used in a home.

chapter 3

I will hire a team of board-certified architects and surveyors to examine my castle and inform me of any secret passages and abandoned tunnels that I might not know about.

Peter Anspach,
The Evil Overlord List

in this chapter

☑ Analog and digital video distribution

☑ Re-architecting consumer television

☑ New PC technologies: Thermally Advantaged Cases

☑ New PC technologies: PCI Express

☑ New PC technologies: Serial ATA

☑ Networked TV software

☑ DVD authoring

IP networks are changing that distribution. The telephone companies learned years ago that it was less expensive and more reliable to run their voice networks using Internet IP packet switching than the older voice circuit switching, and are finally learning that they can benefit by extending telephone service to consumers over IP networks using voice over IP (VoIP) technology. In this chapter, you'll see that although the standards for television over IP aren't as well defined as they now are for voice, you can gain significant benefits by moving your television reception off coaxial cable networks and onto your LAN.

Project Description

Figure 3-1 shows a high-level block diagram of a conventional analog television receiver. The analog signals from the studio camera and sound system are selected by the tuner from among all the ones available, recovered and separated by the demodulator and decoder, then amplified and output in a form you can sense. The entire information path is analog, although it may embody digital controls.

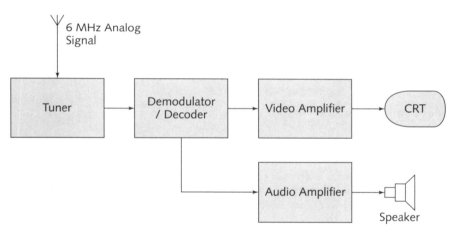

FIGURE 3-1: Analog television receiver

The analog signal format isn't essential anywhere along the signal path except as light coming from the subject or sent to your eye. Cameras using charge coupled device (CCD) sensors output digital images natively, and LCD displays work better with digital inputs than analog ones. Television started in analog form because the available electronics technology could only support analog processing at reasonable cost.

Perhaps the strongest impetus towards digital television was satellite broadcast, because the economic viability of the satellite system is dominated by the number of distinct television channels it can support. Ignoring overlap at the channel edges, the 6 MHz channel required for U.S. analog television permits at most 12 channels in a standard 72 MHz transponder. Wider channel spacing to eliminate interference due to overlap reduces that number noticeably.

A 6 MHz spectrum segment can support 20 to 40 Mbps, however, depending on the waveform, so digital television offers the opportunity for more channels in the transponder so long as one channel fits into no more than 1.6 to 3.3 Mbps. The compression technologies devised by the Motion Picture Experts group (MPEG) solve that problem, reducing the approximately 160 Mbps raw video signal (720 × 480 pixels per frame, 30 frames per second, and an assumed 16 bits per pixel) significantly:

- **MPEG-1** — 1.5 Mbps at VHS video tape quality
- **MPEG-2** — 3-10 Mbps at DVD quality
- **MPEG-4** — 4.8 Kbps to 4 Mbps at varying resolution and quality

The completely digital TV receiver in Figure 3-2 — including a digital display — looks a little different from the analog receiver in Figure 3-1. The tuner still selects a modulated waveform from the available spectrum, but the demodulator outputs error-corrected bit streams rather than analog waveforms. Those bit streams are decoded from the MPEG format to raw video and audio data.

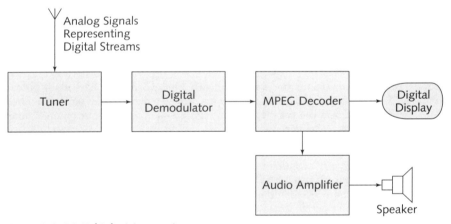

FIGURE **3-2: Digital television receiver**

In the digital receiver of Figure 3-2, there are many ways to transport the signal besides the lossy, inconvenient coaxial cable so common in conventional TV systems.

System Diagram

For example, consider the extended digital television system of Figure 3-3. We've taken some minor liberties in the figure, such as that not all compression is MPEG, and that some digital video (such as from games) will be uncompressed. Don't let those simplifications make you miss the point, however, which is that you really can't pick out the box labeled TV from the figure.

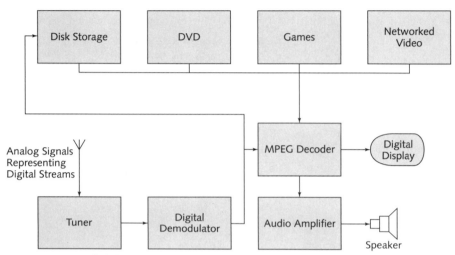

Figure 3-3: Extended digital television system

Depending on what components you're working with, Figure 3-3 could have many different realizations. Use a combination satellite receiver and digital video recorder (such as a DirecTV TiVo) with a television, and you get the setup in Figure 3-4, in which we've grouped functions into blocks representing available consumer electronic devices.

The most interesting aspects of Figure 3-4, though, are the disk storage and networked video functions, because there aren't common consumer electronics devices — other than PCs — for them. If we redraw Figure 3-4 to use a PC, and assign all the functions reasonably done by a PC that way, we get Figure 3-5. Yes, there's another simplification, in that you can use either amplified speakers or an external stereo or home theater amplifier, but again, that's not important. What's important in Figure 3-5 is that, with the exception of a tuner and demodulator, a PC can do everything the system requires. Build the tuner and demodulator into the PC in the form of an add-in card, and the PC does everything.

Not that this plan is without flaws. The most significant one is that you can't get add-in cards that let your PC decode digital satellite or cable TV signals, because those systems use proprietary formats with closed encryption standards. Instead, you have to use one of their set top boxes, but because few set top boxes accept channel change commands from your PC in a convenient way, you'll have a harder problem to solve. We've put some hints in the "Extending the TV Server" section at the end of this chapter to help you get started. If you're using broadcast TV or analog cable, though, you're set.

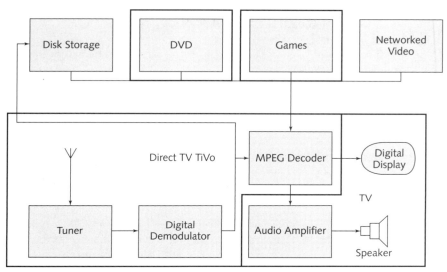

FIGURE 3-4: Digital television with consumer electronics

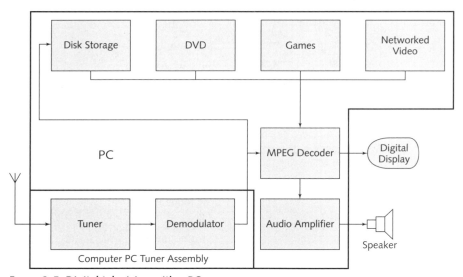

FIGURE 3-5: Digital television with a PC

Digital Cable Adoption

We've seen no end of propaganda saying the future is digital cable, blah blah blah. Perhaps that point of view is somewhat overstated.

We went through literally a decade of being told our neighborhood was to get cable Internet within six months, first by the local cable operator, then by TCI after they bought the system, then by AT&T when they bought TCI, and finally by Comcast. In the meantime, we abandoned cable TV altogether in favor of satellite TV, and disconnected our cable TV feed. We used ISDN and later fixed wireless from Sprint Broadband for Internet access. (Yes, DSL is missing from that list. We'll save the DSL stupidity rant for another book.) In 2004, however, the miracle happened, Comcast upgraded our area, and we installed a cable modem. Service with the cable modem has been fast and dependable.

However, Comcast seems to be incapable of believing we don't want cable TV too, along with Internet access. In that vein, the installation was fascinating in what it unintentionally revealed, because the installers had a list of who had what on our fiber node. Not only were we the first to sign up for cable Internet service — not surprising since it had just become available — there were also literally no digital cable TV subscribers on the node. Not merely just a few, but zero, despite it having been in the area for years.

We did an informal poll of our neighbors to find out why they don't use digital cable, and discovered reasons like these:

- Too expensive altogether, along with constant rate hikes
- Too expensive to have a set top box for each TV
- Ridiculous to sign up for digital cable when the analog cable service has been so bad

Regardless of the reason, cable operators and consumers seem to be at loggerheads. We think cable operators could go a long way towards solving this problem by creating an open standard for digital TV, much as their Cable Labs R&D center (www.cablelabs.com) did for cable modems, which would create consumer-level competition in the cable TV set top box market. If that happened, you'd be able to buy PC add-ins that natively understood how to talk on a digital cable TV system and could deliver all the advanced features those systems were capable of. As it is they haven't done that, so you're forced to kludge a PC together with a set top box. There's no gain for the cable operators keeping set top box capability out of the PC, because you *can* make a PC look like a remote control. There's a big loss for you, because it's a pain to kludge a connection between PC and set top box, and the resulting combination doesn't necessarily let you use all the features the set top box offers.

Stupid. And not in the funny way like in Invader Zim, either ("It's not stupid, it's advanced!").

Returning to Figure 3-5, you can either put all the functions in a single PC or network multiple PCs together across a LAN and distribute the functions. The simplest realization of that idea is to split out the disk storage to a file server with huge drives, letting you share storage and recordings across several PCs and, therefore, several TVs. That approach requires running the coaxial cable to every PC serving as a television, though, which means you're installing single-purpose cabling and have to deal with the noise and losses radio frequency (RF) transmission over coax creates.

There's a better way. You can partition the system as in Figure 3-6, separating the reception and recording functions from the playback and decode ones. Your LAN now becomes the video distribution network, sending error-free streams from one PC to the next; the only PC needing the RF signal is the one with the tuner.

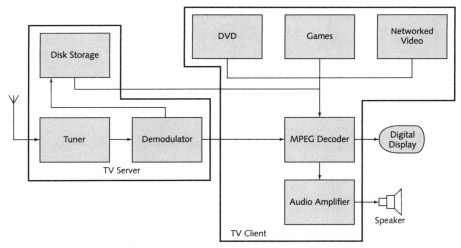

FIGURE 3-6: Networked TV distribution

You can connect as many clients to the server as your LAN can support. You're only looking at 3–10 Mbps for MPEG-2, so in principle you should be able to handle 5 to 25 clients on a 100 Mpbs LAN (assuming no other network traffic and depending on video compression rates) without any collisions or pauses in the video. You can distribute video on a wireless LAN too so long as you scale the number of active clients to the capacity of the system.

The most serious limitation you'll have to resolve with this system design is that you need a tuner for every independent viewer you want to be able to support. If there are three active televisions that all need to broadcast a different channel, you'll need three tuners. You'll see ways to meet that requirement in the next section.

System Design

You can build this project to be anything from simple to sophisticated. The requirements we set for our design were these:

- Receive broadcast video

- Provide full personal video recorder (PVR) functionality, including pause, rewind, and fast forward/reverse, and including selection of shows to record

- Compress recorded video, and provide sufficient storage for many hours of recorded video

- Record video on a server for playback on multiple networked clients

- Play recorded video, MP3 audio, and DVDs

- Provide a client user interface suitable for use on the TV screen, from across the room, via remote control

- Create DVDs from recordings or other sources, including video editing and authoring

If you match these requirements against the key components in Figure 3-6, you get the requirements for those components:

- **Tuner** — The tuner (which incorporates the demodulator function) inputs RF or composite video signals and outputs a compressed digital video stream. The tuner selects the channel you're watching, extracts the analog video signal, and then digitizes it (or a direct composite video signal input) into a bit stream. A compressor (see Video CODEC below) reduces the size and data rate of that bit stream, which then appears at the tuner output.

- **Disk storage** — A standard quality DVD runs at a little over 5 Mbps, or 0.625 MBps. Multiply by 3600 and you get about 2.25 GB per hour, a number you can use to start to size the disk storage you want in your server. You'll want the large disks directly in the server so you can avoid the network traffic you'd see between a file server and the TV server if you put the disks on a remote machine. It's better to save the network bandwidth for video distribution to clients.

- **Video CODEC** — Including both compression and decompression, and indicated as the MPEG decoder in the figure, the video CODEC (coder/decoder) is responsible (in the server) for compressing video headed to disk storage, and (in the client) for decompressing video headed for the display. Compression is typically part of the tuner, because it's usually done in hardware to meet the need to do compression in real time, but faster processors have improved the quality of compression possible in software. The day is not that far off when a PC can do real-time, high-quality MPEG-2 compression entirely in software, although it's less clear why you'd want to use essentially the entire processing capacity of a PC to replace the function of a chip costing about one percent of the price of that PC.

- **Server processing** — The TV server software imposes only a small load on the host processor. Software able to do MPEG-2 compression on the processor would let you use a wider range of TV tuner cards, but will consume even the fastest processor to handle just one stream.

  A more useful way to consume processor cycles is in authoring and burning DVDs. You'll compress raw, uncompressed AVI files, and may need to transcode (decompress and recompress) MPEG-2 files to reduce the data rate. That processing runs on the PC, and although the software we worked with wasn't able to exploit the hyperthreading architecture of the Intel processor we used, the raw speed helps keep authoring time to a minimum.

- **Client processing** — Each television needs client processing in an attached PC to provide the on-screen user interface and to play video stored on the server computer. Playback includes both network access and MPEG-2 decompression (see Video CODEC); MPEG-2 decompression is less demanding on the processor, and although it was a challenge to do in real time with the first Pentium and Pentium II processors, it's easily done now in software on even the slowest processor you're likely to have lying around. Processing on the client PC should also include the capability to play a DVD from the local drive so you don't need a separate DVD player.

- **Remote control** — Even though you can use a wireless keyboard and mouse to control the client software, it's awkward to need all that hardware. More useful is to have a remote control similar to what you'd normally use to control a television. You can use either radio or infrared signals; infrared doesn't go through walls, so is less likely to have inter-room interference issues, but you'll need to be careful if you're also using infrared to control a satellite or cable TV set top box.

We decided to only require reception of off-the-air video for the version we describe here, but the components we used are capable of being adapted to drive satellite and cable TV set top boxes, feeding a composite or S-Video signal into your video capture device.

You'll need to decide how much storage you want. If you follow the lead of the first generation TiVo PVRs, you'll want up to 35 hours of capacity, which translates into 35 hours * 2.25 GB per hour = 78.75 GB. Translate that to disk capacities (which use factors of 1000 and not 1024) and you need 85 GB of space. (In practice, first-generation TiVos shipped with 40 GB disks, but use a range of compression rates — that's why the specification is for *up to* 35 hours.) Table 3-1 uses the same approach, and includes two different compression rates. The 0.625 MBps rate assumes MPEG-2, as above; the 3.614 MBps rate assumes video compressed to an AVI format with little processing and higher quality. Total storage numbers in the table are rounded up.

Table 3-1   Video Storage Requirements

Hours Stored	Date Rate (MBps)	Total Storage (GB)
1	0.625	3
2	0.625	5
4	0.625	9
8	0.625	18
16	0.625	36
32	0.625	71
64	0.625	141
128	0.625	282
256	0.625	563
512	0.625	1,125
1	3.614	13
2	3.614	26
4	3.614	51
8	3.614	102
16	3.614	204
32	3.614	407
64	3.614	814
128	3.614	1,627
256	3.614	3,253
512	3.614	6,506

Table 3-1 notwithstanding, we simply decided to cram as much storage into the box as we could conveniently fit. You'll need Windows 2000 or later to address the very large files and partitions associated with video; depending on the software you use, you may or may not be able to segment the storage into multiple partitions. If you can't, then you'll need to use RAID striping to combine multiple disks together. You can do that with Windows Server, or with hardware.

Server PC

If you're not concerned with video editing and DVD burning, you can skip this section and use most anything you have lying around. The requirements for the Sage TV software we used (client and server) are merely as follows:

- Microsoft Windows 98 Second Edition or Millennium Edition, or Windows 2000 (SP3 or later) or XP. Windows 9X won't handle the large files and disks well.

- 128MB RAM (256MB recommended)

- Intel Pentium III or later, or AMD Athlon. Either way, the processor should run at 600 MHz or faster

- Supported TV tuner card and video card; make sure you have both composite video capture inputs and television outputs to get the most from the system

Being the performance fanatics we are, however, we built up a PC specifically for this project, selecting these components in particular:

- 3.6 GHz Pentium 4 (Prescott) CPU for compression performance when burning DVDs

- Thermally advantaged case to meet the higher cooling demands of the Prescott CPU

- Added fans at CPU air case inlet and case front, including noise reduction gaskets

- Four 200 GB disks. The 250 GB Serial ATA (SATA) disks were hard to get, and 400 GB units didn't ship until after our publication deadline.

- RAID controller on the motherboard to simplify disk integration

Table 3-2 lists the key PC components we included. The processor, motherboard, disks, video card, and case are matched — the motherboard supports the processor power and socket interface, while the case is specifically designed to provide the extra cooling the processor requires. The video card works with the PCI Express graphics port made available by the motherboard.

Table 3-2   PC Components

Component	Source
Processor Intel 3.6 GHz Pentium 4 Processor 560	Intel www.intel.com/products/desktop/ processors/pentium4/index.htm
Hard Disk Seagate ST3200822AS (200 GB SATA) Quantity 4	Seagate Technology LLC www.seagate.com/cda/products/ discsales/marketing/detail/ 0,1081,599,00.html

Continued

Table 3-2 *(continued)*

Component	*Source*

Motherboard
Intel D915GUX
	Intel
	`www.intel.com/design/motherbd/ux/`
	`index.htm?iid=ipp_browse+motherbd_`
	`d915gux&`

Thermally Advantaged Case
Antec SLK2650-BQE
	Antec
	`www.antec.com/us/productDetails`
	`.php?ProdID=92650`

PCI Express Video Card
ATI Radeon X600
	ATI
	`www.ati.com/products/radeonx600/`
	`index.html`

TV Tuner	Hauppauge PVR-250MCE
	`www.hauppage.com/pages/products/`
	`data_pvr250.html`
	
	Packages including the SageTV software, a Streamzap remote control, and one or more of the Hauppauge tuners is available from SageTV at `store.`
	`freytechnologies.com/Merchant2/`
	`merchant.mv?Screen=CTGY&Store_Code=`
	`SOS&Category_Code=SB`

PC-4200 Memory (two 256 MB modules)	Crucial
	`www.crucial.com/store/MPartspecs`
	`.Asp?mtbpoid=B3E1C344A5CA7304&WSMD=`
	`D915GUX&WSPN=CT3264AA53E`

DVD Burner
Sony DRU-710A
	Sony
	`www.sonystyle.com/is-bin/INTERSHOP`
	`.enfinity/eCS/Store/en/-/USD/SY_`
	`DisplayProductInformation-Start?`
	`ProductSKU=DRU710A`

Don't overlook the need for more than standard levels of cooling with the Prescott series of processors — the heat sink and case must, collectively, be able to dissipate 115 watts from the processor alone, and the power supply must meet that requirement along with the requirements of the memory, motherboard, and disk drives.

The PC industry refers to cases designed for these processors as Thermally Advantaged Cases (TAC). The key difference you'll see looking at a TAC unit is the presence of an air inlet on the side of the case directly in line with the CPU. Using the standard power supply and case rear fans, and adding fans for the CPU air inlet and case front, we measured the processor temperature to be no higher than 63°C under all processing loads.

We used four disks simply because that's how many SATA drives the motherboard supports. The RAID hardware controller on the motherboard only supports RAID striping for pairs of drives, however, so we used it to create two arrays. Those arrays show up in Windows as 372 GB each, reflecting the factor of 1000 disk makers use to convert bytes to KB, MB, and GB versus the factor of 1024 Windows uses. We set the second RAID array as a folder in the first because we dislike drive letters, but you could equally well make them independent drives.

We're assuming that readers of this book know how to build PCs and install Windows, so in this section we're only going to highlight parts of the server PC we built that are different than common practice. If you need more details on how to assemble and start up a PC, please see our *PC Upgrade and Repair Bible* (Wiley, 2004).

The first difference you'll see is the hole in one side of the case. There's a duct attached to the hold inside the case to direct cool air from outside the case straight to the CPU cooling fan. We interposed an 80 mm fan between the case side and the duct (Figure 3-7) to increase the air flow onto the CPU cooler. (As it happens, we used an Antec fan with blue LEDs, and wired it to a pulse width modulated fan connector on the motherboard. The result is that the LEDs flash and stay on more the hotter the system is.)

FIGURE 3-7: CPU cooling air duct with fan

We also used a soft gasket between the fan and the case side to help reduce noise from fan vibration. Figure 3-8 shows the details of the installation — the gasket is between the fan and the case side panel; fan screws inserted from the outside of the panel anchor the fan to the metal. Another set of screws anchor the duct to the fan. We used soft washers between the fan and the duct to further reduce noise.

FIGURE 3-8: Fan noise reduction gasket assembly

The case provides noise isolation mounts for the disk drives too. Figure 3-9 shows the stack of four drives we used for an aggregate 800 GB capacity.

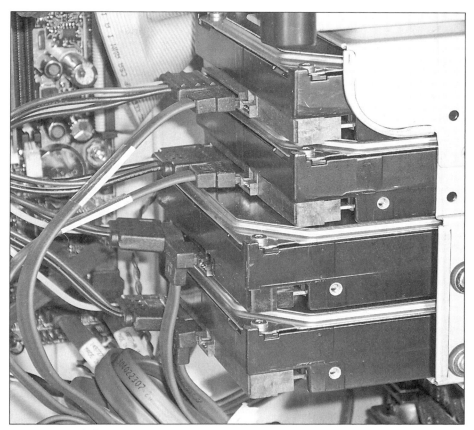

FIGURE 3-9: Disk drive mounting

The D915GUX motherboard (Figure 3-10) is somewhat different from the usual micro ATX board too — the processor socket is more dense, and the board hosts PCI and PCI Express sockets (but no AGP socket).

FIGURE 3-10: D915GUX motherboard

Figure 3-11 is a close-up view of the processor socket. Each of the little pads in the socket contacts a point on the processor. You must be extremely careful not to touch or bend the pads, nor to damage the contacts on the processor.

FIGURE 3-11: Pentium 4 LGA775 socket on D915GUX motherboard

Figure 3-12 shows the processor after installing it in the socket and closing the retention clamp. You ensure the processor is properly oriented, gently drop it straight down into the socket, verify it's located right, and latch the clamp down.

FIGURE 3-12: Pentium 4 processor installed in LGA775 socket

Figure 3-13 shows the PCI Express X1 connector, shown next to PCI connectors for size comparison.

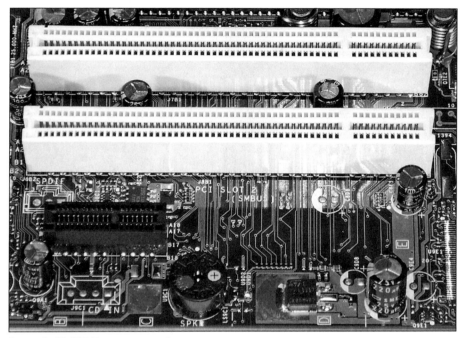

FIGURE 3-13: PCI Express connector

It's easier to mount the processor when the motherboard is outside the case, but you'll want to mount the CPU cooling fan after you install the motherboard. Figure 3-14 shows the cooling fan and heat sink.

FIGURE 3-14: CPU cooling fan

There's a specific process for attaching the cooling fan assembly to the motherboard involving turning the retention clips. It's important you get that process right, because if you don't the clips won't be secured properly and the cooling fan will either not be in tight contact with the processor, so it won't perform properly, or — far worse — it will fall off. Figure 3-15 is a close-up of the retention clip.

The Intel D915GUX motherboard follows a new interface specification (ATX12V 2.0) for the power supply too, adding four pins to the motherboard power connector (Figure 3-16). Keyed (shaped) sockets on the connector help make sure you'll orient the power supply connector the right way.

Many cases and power supplies — including the ATX12V 1.2 supply in the Antec case we used — don't have the necessary newer connector, so in addition to the now-common 12-volt auxiliary power connector, the D915GUX adds a disk drive–type connector to bring more power onto the motherboard. Figure 3-17 shows both the 12-volt auxiliary power connector (on the right) and the disk drive connector (on the left). We connected both to the power supply to provide the necessary additional power the motherboard and processor require.

FIGURE 3-15: Cooling fan retention clip

FIGURE 3-16: 24-pin motherboard power connector

FIGURE 3-17: Additional D915GUX power connectors

Figure 3-18 shows the motherboard PCI Express X16 connector above a PCI connector for comparison. The PCI Express X16 connector, which provides more bandwidth to the video card than PCI or even 8X AGP, is similar in size and position to the older AGP connector, and significantly longer than the PCI Express X1 connector in Figure 3-13. There aren't many PCI Express video cards on the market as we write this — the ATI Radeon X600 is one of only a few — but the market should expand rapidly as more machines with PCI Express motherboards are deployed.

You'll get the best TV video quality using an S-Video output from the video card to the television. We suggest setting the video card at 800 × 600 resolution, and 32-bit color. Don't forget a screen saver, particularly if you're using a large-screen projection TV subject to burn-in.

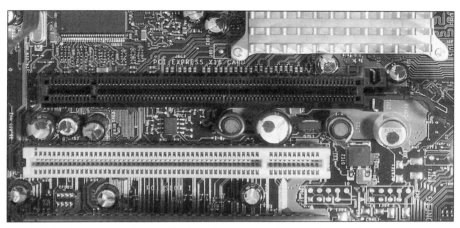

FIGURE 3-18: PCI Express X16 motherboard connector above PCI connector

Software

The hardware you choose will affect the capacity of your system, the number of simultaneous channels you can watch or record, and the quality of the video you see, but it's the software that determines how much you like the end result. Media Portal is available as open source on SourceForge.net (mediaportal.sourceforge.net), and looks very capable. If you're looking for a more ready-to-go software suite, however, SageTV is what you'll want. The software gives you capabilities similar to TiVo (Figure 3-19), including the ability to schedule future recordings by specific times or by what shows you want (Figure 3-20). In full-screen mode, the user interface is well suited to display on a television and control with a handheld remote.

FIGURE 3-19: SageTV recording options

The software not only gives you the client/server structure we've designed into the hardware, it extends that design to let you play MP3 playlists and DVDs, and to run multiple TV tuners in networked PCs. You'll start to see more network traffic into the server as well as out from it, so you'll want to make sure your LAN has the necessary bandwidth.

Multiple tuners, something we'd previously only seen on the DirecTV TiVos, give you more options when you're watching. Even if there's only one TV in use, multiple tuners can be useful when there are shows you want recorded while you watch something else, or when there are several shows you want to flip among. The presence of multiple tuners does more for watching multiple live channels than skip commercials, because it lets you pause playback, shift to other channels, and then return — because the video was on pause, you miss nothing in the process.

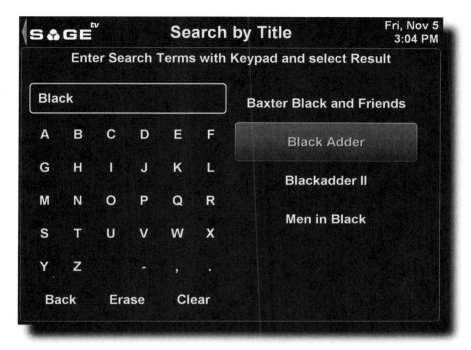

FIGURE 3-20: SageTV search by title

Video Edit and Authoring

Video editing and recording onto DVD (called *authoring*) remains one of the best applications of a fast, capable PC. You can do everything you used to do with a VCR, including preserving both off-the-air broadcasts and camcorder video, but do it with better quality and with editing to select just the parts you want. Your PC can do more than the standalone DVD recorders, too, because you can get software that's more capable than what's hardwired into the standalone units. You can now get dual-layer DVD burners too, enabling you to store about 9 GB (about 2 hours of standard quality compressed video) on a single disk.

That's the good news.

The bad news is that, despite having tried a number of programs, we've not found reasonably priced editing and authoring software we can recommend unconditionally. Here's our take:

- **InterVideo WinDVD Creator 2** — With a user interface (Figure 3-21) similar to that of Pinnacle Studio, we were prepared to like WinDVD Creator as much as we like WinDVD, which is our favorite DVD player software. Our initial work with it went well, but after we discovered it crashed regularly on files we'd pulled in with another manufacturer's video capture card and codec, we gave up. If you can be sure you'll never need a foreign codec, you might like WinDVD Creator. You can find the software at www.intervideo.com/jsp/WinDVDCreator_Profile.jsp.

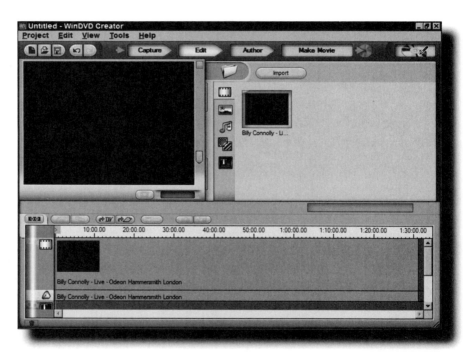

FIGURE 3-21: InterVideo WinDVD Creator 2

- **Pinnacle Systems Studio and Expression** — We've used Studio since we started making DVDs, and like it a lot. Unfortunately, we've had problems with it, too. The version of Studio we use, Studio 8, often fails to keep the audio and video in synchronization, and has a relatively slow MPEG-2 encoder. It's possible those problems have been fixed in Studio 9, but when we read part of the license agreement that gave them unlimited permission to make changes to our computers remotely, with no liability to them for problems created, we terminated the install. Pinnacle Expression is a basic authoring package and doesn't seem prone to the synchronization problems Studio has, so the pair give you the total capability you need. You can find the current versions of the software at `http://www.pinnaclesys.com/ProductPage_n.asp?Product_ID=1501&Langue_ID=7`.

- **Ahead Software NeroVision Express 3** — As we've come to expect from Ahead Software, NeroVision Express 3 was a solid, reliable program that on installation recognized and was compatible with the dual-layer Sony DVD burner we used. We found the user interface (Figure 3-22) a little clunky and dumbed down as compared to Pinnacle Studio, but if you can work past that, this might be the one to choose. You can find the software at `www.nero.com/us/NeroVision_Express_3.html`.

FIGURE 3-22: Ahead Software NeroVision Express 3

Regardless of the software you use, making a DVD consists of these steps:

1. Capture the source video as one or more clips. Use the best source format you can, such as S-Video, and — ideally — capture to disk with no compression or lossless compression. You'll want to preserve the choice of compression parameters for when you write the DVD, and multiple compression cycles only reduce the video quality.

2. Edit the video into a complete program. We generally combine all the clips together, leaving breaks only where we want menus to go on the DVD. Add any necessary sound tracks and transition effects.

3. Render the completed program to disk. Strictly speaking, you don't have to do this before you burn the DVD, but we've encountered enough problems in the authoring steps following this one that it's a time-saver to keep a copy of the final version. Editing and rendering go much faster if the source and destination files are on local disks, and faster yet if they are themselves on different physical disks.

4. Build the DVD menu (or menus if you have so many clips you're setting as chapters that you need to segment them) in your authoring software. Set a background image, number of menu items, item formats, and item images as you want, then test the menu operation. Testing is useful to make sure you've defined the menu the way you want.

   If you extract short video segments from the program or another source — say, 10 to 20 seconds — some programs let you set them as the menu item or screen background.

5. Burn the DVD and test it in a DVD player. Set the compression so the program adjusts the degree of compression to make the overall program just fit on the DVD, which will give you the least degree of compression and the highest video quality that fits on the DVD.

Extending the TV Server

Much to our surprise, we didn't think of many variations on this project, which probably reflects how well the version we describe turned out. The ones we came up with are:

- **Play DVDs from a remote drive.** The SageTV software only plays DVDs from a local drive. If you used the Media Portal software, you could make whatever modifications required so it would play from a remote drive shared on another PC, too.

- **Use multiple tuners.** You might do this on multiple PCs. Recording multiple streams at once is relatively simple — the only real complexity is that you'll need the SageTV Recorder software to control remote tuners on other PCs. The biggest issues in the entire effort will be getting the video signal to all the tuners and making sure you have your network equipped with switches and enough bandwidth.

- **Set up IR remote transmitters so SageTV can control set top boxes.** You can get many more channels on cable TV or satellite, but (because the data streams are encrypted and must be decrypted against data stored in a smart card) digital cable TV and satellite require you to use the provider's set top box. SageTV can control those boxes using infrared signaling through a transceiver you attach to the corresponding PC. We suggest using the USB-UIRT infrared transceiver (www.usbuirt.com, also available from SageTV at store.freytechnologies.com/Merchant2/merchant.mv? Screen=PROD&Store_Code=SOS&Product_Code=UIRT&Category_Code=HD).

Summary

TV doesn't have to be the constrained, simplistic enterprise most people are accustomed to. You can centralize the recording and video operations, distributing compressed video over your network. The result is a far more flexible system with which you can not only watch what you want, but also watch it where you want it.

Security Monitoring

More people than we thought seem to have vacation cabins. Not expensive, grandiose second homes, but literally cabins or small homes in remote places they use to escape the city they live in. These places are by their nature seldom occupied, making them more inviting targets for break-ins or vandalism than you'd like. There's good reason for security monitoring.

Project Description

Enter, however, your inner geek. Home security services may have their place, if you're careful to research the company, read their contract carefully, and test their response regularly, but paying someone else to provide and install monitoring electronics? Oh, please.

A security monitoring system is merely a collection of sensors driving a mechanism to generate an alert. There's a huge variety of sensors you can use, many kinds of alerts, and lots of techniques to prevent accidental triggering or hostile takeover. Nevertheless, at the core, a security system is just sensors, processing, and alarms. This project shows you the common sensors you have available (for more sophisticated sensors, see Chapter 6 on video surveillance in *PC Toys,* Wiley 2003), how they can be used, and some options for how you can generate alerts based on those sensor inputs.

System Diagram

Figure 4-1 illustrates the sensors and alerts idea. Sensors detect a condition and either close or open a switch; the switch closure triggers the processor and, depending on decisions software might make, can generate any of several alerts.

If my surveillance reports any un-manned or seemingly innocent ships found where they are not supposed to be, they will be immediately vaporized instead of brought in for salvage.

Peter Anspach,
The Evil Overlord List

in this chapter

☑ Monitoring a building

☑ Security system elements

☑ Sensors, processors, and alerts

☑ Interfacing to a PC

☑ Hardware interface software

☑ Generating e-mail automatically

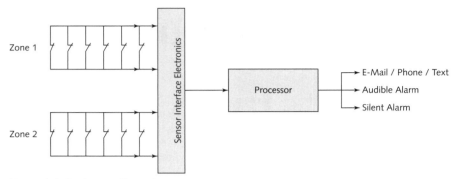

FIGURE 4-1: Basic security system

Basic security requires monitoring for unauthorized entry, so every potential entrance to the structure — windows and doors in most buildings — requires a sensor to detect an opening. That's potentially a lot of switches in even a relatively small building, because buildings often have many doors and windows, so to save money it's common to connect sensors into related groups called *zones*. You connect normally open switches in parallel (as in Figure 4-1), or normally closed switches in series. If any switch changes state, the interface detects it and notifies the processor. There's no way to tell which switch in a zone tripped, but you have localization to the level of the zone.

Sensors

Ignoring direct audio or video monitoring, security system sensors act to convert conditions to on/off representations, typically as switch closures or openings. You can build sensors for nearly anything; here (in no particular order) are the types we found readily available on the Internet:

- **Door and window** — Perhaps the easiest sensor type to build, door and window opening sensors work using either mechanical or magnetic switches. Pressure from the door or window frame holds a mechanical switch against a spring; opening the door or window releases the pressure and actuates the contacts. A permanent magnet mounted on the moving part of the door or window holds a small reed switch actuated; opening the door or window releases the reed switch.

- **Floor** — You can detect weight on floors with pressure-sensitive switches. The ones you can buy are relatively small — just a few square feet — so if you need to cover a larger floor space, you'll need to be inventive. Suspending a large floor on pressure switches probably isn't practical, particularly in existing buildings, but Hollywood-style infrared lasers or other optical sensors may be. If you have a large area to cover, however, you'll probably want to use motion detectors.

- **Motion** — Detecting motion is a good solution for seeing intruders in relatively large spaces, particularly ones where it's impractical to monitor the entire perimeter. The most common motion detectors use *passive infrared (PIR)*, a simplified form of imaging sensor that maps out the heat levels across the scene. PIR sensors have a specific field of view, and you may need multiple sensors to adequately cover an area. PIR sensors are subject to false alarms from medium to large size pets and other animals, something you'll have to consider in your overall system design.

More sophisticated motion sensors process live video, looking for changes in the image, and can track the moving elements with a motion camera pedestal. We described how to use a TrackerPod (www.trackerpod.com) that way in *PC Toys* (Wiley 2003).

- **Smoke or carbon monoxide** — There are many concerns you might monitor for besides break-ins, including fire and heater malfunction. The same sort of smoke and carbon monoxide detector technology you use in your home can trigger switches that feed your remote security system. If you use battery-driven units, be sure to replace the batteries regularly, because there's no practical way for the security system to test them. (What you *could* do, though, is to program your software to send you reminder e-mails periodically.)

- **Glass breaking** — One of the ways to circumvent a window alarm switch is to break the glass, entering without opening the window frame. Breaking glass creates high-frequency sound with well-known characteristics distinct enough that you can get sensors to listen for those sounds. The sensors will close a switch when they hear the right noise, triggering your alarms.

- **Wind, water, and temperature** — High wind, flood water or water in the basement, and freezing temperatures can all do significant damage. Measured data doesn't itself fit the on/off switch model directly, though, so you'll want to pick sensors that compare the measured value against a threshold and trigger switches based on those decisions.

- **Vehicle** — Your security system need not stop at the building walls. Vehicles that don't belong are one good indication of a potential problem, and can be detected with a low false alarm rate. Motion detectors are another good way to monitor outdoor areas, but are much more likely to generate false triggers.

- **Power failure** — It's not hard to generate an alert when an electrical circuit loses power. You can get monitors that generate a switch action, or can receive the warning in software from an uninterruptible power supply (UPS).

Monitoring for trouble and sending alerts is harder if all the power goes out. You'll need at least a UPS to make sure your power failure message gets out (we use APC units such as those at www.apc.com/products/family/index.cfm?id=23), but if you're *really* intent on having all the power you need no matter what, consider something like the Generac Guardian Air–Cooled 12KW Standby Generator (www.guardiangenerators.com/products/guardian7_15kw.asp), about $3,200. Connect it to a natural gas supply and you could probably run all winter long no matter how bad the local power.

Either way, make sure both your communications equipment and your computers still have power after the UPS kicks in, and test the system with the power cut to make sure you haven't overlooked anything. Test that the system powers up and resumes normal operation without any user interaction after power is restored, too.

Perhaps the least obvious sensor technology — one you're near constantly but never think about — is the vehicle detector. People tried many different technologies, including treadles to sense the weight on the tires, before settling on a coil buried in the pavement. A large enough mass of metal near the coil alters its magnetic properties enough to change the frequency at which an oscillator connected to the coil runs, a change you can detect with a frequency counter. There's some good discussion of how vehicle detectors work at both `www.tfhrc.gov/pubrds/septoct98/loop.htm` and `www.its.berkeley.edu/techtransfer/resources/pub/nl/01fall/loop.html`.

Processors

You have two fundamental options for the processor you use to control your security system. Commercial alarm manufacturers use dedicated processors, but you don't have to:

- **Dedicated** — A dedicated processor generally runs either no operating system or a real-time operating system designed for fast boots and without the complexity of Windows or Linux. The reduced complexity, combined with the ability to run nothing but your security software, makes them easier to make highly reliable, a valuable characteristic for a security system. The very simplicity of dedicated processors causes many of them to lack facilities useful in a security system, such as built-in Internet connectivity.

  Dedicated processors often have electrical interfaces designed for reading and writing digital and analog ports, reducing the cost of the overall system, and typically have software built in to manage those ports.

- **PC, Linux or Windows** — PCs are far more complex than dedicated processors, but in return offer far more capabilities and resources. Foremost among those are more sophisticated options for software development, including software libraries, and built-in Internet access. The more sophisticated hardware and software architecture comes at a price, though, in that it's harder to directly attach digital or analog devices, and harder to write software to work with those devices.

Despite the disadvantages, we chose to use a PC for the security system largely because it simplifies the job of issuing the alerts we thought appropriate for a remote building (see the next section). Given that decision, the key architectural question becomes how to interface the switches in the alarm sensors to the PC. Again, there are two fundamental options:

- **Take over existing signals** — You can adapt signals in the serial or parallel ports on a PC for digital inputs without an intervening processor. The parallel port can run in several modes, including a bidirectional mode that lets you input eight signals as a byte. You could use each of the eight signal lines to input a zone of switches; use a pull up resistor in each line and let the switches pull the line to ground. The Web site at `www.lvr.com/parport.htm` has extensive coverage of how to use parallel ports.

  You can use a serial port in much the same way, but (assuming you want to read asynchronous digital lines without an interface processor) the receive data line itself isn't useful for that purpose because the PC electronics expect to see framed characters on the line at specific data rates (see `www.lvr.com/serport.htm`). The input control lines — Data Set Ready, Data Carrier Detect, and Clear to Send in particular — will input an asynchronous level, but because serial port signals are nominally at ±12 volts, with a dead zone between ±3 volts, you can't just use the switches and pull up resistors directly. Instead, you'd need RS-232 receivers (there's a selection guide for Maxim parts at `para.maxim-ic.com/compare_noj.asp?Fam=RS232&Tree=Interface&HP=Interface.cfm&ln=`) at the interface. When you consider how few signals you get, the difficulties of writing appropriate software, and the need to create an interface board to host the level shifter chips, it's more pain than it's worth.

■ **Use an interface board** — The easier, and more flexible, alternative for interfacing sensors is to use a board with enough electronics to interface to the digital and (perhaps) analog sensors you're using on one side, and to a standard PC interface (USB or serial port, for example) on the other. This approach has the advantage of not being inherently limited in the number of signals you can tie to, and if you use an existing commercial product, you're likely to have a software interface library available. We like USB interfaces when there's a choice between that and serial ports, because USB is faster with lower latency, and because serial ports are more prone to configuration problems.

Alerts

How you handle the output side of your security system depends on what you're trying to accomplish. Systems have used a siren or a combination of sirens and remote monitoring for years; that remains a viable approach today. There may not be enough people near a home in a remote location to even hear a siren, though, so in this application you'll need remote monitoring.

There are two basic ways to do remote monitoring — you can receive a notification when something needs attention or you can check in on the site periodically. Combinations of the two are perfectly reasonable, and there are many ways to do each:

■ **Notification** — The most common approach to remote monitoring is to send notifications to a person or site when the on-site system detects something of importance. For many years, nearly the only communications option was a direct modem-to-modem phone call to the monitoring point. Today, using the Internet, your options range from e-mail and instant messaging to VoIP telephony and custom client/server applications.

■ **Polling** — On-site processing and detection is required to generate notifications, but some conditions, such as nearby flooding or piling snow drifts, are simply very hard to detect automatically. Video cameras stationed around the property that you can access remotely through a broadband Internet connection let you look in whenever you choose; microphones let you hear any ambient sounds.

■ **Combined polling and notification** — One of the weaknesses of notification systems is that they can only tell you what condition they sensed, not the cause. Polling systems have a complementary weakness, in that with one you can readily determine what's happening, but you can't know when something is happening. The combination of the two — notification and polling — is very effective, because you can use the notification to connect in to the polling sensors and analyze the situation.

We're only describing a notification system in this chapter; the TrackerPod chapter in *PC Toys* should give you everything you need to get started on the complementary polling system.

Parts and Designs

The simplicity of the open/closed switch sensor interface means there's literally no end to the number or type of sensors you can attach to your system. We've described a selection of sensors in this chapter, but perhaps even more useful is that we've given you leads to several sources for sensors. We've worked with Smarthome (`www.smarthome.com/securmap.html`) and Winland (`www.winland.com/security`) for some time, and had a successful relationship with Phidgets while we wrote this book, but there are many, many other sites on the Internet, such as the Home Security Store (`homesecuritystore.com`), you'll want to look into.

Systems

We'd anticipated, when we started writing this chapter, that the alerts would inevitably be e-mail or phone calls you'd receive from the system, because all the large alarm monitoring companies expect to sell you equipment, installation, and a lock-in contract for monitoring services.

We were wrong. Pleasantly surprised, but wrong. Smarthome apparently sells a lot of security systems, and in response to customers wanting a central monitoring service, has arranged to provide just that (see `www.smarthome.com/alarm.html`). You have to use one of the specific alarm controllers they sell, or verify the one you have is compatible with their service. With that constraint — which means you won't be doing your own processor or software — the installation, sensors, and power line backups are your design.

Sensors

Table 4-1 lists sources for representative sensors. We've assumed you'll want to use hardwired sensors — ones that use pairs of wires between the sensor and the processor — because they're more reliable (and often less expensive) than wireless ones. Many of them require a power source; if you don't use an uninterruptible power supply to drive them, you'll want to be sure you're warned about power failures.

Table 4-1 Security Sensors

Sensor Type	Sources
Door and window	Magnetic sensors—Smarthome www.smarthome.com/7352.html
Floor	Smarthome www.smarthome.com/5195.html www.smarthome.com/790901.html
Garage door or gates	Smarthome http://www.smarthome.com/7455.HTML
Glass breaking	Smarthome www.smarthome.com/glassbreak.html
Motion	Smarthome—indoor www.smarthome.com/secpirmotion.html Smarthome—outdoor www.smarthome.com/outdoormotion.html
Power failure	Winland www.winland.com/security/products.php?category_id=3
Smoke or carbon monoxide	Smarthome www.smarthome.com/7309.html www.smarthome.com/7497.html www.smarthome.com/79717.html
Vehicle	Smarthome www.smarthome.com/secvehicle.html Winland www.winland.com/security/products.php?product_id=18
Wind, water, and temperature	Smarthome www.smarthome.com/sectemp.html Winland www.winland.com/security/products.php?category_id=1 www.winland.com/security/products.php?category_id=2

Figure 4-2 shows the Winland Vehicle Alert system, consisting of the sensor embedded in PVC pipe, the control box, and the cable to run between the two. The sensor is protected in a pipe filled with sand, so you can directly bury it in a gravel drive. Put the sensor 6–8 inches down, regardless of whether it's in the drive or along it.

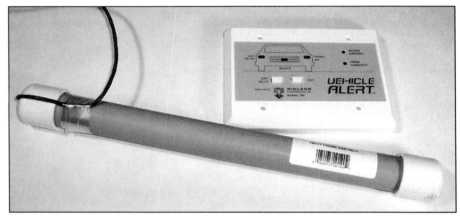

FIGURE 4-2: Winland Vehicle Alert

Figure 4-3 shows the interior electronics, including the connection points for the power supply, sensors (you can use two in parallel), and alarm contacts. The contacts are normally open, closing when a moving vehicle is detected. There are two sets of contacts, which would let you drive an X-10 Powerflash module as well as the security processor.

FIGURE 4-3: Vehicle Alert interior connections

Figure 4-4 shows your options for how to locate the sensor pipe to monitor a driveway. If you install a pair of alerts (this only works on a sufficiently long driveway), you can use the sequence of contact closures to detect whether the vehicle is coming or going. You'll need two control boxes to do that, not one box with two sensors, because you need a separate set of alarm contacts for each sensor.

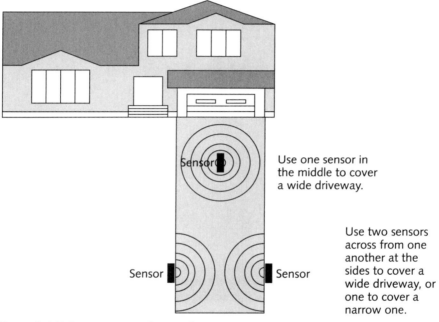

Use one sensor in the middle to cover a wide driveway.

Use two sensors across from one another at the sides to cover a wide driveway, or one to cover a narrow one.

Sensor

Sensor

Sensor

FIGURE 4-4: Driveway sensor placement

Figure 4-5 shows the Winland WaterBug, a moisture sensor you can use to detect either flooding or too-low levels in a water tank. The sensor at the bottom of the photo is upside down to show the four water contacts. Any conductivity between any pair of the contacts will trigger the sensor. The sensor detects basement flooding by placing it on the normally dry floor, and detects lack of water by mounting it underwater, making sure the lowest pair of contacts (or all four) are at the minimum desired water line. The contacts on the control module, from left to right, are input power, ground, two for the sensor, contact common, and the normally open and normally closed relay contacts.

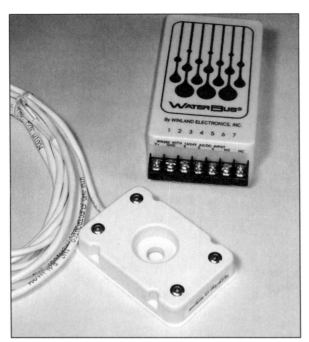

FIGURE 4-5: Winland WaterBug

Figure 4-6 shows a typical magnetic door switch installed on a sliding glass door. The switch is in the upper corner where the door opens, with the wires trailing into the wall. The magnet is mounted on the door, and slides to the left away from the switch. The installation wasn't difficult, because careful removal of the molding above the door provided a place to work to get the wires pulled through.

FIGURE 4-6: Magnetic door switch

Figure 4-7 shows a collection of analog sensors built for the PhidgetInterfaceKit described in the next section. The pipe section at the top encloses a passive infrared motion sensor in a form (if you attach more pipe to the back and terminate in a proper enclosure) sealed against the environment, while the boards at the bottom are a light sensor and temperature sensor on the left and right, respectively.

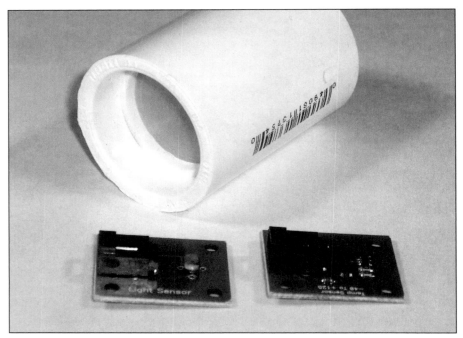

FIGURE 4-7: Phidget analog sensors

Hiding the wires running from sensors to the processor is an art. You'll probably need to make and repair holes in walls; multiple Internet sites offer help on how to do the repairs. There's an entire collection of tutorials on drywall repair at www.diynet.com/diy/wa_drywall/ 0,2036,DIY_14407,00.html; we also found doityourself.com/wall/drywall repairs.htm useful.

Plan the installation carefully to keep wires out of site and minimize the amount of wall repair you have to do. It's easiest to run wires through an attic or unfinished basement; but you'll have to use at least in-wall rated wire (www.smarthome.com/8460.html), and you should use plenum rated wire if the cables go through areas that are part of the ventilation/heating/air conditioning airflow path. You may be able avoid running wires inside walls using flat wire (www.smarthome.com/8470.html)—a little patching compound and paint over the tape should make it invisible.

Processors

A PhidgetInterfaceKit 8/8/8 (www.phidgets.com/index.php?module=pncommerce &func=itemview&KID=Admin&IID=85), shown in Figure 4-8, connects sensors to the PC. The terminal block on the left ties to eight digital inputs, with ground terminals at either end of the block. The terminal block on the right connects to eight digital outputs, also with grounds on either end, and with pull up resistors on each output. Eight analog output ports are along the bottom, while the top has DC power input and output connectors on the left, a two-port USB hub in the middle, and the USB connector to the PC on the right. You only need to power the device separately if you plan to use the USB hub; otherwise, the interface draws all required power from the PC USB connection.

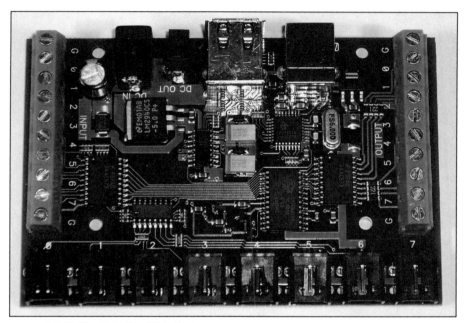

FIGURE 4-8: PhidgetInterfaceKit 8/8/8

Figure 4-9 shows the processor core of our system design. If you don't want to use a pre-built temperature warning sensor, you can read a thermistor directly into any of the Phidget analog inputs — see Chapter 8 for how to convert a resistance into a voltage reading and how to convert that voltage reading into a temperature measurement.

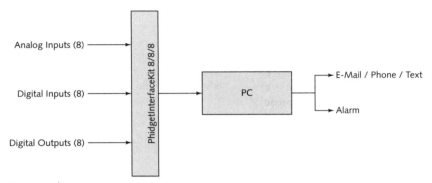

FIGURE 4-9: Security system design

Any PC that can run the version of Linux or Windows you choose has enough capability to run an alarm system (after all, you can run one on a simple, low-speed embedded processor — see the sidebar *Choosing an Embedded Processor*). Wipe the PC's hard disk clean, and install just the software you need. Minimizing what's on the machine will make it more reliable, and reduce the opportunity for software conflicts. Don't forget to protect the machine with a hardware or software firewall, and good anti-virus software if you'll connect it to the Internet. Don't use the machine for anything else — have a second machine if you need to, and keep this one in a closet. E-mail and Web browsing are the most likely ways to bring in spyware and viruses, things you really don't need to have on a machine you're counting on as part of a security system. Don't think of it as a PC, think of it as the processor running the security system.

Choose the location where you install your processor so all the wires can easily run back to there. Pick an out-of-the-way place with adequate space, ventilation, power, and communications.

Choosing an Embedded Processor

You have many options if you decide to build your system with a dedicated processor instead of a PC. There's a good list of embedded Java boards on the Internet (java.fritjof.net); included there is the Parallax Javelin Stamp (www.parallax.com/javelin/index.asp) we use in Chapter 8 for controlling a barbeque to smoke ribs. The Javelin Stamp would work well for this application—you could use its embedded UART virtual peripheral and supporting classes to communicate through a modem, for example—as would the Parallax Basic Stamp (www.parallax.com/html_pages/products/basicstamps/basic_stamps.asp) should you be more at home with that language.

Alerts

Installing a siren, if you choose to use one, is a matter of placing it where it can be heard and running wires back to the interface. You can drive a siren from one of the digital outputs, but because the output can pass no more than 20 milliamps, you'll need to use a relay or transistor to buffer the higher power needed to drive the siren. Figure 4-10 shows a sample drive circuit for a DC siren using the same approach we use to drive the fan in Chapter 8. Even if it requires more interface hardware to remote it, consider locating the siren away from the PC, and out of reach, to make it harder for an intruder to disable.

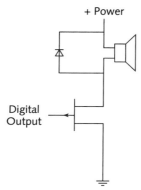

FIGURE 4-10: Siren drive
circuit

The Home Security Store has a page of sirens on their site (homesecuritystore.com/ ezStore123/DTProductList.asp?p=2_1_1_1_0_0_17). The loudest ones on that page work at 12 volts, and require no more than 1.5 amps. Choose a relay or drive transistor to fit those parameters and you won't have to worry about overdriving your system should you connect a different siren later. If you might ever connect multiple sirens in parallel, use an appropriately larger driver and power supply. Don't forget to count the power required by the siren when you're calculating the size you need for a UPS.

Software

We wrote a simple Windows dialog application, using the Microsoft Foundation Classes (MFC), to control the security system, patterning its functionality on that of a simple dedicated alarm system. The requirements we set were these:

- Monitor zones corresponding to contact closures on any of the eight Phidget digital inputs.

- Assume the Phidget interface board is and remains connected while the software is running.

- Track the time of last change on every zone.

- Generate an e-mail to a specified address any time there's a contact closure.

- Include the zone generating the alarm and the date/time in the e-mail.

There's a lot more you can do in the software. We've described some enhancements you might take on at the end of this chapter.

Hardware interface

The PhidgetInterfaceKit 8/8/8 (which we'll call an 888) connects up to eight zones to a PC through a USB port. The 888 uses the Human Interface Device (HID) standard USB protocol and drivers built into Windows, eliminating any requirement to install system-level software. The HID standard was designed to support mice, keyboards, joysticks, and similar devices. If you think about the 888 in that light, it looks like a *very* capable joystick having lots of switches (digital inputs), axes (analog inputs), and indicator lights (digital outputs). The fundamental Phidget HID message interface is documented on the Web site (`www.phidgets.com/modules.php?op=modload&name=Sections&file=index&req=viewarticle&artid=34&page=1`), while Microsoft documents the programming interface to HIDs on their Web site (`msdn.microsoft.com/library/default.asp?url=/library/en-us/intinput/hh/intinput/hidclass_cea65f4b-2fd8-43f2-a658-c5bed4a19e91.xml.asp?frame=true`).

Programming to the HID specification is somewhat complex, so we used the `phidget20` library (`www.phidgets.com/modules.php?op=modload&name=Downloads&file=index&req=viewdownload&cid=1`), which encapsulates the interface to the HID device into a collection of functions. There are two elements of the `phidget20` interface you could use — the `PhidgetManager` identifies the connected Phidget devices and will notify your code when one is attached or detached from the USB bus, while the `PhidgetInterfaceKit` operates the device itself. We assumed the 888 was always connected in our code; see the discussion later for how you might extend the code to detect attach and detach operations.

The HID protocol is not interrupt driven — you have to poll the device for status. The `PhidgetInterfaceKit` application programming interface (API) follows the usual open/read/write/close pattern; we open the device and keep it open, then read it in a polling loop, sleeping between reads. There are three ways to implement that pattern in MFC:

- Override the application's OnIdle method, so your routine can be called when the application message queue is empty. We wanted to control how often we polled the 888, which could be done this way by monitoring the clock, but it's clumsy.

- Use a Windows timer (via the WM_TIMER message) to periodically invoke a processing routine. This is a good approach, which we discarded only because we had no data on how long the calls into the phidget20 library might take, and don't want to keep the main application thread running for any significant time.

- Create a worker thread using AfxBeginThread whose responsibility is to loop continuously polling the interface. This is the approach we used.

We encapsulated the entire Phidget interface in the CPhidgetInterface class, including the worker thread creation and management. Creating the thread within an object is simpler than often thought — we defined the thread procedure as a static member function:

```
//--------------------------------------------- ReadThreadProc -----------
static UINT ReadThreadProc( LPVOID lpParam )
{

    CPhidgetInterface* cpi = (CPhidgetInterface*)lpParam;
    int nResult;

    cpi->m_ThreadResult = 0;
    while (!cpi->m_ExitThread) {
        if (!cpi->m_bPause || !cpi->m_hParent && cpi->m_cpikInfo) {
            nResult = CPhidgetInterfaceKit_read( cpi->m_cpikInfo );
            if (nResult) {
                cpi->m_ThreadResult = nResult;
            }
        }
        Sleep( 100 );
    }
    cpi->m_ExitThread = FALSE;
    return( cpi->m_ThreadResult );
};
```

You have to include the function in the class declaration (within the .H file), not in the implementation (.CPP) file unless you choose to exploit one of the Microsoft language extensions. We put it in the declaration.

A static member function can, by itself, only reference static members of the class. We used the parameter passed to the function to provide the address of the parent CPhidgetInterface object, giving us a way to access all parts of the object, including flags, to pause the polling or cause the thread to exit, and a variable to allow monitoring for errors from the device read. The loop runs until told to exit, pausing 100 ms between polls.

What the loop doesn't do, however, is examine and act on any data received by the read operation. That's because we've used the ability of the `phidget20` library to install callback routines that serve to notify the application when there's been a change in the device state. We installed callbacks for both digital and analog (sensor) input changes, and wrote those callback routines (also static member functions) to post messages to the main application window's message queue. Those callback functions are almost identical:

```
//---------------------------------------------- IK_DIChangeHandler -------
static int IK_DIChangeHandler(struct __CPhidgetInterfaceKitInfo *IFK,
                             void *userptr, int Index, int Value)
{
    CPhidgetInterface* cpi = (CPhidgetInterface*)userptr;

    // Signal the digital change
    VERIFY( PostMessage( cpi->m_hParent, WM_DIGITALCHANGE, Index, Value ) );
    return 0;
};

//---------------------------------------------- IK_SIChangeHandler -------
static int IK_SIChangeHandler(struct __CPhidgetInterfaceKitInfo *IFK,
                             void *userptr, int Index, int Value)
{
    CPhidgetInterface* cpi = (CPhidgetInterface*)userptr;

    // Signal the sensor change
    VERIFY( PostMessage( cpi->m_hParent, WM_SENSORCHANGE, Index, Value ) );
    return 0;
};
```

The messages we post are in the user-defined application message space (that is, above 0x8000). We connect them in the application using an MFC macro in the message map:

```
ON_MESSAGE(WM_DIGITALCHANGE, OnDigitalChange)
ON_MESSAGE(WM_SENSORCHANGE, OnSensorChange)
```

The processing routines get the standard wParam and lParam parameters, having these declarations:

```
void CGeekSecurityDlg::OnDigitalChange( WPARAM wParam, LPARAM lParam );
```

where wParam is the zero-based index of the zone that changed and lParam is the new Boolean value, and

```
void CGeekSecurityDlg::OnSensorChange( WPARAM wParam, LPARAM lParam );
```

where wParam is again the zero-based index of the zone that changed and lParam is the new sensor reading. Our code only acts on the digital input changes, ignoring the analog ones. OnSensorChange is where you'll hook in new code to process data from analog temperature sensors, light sensors, motion sensors, and the like; in general, what you'll want to do is to define minimum and maximum threshold values for each analog sensor, and then report out an alarm condition from OnSensorChange if the reading goes outside those limits.

Filtering inputs

The software has to filter the changes reported by the hardware, because you only want certain changes to trigger an alarm. In the current software, for example, only switch closings generate the alarm; opening the switch back up does not. We implemented that filter directly in the code in the last few lines of the processing for WM_DIGITALCHANGE by testing the new zone status value:

```
//----------------------------------------------- OnDigitalChange --------------
void CGeekSecurityDlg::OnDigitalChange( WPARAM WParam, LPARAM LParam )
{
    int nIndex = (int)WParam;
    BOOL bValue = (LParam ? 1 : 0);

    ASSERT( nIndex < MAXZONES );
    m_zcgLines[nIndex].SetCheck( bValue );
    m_zcgLines[nIndex].SetTime( CTime::GetCurrentTime() );
    UpdateWindow();
    if (bValue)
        SendAlarmMessage( nIndex, bValue );
}
```

We didn't filter multiple triggers of the sensor, so if you happen to use a switch with very slow bounce characteristics — slower than the 100 ms loop time — you might want to either slow the polling loop or filter so you don't send multiple e-mails when the switch bounces. Similarly, if you do slow the loop a lot, you might want to combine multiple e-mails into a single one reporting all the zones that are triggered.

Sending e-mail

There are (at least) two approaches for sending e-mail in Windows: the Messaging Application Programming Interface (MAPI) and direct implementation of the Simple Mail Transfer Protocol. MAPI has some advantages, such as the ability to use its address book, but we decided not to use it because it may not be installed on all machines, and because recent Office security patches from Microsoft change MAPI so that user intervention is required before an application like GeekSecurity can actually send a message, something inappropriate for unattended operation.

SMTP is complex to implement, however, so rather than do that we used a nice class written by PJ Naughter (www.naughter.com/smtp.html). We didn't need all the functionality of his class, though, and wanted to provide persistent storage of the addressing and server parameters. We therefore encapsulated his code with a class of our own, requiring only code such as this to send a message:

```
//----------------------------------------------- OnTestemail -----------------
void CGeekSecurityDlg::OnTestemail()
{
    CEmailNotification emnTest;

    emnTest.SetSubject( "Test alarm system e-mail" );
```

```
emnTest.SetBody( "If you can read this\nthen the send worked.\n" );
if (emnTest.Send())
    MessageBox( "Test e-mail sent successfully." );
else
    MessageBox("Test e-mail send failed.", NULL, MB_ICONHAND );
}
```

All the other message parameters, including server, authentication, addressee, and sender, are maintained in the registry and configured via a dialog box. The constructor for the CEmailNotification class reads the registry, while the destructor writes changed values to those parameters back to the registry.

User interface

Figure 4-11 shows the main dialog window for the GeekSecurity application. For each of eight zones, it gives the zone name (included in the alarm e-mail), a checkbox to indicate if the zone has tripped the alarm, and the time the zone last changed status.

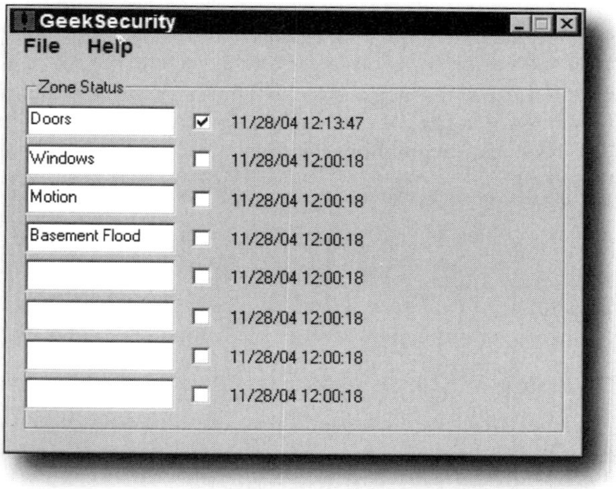

FIGURE 4-11: GeekSecurity user interface

We built the CZoneControlGroup class to manage rows in the window, and then created an array of elements of that class, one per row. We save the zone names into the registry in the OnExit method, and read them back in the OnInitDialog method.

Extending the System

There are many ways to extend the security system beyond what we've shown in this chapter. From a hardware perspective, you can add different kinds of sensors for specific applications. Don't be limited by conventional thinking — for example, you could use a sensor like the Memsic 2125 Dual-axis Accelerometer (www.parallax.com/detail.asp?product_id=28017) to detect when someone picks up or moves an object, possibly linking the sensor readings in wirelessly.

The software we wrote is relatively simple. Here are some ways you could extend it:

- A Phidget digital output will let you turn on a siren using the circuit in Figure 4-10. You'll use the write function from the `PhidgetInterfaceKit`, and should synchronize the write call with the operation of the worker thread, because you can't assume the library is re-entrant.

- The GeekSecurity code assumes a persistent connection to the Internet. You could revise it to automatically dial a connection if necessary, send the e-mail, then disconnect. The WinInet functionality in the Microsoft Platform SDK provides what you need — see the MSDN article Establishing a Dial-Up Connection to the Internet (msdn.microsoft.com/library/default.asp?url=/library/en-us/wininet/wininet/establishing_a_dial_up_connection_to_the_internet.asp). You'll likely want to focus first on the function `InternetAutodial` (msdn.microsoft.com/library/default.asp?url=/library/en-us/wininet/wininet/internetautodialhangup.asp?frame=true), using the `INTERNET_AUTODIAL_FORCE_UNATTENDED` flag.

- PJ Naughter wrote another useful class, one to send Short Message Service (text) messages (www.naughter.com/mfcsms.html). Using a cell phone enabled for SMS service, you could send alarm notifications to the cell phone you carry.

- Our code assumes the 888 is connected when the software starts up, and that it remains connected as long as the software is running. You could use the `CPhidgetManager` to detect attach and detach events, which would allow handling accidental or intentional unplugging of the interface. Attach and detach events would have to be coordinated with the `CPhidgetInterfaceKit`, since opening or holding open a device that's not connected doesn't work very well.

- Our implementation assumes eight digital input ports. You can extend the code to use a 16-port interface just by changing the `MAXZONES` constant, extending the dialog box, and recompiling. More difficult is to handle more than one PhidgetInterface; we'd approach that by using the board serial numbers, which are passed to the `PhidgetManager` attach and detach handlers.

- The code stores e-mail authentication for username and password in the registry. That's insecure; better would be to keep them in encrypted form.

- The GeekSecurity software receives changed Phidget analog sensor readings, but currently throws that information away. If you wanted to process information from temperature, light, motion, or other analog sensors, you'd need to establish thresholds to categorize readings into normal or alarm states. That requires code to store thresholds, compare new readings against the thresholds, and send alarms if necessary. You calibrate some of the sensors (such as temperature) for readings based on absolute value, while the direction of change of the analog values is the useful information for some of the sensors; for example, the motion sensor (which detects movement in one axis across the sensor) values indicate which direction the movement is in, while the light sensor values get higher for brighter light.

- Our implementation sends an e-mail immediately when a zone triggers, which allows no time to disable the alarm when you enter the building. You'd fix that by adding a delay from when the alarm triggers to when the software sends e-mail, along with an alarm disable button (perhaps with a password) in the user interface. You might want to add alarm enable and disable states, along with an exit delay once you arm the system.

- Zones are assumed to be normally open in the software. You could add a checkbox for each zone defining whether it's normally open or normally closed, and generate the alarm e-mail when the state changes from normal.

Summary

Security systems all consist of sensors, processing, and alarms. You can use a simple USB interface to tie sensors to a PC, and then apply as much sophistication in the processing software as you need. The sensors you choose are limited only by your imagination, as are the ways in which you generate and transmit alerts.

Television Mute on Phone Ring

Telephones aren't always where you can hear them readily — less so if the television is turned up loud — and even reasonable volume on the television can lead to missed calls. It's easy to detect rings, though, and with the right electronics you can turn off the television sound when a ring happens.

Project Description

This project combines some simple modules together, one to detect telephone rings, and one to pass or mute sound. Hooked together, they're a complete device and one you can use anywhere. Figure 5-1 shows the system concept — the ring detector monitors the telephone line and, when a ring signal is sensed, outputs a control signal to the actuator. The actuator determines how long to keep the sound muted, and connects to the audio subsystem of the television to accomplish the muting operation.

There are many ways to implement the system, such as the following:

> **Ring Detector** — The detector can sense the ring signal on the telephone line, or could sense the ring sound from telephones connected to the line. A more extreme approach would be to sense the ring waveform sent to wireless telephones.

> **Actuator** — The actuator can mute the amplifier itself, change the volume of the signal input to the amplifier, or interrupt the signal before it gets to the speakers. It can use several different control paths to accomplish its task, including wireless, direct wiring, or power line control wiring.

You can do more than connect the project to your television — it connects equally well to your home theater or stereo, and is useful for muting games as well as video and audio.

Despite its proven stress-relieving effect, I will not indulge in maniacal laughter. When so occupied, it's too easy to miss unexpected developments that a more attentive individual could adjust to accordingly.

Peter Anspach,
The Evil Overlord List

in this chapter

☑ Telephone signals

☑ Detecting the ring

☑ Designing a complete muting system

☑ Circuit diagrams

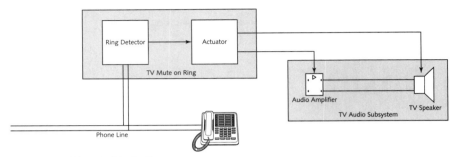

FIGURE 5-1: TV mute block diagram

Parts and Designs

The most constrained part of the design is the ring detector, because the telephone company supplies a standardized signal on the line, and all connected equipment must conform to that interface. Both voice and ring signals are alternating current (AC) signals; voice is up to about 4 kHz and a few volts, while the ring signal will be between 20 and 86 Hz, and between 40 and 150 V.

Ring detector

The first question, therefore, is how you will detect the ring signal. A simple way, if you're willing to dedicate the modem on a PC to the task, is to let the modem do the work. Windows will tell your application when a ring occurs with the Telephony Application Programming Interface (TAPI) `LINE_LINEDEVSTATE` message. If you're writing in C++, you can use MFC (as we've done in this book). Microsoft's "Creating a TAPI Connection Using CTapiConnection" article at `msdn.microsoft.com/library/default.asp? url=/library/en-us/dntapi/html/msdn_ctapic.asp` will get you started with TAPI and MFC. Your program will have to use the ringing information to get the control signal to the television, but there are several good ways to do this that we discuss later in this chapter.

Alternatively, you can use a circuit to detect the ring independent of any PC. The left-hand image in Figure 5-2 shows the Radio Shack Fone Flasher 2, which provides a loud ringer, a flashing light, or both when the phone rings. The right-hand image shows the connection to the piezoelectric module, across which you could tap to generate a control signal. The device connects to the power line as well as the telephone line, so there's no high voltage inside — you might want to think twice about modifying one of these for your ring detector.

FIGURE 5-2: Radio Shack Fone Flasher 2

We also found modules on the Internet designed for use as ring detectors. Figure 5-3 shows the ELK Products model ELK-930 doorbell and telephone ring detector. If you look closely at the figure, you'll see the board is perforated to let you separate the three modules (two doorbell and one telephone) into individual elements. Each has four connections, and requires no external power. The doorbell modules connect to the 24 VAC signal in parallel with the doorbell itself; the telephone ring detector connects across the phone line. Both module types provide an open collector transistor output you can use for the control signal.

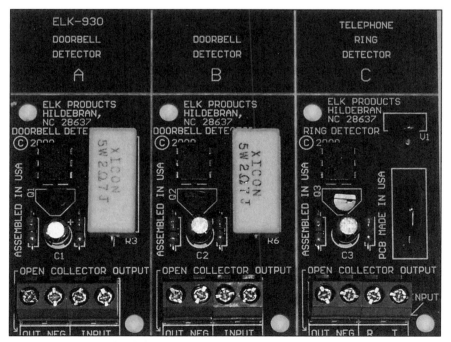

FIGURE 5-3: ELK-930 doorbell and telephone ring detector

Table 5-1 shows you where to find both units.

Table 5-1   Telephone Ring Detectors

Ring Detector	Source
RadioShack 43-178 Fone Flasher 2	Radio Shack www.radioshack.com/product.asp?catalog% 5Fname=CTLG&product%5Fid=43-178
ELK-930 Doorbell and Telephone Ring Detector	Smarthome www.smarthome.com/1221.HTML

Alternatively, you could also design your own circuit, such as the one in Figure 5-4. The incoming telephone line signal is applied across the series stack of a capacitor, pair of Zener diodes, signal diode, and resistor. The capacitor blocks all DC from the circuit, and should be rated to withstand the high input voltages. The back-to-back Zener diodes block any AC signals (such as audio) smaller than the ring signal, and should be rated at 10–20 V. The optoisolator ensures that the high voltages on the telephone line do not appear on the control circuit, while the diode cross connected across the optoisolator limits the voltage the optoisolator sees when reverse biased.

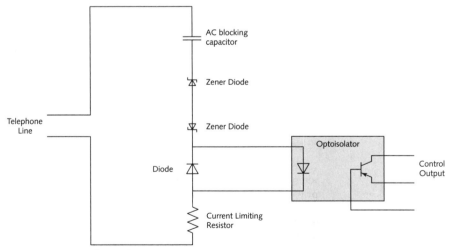

FIGURE 5-4: Typical ring detect circuit

The end result of the circuit is that the optoisolator output turns on whenever a ring voltage is present, much as the ELK unit open collector output does.

Actuator

Once you have a signal activated on ring, be it in software or hardware, you must use that signal to mute the television output. There are many ways to mute the sound. Here are three:

- Transmit an infrared muting command to the television.
- Interrupt the signal between the tuner and audio amplifier.
- Interrupt the signal between the audio amplifier and speakers.

Another approach would be to interrupt the power to the audio amplifier, but that's relatively hard on the equipment. We don't recommend it.

Perhaps the easiest way to implement the actuator (Table 5-2) is with an infrared command to the television. You could couple the Javelin Stamp (Chapter 8) or Basic Stamp (Chapter 1) to your ring detect signal and to a serial port infrared transceiver, and use the processor to both learn the mute code and transmit it. If you have a digital video recorder (DVR), such as a TiVo or the system in Chapter 3, you could pause the playback the same way.

Table 5-2   Actuators

Actuator	Source
Jon Rhees USB Universal Infrared Receiver Transmitter	Jon Rhees `www.usbuirt.com`
Luc Degrande. Serial Universal Infrared Receiver Transmitter	Luc Degrande `users.skynet.be/sky50985`
X-10 PF284 Powerflash	X-10 `www.x10.com/security/x10_pf284.htm`

X-10
UM506 Universal Module
	X-10
	`www.x10.com/automation/`
	`x10_um506.htm`

If you're using the TAPI modem interface instead, you could use the USB infrared transceiver in much the same way, except you'd use a software interface instead of a control signal, letting you implement the entire project with just a PC, some plug-in hardware, and some software. Using the mute command, incidentally, solves a knotty design problem, which is how to decide when to restore normal sound. Using the built-in mute function lets you restore sound with your normal remote control, while using a direct electrical interface requires you implement the mechanism to restore sound yourself.

You can also combine a hardware ring detect with a PC-operated infrared transceiver. The USB or serial port infrared transceiver still works in that design; the issue becomes how to interface the ring detect circuit into the PC.

- If you use one of the open collector signal devices, such as the ELK-930, a pull up resistor completes a circuit from the positive power line, through the resistor and open collector driver, to ground. You can tie a standard digital input to the open collector/resistor junction.

- If the digital input you connect to the junction is that of an RS-232 transmitter, you can tie the RS-232 signal into the ring detect or data set ready line of a serial port.

- Alternatively, if you use the junction signal to drive a standard TTL logic buffer, you can toggle the paper out signal line on a standard parallel port.

- A USB interface is much more complex, but there are interface chips to help you there too, such as those from Future Technology Devices International (www.ftdichip.com/FTProduct.htm). If you provide external power to the USB interface, you can probably avoid needing an embedded microprocessor (USB has very strict power management requirements if you're drawing power from the bus).

You don't, however, have to use infrared and mute the TV. Assuming a stereo television, a pair of relays wired into the audio signal path will do the job too. Your design has to connect the ring detect signal to the relays, and has to maintain the integrity of the audio circuits to preserve sound quality. Here are some ideas:

- If you don't have a telephone line connection near the television, you'll need to remote the signal. You could use the same radio technology as for the Wireless RS-232 Link (Chapter 2) or the Remote Control Finder (Chapter 4), because all you need to do is carry one signal from one point to another.

- Instead of a radio connection, you could use X-10 power line technology. In its simplest form, you'd use the PF284 Powerflash to create a power line transmission when the ring detector fires, and the UM506 Universal Module to open and close the audio circuits. You'll need two UM506 modules for stereo, one for each channel.

Figure 5-5 shows the X-10 approach. If the PF284 sends the same house code and unit code (that is, address) as is received by both UM506 modules, the ring detector will control the television directly, so you'll only get a brief sound interruption when there's really a ring sounding. If you set them to different addresses, you can use software in the control PC, such as HomeSeer (Chapter 9), to decide how long to keep the sound turned off.

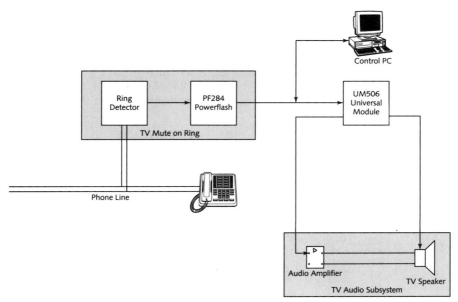

FIGURE 5-5: X-10 television muting

Modifying the inputs to the audio amplifier within a television is likely to be difficult. A better alternative is to open the connection to the speakers. Keeping a proper load on the amplifiers is a good idea, so you could use a double pole, double throw relay with load resistors. Figure 5-6 shows the idea; make sure the load resistors are sized for the amplifier power output levels. Be very careful working inside a TV (or don't do it) — televisions with picture tubes contain lethally high voltages that persist well after the TV is shut off or unplugged.

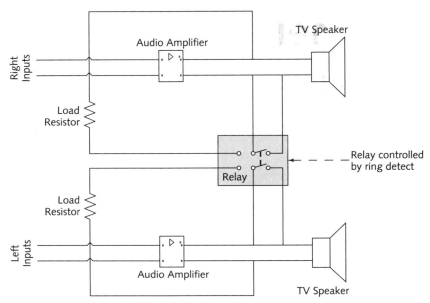

FIGURE 5-6: Speaker muting

You could use a similar circuit, and one that's far easier to install, to interrupt the line-level signals between the television and your stereo or home theater pre-amplifier, although in that case (instead of load resistors on the amplifier output) you'd want to connect a 600–1000 ohm resistor across the pre-amplifier inputs when muted to make sure the amplifier stays silent and doesn't pick up noise or hum.

Summary

Using the telephone ring signal to mute the television (or stereo — it works the same way) is a perfect example of how, in a Geek House, you can make things work the way you want. You don't have to keep the volume down because you're expecting a call — you just have to have the right electronics, ones you can readily design and build yourself.

In the Kitchen and Dining

part

III

Anything Inventory

We have a lot of conversations where one of us is at a store calling back home to ask "Do we need anything else from here?" Whether the topic is DVDs, groceries, wine, or anything else, the answer given usually depends far too much on the vagaries of memory, because in addition to needing to know what's required for some upcoming event or project, answering requires knowing what we already have.

Project Description

Given a little discipline, life can be far more organized. Virtually everything manufactured and sold at retail has a unique identifying number, its Universal Product Code (UPC), and is marked with a barcode image (see Figure 6-1) to let optical scanners read the code. Barcodes themselves are simply an optical encoding for information — it's the combination of barcodes and a standardized information format, the UPC, that lets a scanner recognize objects from their barcode. The characters are encoded by the width of the vertical lines and spaces in most barcodes; the type shown in Figure 6-1 is a two-dimensional barcode. The differing line heights in the figure have no significance to the scanner.

The Anything Inventory project lets you inventory anything that has a UPC barcode, giving you the tools to read the barcode, identify the item, and store it in a database. Use it for your kitchen pantry, DVDs, CDs, bottles in the wine cellar, books in your library, a house insurance inventory, or most anything else. You can count how many of each item you have, and export your database in a format you can process with Microsoft Excel or most database programs.

I will not use any plan in which the final step is horribly complicated, e.g. "Align the 12 Stones of Power on the sacred altar then activate the medallion at the moment of total eclipse." Instead it will be more along the lines of "Push the button."

Peter Anspach, *The Evil Overlord List*

in this chapter

☑ Barcodes and UPC codes

☑ Internet UPC lookup

☑ Barcode scanners

☑ Applications, including collections, inventories, and stores

☑ Implementing and extending the software

FIGURE **6-1: Barcodes identify everything**

System Diagram

Figure 6-2 shows the essential components of the Anything Inventory system: a barcode scanner, software, and a data source so you can readily look up scanned UPC codes. The components in the figure are the barcode itself; the barcode scanner, which reads the optical barcode and outputs its electrical equivalent; the PC and software, which control the entire system; and the Internet and a remote database, which provide information letting you look up barcodes you've not scanned previously. Barcodes are unfortunately most often on the packaging but not on the actual item itself, meaning once you discard the packaging you've lost the ability to scan the item.

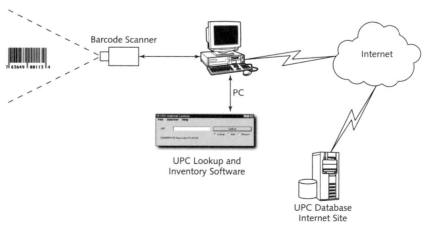

FIGURE **6-2: A barcode scanner, software, and your PC do the work**

Here's more detail on what each component does in the overall system:

- **Barcode Scanner** — In principle, you could simply type the UPC codes for inventory items into your PC, but that's tedious and unreliable. If you're like us, those two problems are enough to kill the idea of having an inventory (we're not terribly patient). The barcode scanners we found, including the modified CueCat scanner we describe later in the chapter, enter the scanned data in as if you'd typed it yourself.

- **PC and Software** — Our idea is that the PC maintains one or more inventory files listing what you've scanned, how many you have on hand, and other information. Actually reporting out your inventory is easier done in a spreadsheet or database office automation program than by writing reporting software, so we kept the software small and simple with an export function.

- **UPC Database** — It's also tedious and unreliable to have to enter the description of every item you scan for the first time, so the project needed a data source against which the software can look up items not already in the local database. The *Internet UPC Database* (www.upcdatabase.com) is an open source group effort to provide just that, so we've integrated its use into the software.

Barcodes and UPC codes

A one-dimensional, or *linear*, barcode is a sequence of vertical lines — bars — and spaces used to represent numbers or alphanumeric characters. In some ways, the electrical signal corresponding to a barcode's sequence of light and dark as you scan from the start to the end of the barcode is similar to the signals you find on a serial (RS-232) data line. A barcode has a start code, the encoded data, and a stop code that corresponds to the start bit, data bits, and stop bit on a serial line.

Barcodes are also similar to serial port data in that there are message structures imposed on the raw data encoding. For barcodes, those message structures are called *symbologies*, and they define how much and what type of information the barcode carries. Of the many different barcode symbologies, there are two specific ones, with some variants, that you're most likely to need to process in a home inventory application, and which our Anything Inventory software processes:

- **UPC** — The grocery industry in the United Stated adopted the first widespread barcode, the Universal Product Code (UPC), in 1973. The most common version of UPC, called UPC-A, consists of 12 digits broken down as shown in Figure 6-3. Starting at the left of the number, the first digit identifies the number system code. The next five digits identify the manufacturer, using code assignments defined by the Uniform Code Council (UCC, www.uc-council.org). The next five digits identify the specific product using codes assigned by the manufacturer, while the final digit is a check digit used to ensure that the barcode scanner reads the sequence correctly. There's no necessary physical or positional correlation between the digits and the bars; the barcode scanner only sees the widths of the black and white areas, ignoring their height and any printed elements.

The UPC-E variant is a fixed-length abbreviation of UPC-A including only a total of eight digits. Six of the UPC-E digits are derived from the UPC-A code.

FIGURE 6-3: UPC-A structure

■ **EAN** — The European Article Numbering (EAN) standard is based on UPC (indeed, UPC is the subset of the thirteen-digit EAN-13 standard formed by eliminating the first digit). EAN is widely used outside the United States, and for some applications, such as books, in the U.S.A. The first 2 or 3 digits of the EAN-13 barcode are a country code, followed by 9 or 10 digits for the item code and a check digit. The 978 country code indicates that the item code holds 9 digits of an ISBN (International Standard Book Number). In deference to the country code terminology, 978 is often said to refer to Bookland. The ISBN check digit, completing the usual 10-digit number, is omitted, but the EAN check digit performs the same function, and the ISBN check digit is readily recomputed from the 9 digits themselves.

PC and software

Guided by the Anything Inventory software, your PC will record what you scan. We set these requirements for the software before we wrote it:

■ Permit barcode entry from the keyboard or a barcode reader that generates what looks like keyboard input.

■ Record each item's barcode, description, and the inventory quantity in a database.

■ Add and remove items from inventory, and look up codes without adjusting inventory.

■ Record the dates when each item is originally entered, last added to inventory, and last removed from inventory.

- Look up the item description for scanned barcodes on the Internet if a connection is available.

- Export the inventory data in a format suitable for processing and reporting by other programs.

Figure 6-4 shows the user interface for the software. We took a minimalist approach — you pick the function you want (Lookup, Add, or Remove), enter the UPC or EAN-13 barcode number (you can have either or both in the database), and either press Enter or click the button in the window. The modified CueCat barcode scanner we use (see "Parts and Designs" later in this chapter) enters the barcode data as keyboard input and follows it with an Enter, so once you set the function a swipe of the scanner enters the data and performs the operation.

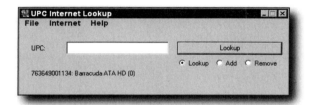

FIGURE 6-4: Anything Inventory UPC Internet Lookup software

Figure 6-4 shows the result after we scanned the barcode on the package from a Seagate hard drive. The digit sequence 763649001134 is the UPC-A barcode, and breaks down like this:

- 7 — The number system code

- 63649 — The five digit manufacturer code (which corresponds to Seagate Technology LLC)

- 00113 — The manufacturer's product identification number, corresponding to the specific drive

- 4 — The barcode checksum

The software's File menu contains the following commands, most of which should be familiar from other Windows software:

- **Open** — Inventory files created by the Anything Inventory software have the extension .upc. If you've previously saved an inventory file, you can reload it with the File Open command, or by double-clicking on it. (You'll have to configure Windows to link the UPC extension to the EXE file for the latter to work.)

- **Save** — You save or update an inventory file with the File Save command. If you've not yet defined a name for the inventory file, the program invokes the File Save As command for you.

- **Save As** — You initially save an inventory file with the File Save As command, or save an existing file with a different name. File Save As will warn you if you attempt to save over an existing file.

- **Load CSV** — The Internet site hosting the online database the Anything Inventory software uses also offers a subset of its entire UPC database for download to your PC. The download provides you a text file in the usual Comma Separated Value (CSV) format; the File Load CSV command will load that file into the program. You can save the result in the Anything Inventory native format with the File Save or File Save As commands.

- **Export Inventory** — You can write your inventory to a CSV file with the File Export Inventory command. The format is not the same as that used by Load CSV; and the first line in the file is a header identifying the contents of each column. Because it's possible to load a very large number of otherwise unused items into the inventory through the File Load CSV command, the File Export Inventory command filters the items exported to be just those whose last modification time is different from the creation time or which have been looked up on the Internet and not loaded from a file.

- **Exit** — The program closes. You'll be asked if you want to save your changes to an inventory file.

The file extension for the export file is intentionally `.INV` to prevent Microsoft Excel from auto-parsing the file as it would do if the extension were the more conventional `.CSV`. You can convert the CSV format to columns in Excel using the Data Text-to-Columns command; import the first column (the UPC) as text to avoid truncating leading zeroes in all-numeric codes.

The software holds the entire inventory in memory, presuming you'll not be tracking hundreds of thousands of items. That's not a great assumption if you load a data file from the UPC Database Web site — when we loaded the complete file (475,617 items as of mid-2004), the memory required ballooned to 150MB, while the saved inventory file grew to 32MB. If you plan to use a downloaded database as a pre-load, which you might want to do if you don't have continuous Internet access, one of the useful projects you could undertake would be to modify the software to couple it to a file-based database.

The Anything Inventory software processes both UPC-A codes and books. Figure 6-5 shows the difference, using our *PC Upgrade and Repair Bible Desktop Edition* as an example. The left image in the figure shows the product UPC-A; it's a generic code for a book from Wiley at a specific price. The right image in the figure is unique to the specific book, and is an EAN-13 code.

FIGURE 6-5: Book UPC-A (left) and EAN-13 ISBN (right) barcodes

The first 3 digits of the EAN-13 code are 978, for Bookland, followed by the first 9 digits of the ISBN (076455731) and a check digit (6). The software ignores the second set of bars appended on the right. The software forms the complete ISBN by taking the first 9 digits and appending a proper ISBN check digit, which for this ISBN is the digit 9.

The Internet menu contains these commands:

- **Enable** — You may or may not have an Internet connection when you're using the software. The Internet Enable command lets you control whether or not the program attempts to look up unknown scanned barcodes on the Internet. If there's a check next to the Enable item in the menu, Internet access is enabled and the program will try to do lookups. The check mark changes on/off status each time you select the command.

- **Force** — Items the program has looked up on the Internet are not looked up again when you later scan them. Enabling the Internet Force command ensures new lookups, letting you access new or changed data on the Internet.

The Help menu contains only an About command. You could write your own help file if you wanted.

UPC Database

The final system component is the online data source. Having to enter all the item descriptions manually would make the program too tedious to be useful, so we needed a database. All the databases we could find as files are neither free nor easily available, and updating them becomes a chore. Those factors drove us to look for online databases, a search that ended when we found the UPC Database site at www.upcdatabase.com.

The UPC Database is a public source for UPC lookups. The plain, unadorned page at www.upcdatabase.com/item.pl lets you look up individual UPC barcodes, returning an equally simple page with the item description or a message that the item is unknown. The site lets — and encourages — you to enter descriptions for unknown items, which is the primary way the database expands to include more items.

Our Anything Inventory software uses the Web pages directly to look up an item, passing the same URL to the server as the lookup page itself would generate if you entered the UPC there. The software then waits for the response page and picks out the result.

The UPC Database includes food, DVDs, and many other kinds of items, but doesn't include books. We puzzled for a while how to solve that problem, had the epiphany, smacked foreheads, and wrote the code to look up books through Amazon. Doh!

Parts and Designs

Literally any PC running Windows 2000 or later with an Internet connection will do for the Anything Inventory, although substantially more memory than the minimum for Windows is a good idea for large inventories. In its simplest form, all the hardware you need for the Anything Inventory beyond the PC (and its Internet connection) is a barcode scanner. The barcode scanner hardware we used, called a CueCat (Figure 6-6), works reasonably well and is widely sold on eBay for $5–$10. The scanners were available in both keyboard serial port and USB versions, and were originally given away for free (RadioShack had them). Figure 6-6 shows a serial port version; the dark square at the cat's mouth is the scanning aperture.

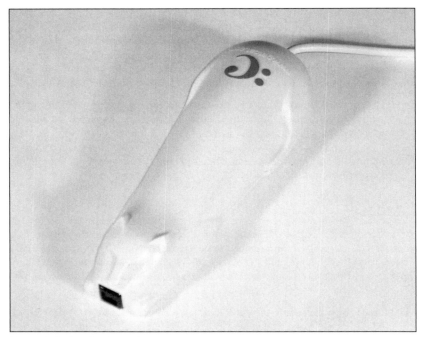

FIGURE 6-6: CueCat barcode scanner

Sadly, the scanners were free as in free lunch — neither one worked out too well. CueCats were originally produced by a deservedly defunct company called Digital Convergence, whose plan was to give the CueCats away, but then relay everything you scanned back to their servers. Using that information to gauge your buying habits, they expected to make money through the universally popular idea of targeted marketing campaigns. Not that they *told* you that was the plan, they just had you install their spyware software and assumed all would be well.

We may never know whether that plan was based on stupidity or arrogance, but doomed it was. People soon discovered the uploads to the Digital Convergence server, after which it was only a matter of time before someone reverse engineered the software or hardware, after which all was lost. Much of the history of Digital Convergence and the CueCat is recorded at www .fluent-access.com/wtpapers/cuecat, and it's a great read. It should have been titled "Hubris and How It Works for You," but it's nevertheless a great read.

In practice, reverse engineering of both the software and hardware happened. People built software drivers to undo the encryption the hardware applied to the barcode; see these sites:

- `cuecat.bearsoft.com/cuecat_source.html`
- `cuecatastrophe.com`
- `www.beau.lib.la.us/jmorris/linux/cuecat/DeCat.exe`
- `www.cedmagic.com/cuecat/cuecat.html`
- `www.download.com/3302-2110-3682158.html`
- `www.netaxs.com/joc/perlwin33.html`

Or, run a Google search on "cuecat software decrypt". We've not tested any of the software at these sites, however, because people also figured out how to modify the CueCat hardware so it outputs the barcode result as keyboard input, free of encryption and without the device serial number incorporated by the unmodified scanner. You can find directions on how to modify the CueCat hardware at these sites:

- `mavin.com/cuecat_flyer.html`
- `oilcan.org/cuecat/decrypt.html`
- `www.airsoldier.com/~cuecat/hardware-decrypt/cuecat_mods.html`
- `www.cexx.org/cuecat.htm`
- `www.dynasytes.com/cuecat`

There are a lot more sites (Google on "cuecat hardware decrypt"), but these are enough to get you going. Collectively, the sites above include directions for modifying both serial and USB port versions of the CueCat. We prefer the USB version, because we don't like dongles on either keyboard or printer ports, because the USB version powers down its LED, going dark after a few minutes of disuse, and because we don't have enough serial ports on our PCs to dedicate one needlessly.

Full disclosure being what it is, we didn't bother to do the hardware modifications ourselves — we bought a CueCat on eBay with the mods already installed. If you want one (or many) without modifications, you can get them from the retailer that bought up the inventory when Digital Convergence went under at `www.mavin.com/computermice.html`.

Wireless or Remote Barcode Scanning

You'll see in the next chapter how to use a barcode scanner in your kitchen to track what's in stock and know what you have to cook with. Making that work requires you to scan everything you put into and take out of the pantry, which could be inconvenient if you've not built a kitchen PC and your desktop PC is across the room (or house).

There are several ways to address this problem:

- You could run the software on a laptop. If you keep the actual data files elsewhere, a wireless LAN would give you access to those files.

- You could port the software to a handheld computer (see "Port the Software to Run Under Other Operating Systems" below) so you can bring everything to where you are.

- You could run the software remotely on a desktop and use a long cable or wireless link to span the distance. We built sounds into the software so, with the volume high enough, you could hear if a scan was successful or if it failed. Chapter 2 (Wireless RS-232 Link) shows you how to build a wireless link you could use with a serial CueCat or other scanner using a serial interface; remember that the standard PS/2 keyboard port is just an RS-232 port itself, so you can use the wireless link there, too. Figure 6-7 shows how to modify the system — the wireless link literally extends the serial port cables, so neither the PC nor the Anything Inventory software should be the wiser when you're done.

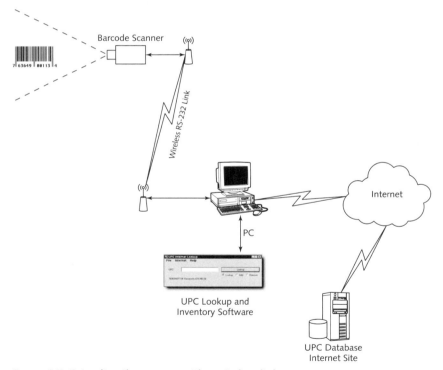

FIGURE 6-7: Extending the scanner with a wireless link

Using External Software

We built the Anything Inventory software assuming you'd use some other software to analyze the inventory and build reports. The File Export Inventory command generates the file you use for import into other applications. Although the resulting file has the standard comma separated value (CSV) format expected by many programs, we chose to give it the extension .INV to preclude automatic conversion. (For example, if you read a .CSV file into Microsoft Excel, the program automatically makes some assumptions and parses the file.) Automatic conversion likely parses the first column—the barcodes—as a number, which won't look the way you want; you'll lose the leading zeroes. Figure 6-8 shows what happens when you open the .INV file in Microsoft Excel—each line reads in as the leftmost cell, as text. The first line is a header, so you know what the fields are in each subsequent line. You use the Data Text to Columns command to parse the line into columns at the commas, controlling the conversion so the first column comes in as text.

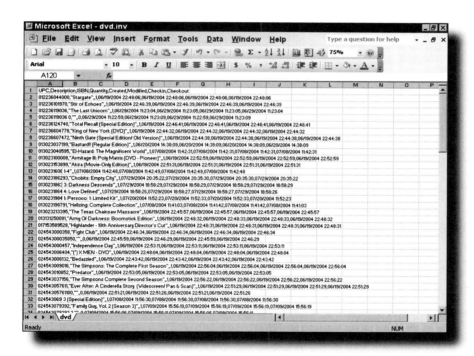

FIGURE 6-8: .INV file after opening in Microsoft Excel

Figure 6-9 shows the result in Microsoft Excel once you complete the conversion and after sorting the database by the description.

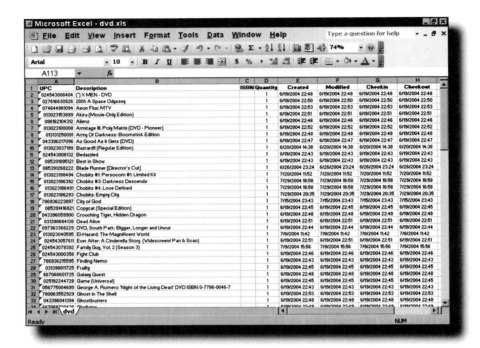

FIGURE 6-9: .INV file in Microsoft Excel after conversion to columns and sorting

You could import the file into Microsoft Access instead, with the result shown in Figure 6-10.

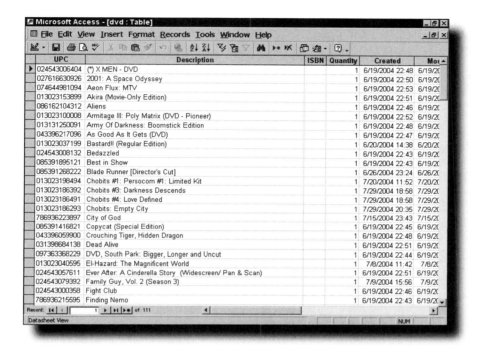

FIGURE 6-10: .INV file in Microsoft Access

Applications

The following sections describe several applications around the house and home office for a barcode reader, and although we had a reasonably large group to suggest these, we're sure you'll come up with your own in almost no time.

Book, DVD, CD, and video game catalog

Two of the key advantages you get from making an inventory of your collection are that it helps you remember what you have, and it helps you remember to whom you've loaned what. We have thousands of books, and something between 400 and 500 DVDs, CDs, and video games. Ours is a small collection compared to serious collectors. We've accumulated it over decades, making it hard to remember what we actually have. There are apparently a lot of people in the same situation, because everyone we asked suggested a book, DVD, and CD catalog as the first application, an idea that readily extends to video games on DVD or CD.

You can combine everything in one inventory or maintain separate ones as you prefer. The inventory is easy to set up, because books, DVDs, and CDs usually, if not always, have the UPC-A barcode printed on the cover where you can still find it long after it's been filed on a shelf.

The Anything Inventory software should do everything you need if all you're doing is cataloging what you have and when you acquired it. If you're also going to track what you loan and to whom, you'll want to add a field for notes or a field to record who has the item, and you might want to add a field for when you loaned it out. The section "Add Other Data Items" will get you started on how to modify the software for that purpose. We're assuming you'll use other applications (such as Microsoft Excel, Figure 6-9, or Microsoft Access, Figure 6-10) for reporting; if you want reports directly from the software, you can add that functionality to the software as described later in this chapter in the section "Display a Simple Real-time Inventory Report."

CDs contain individual tracks, of course, and it's very useful to have the track names in your database as well as the album titles themselves. You could enhance the software for your CD catalog by looking up the album in the FreeDb database (www.freedb.org) using a class available at The Code Project to query FreeDb (www.codeproject.com/cs/media/freedb.asp); however, that library uses the disc ID for the lookup and may need enhancement to support looking up album titles. Moreover, the album title you retrieve from the UPC Database or that you enter yourself may not be phrased precisely as stored in FreeDb, so you could have some interpretation to work through.

Similarly, you could look up DVD movies by title in the Internet Movie Database (www.imdb.com).

Kitchen pantry and cooking

You'll read about this application in much more detail in Chapter 7, "Kitchen PC." The inventory part of the Kitchen PC tracks what you have in stock to cook from. That's a simple beginning but, depending on how much work you're willing to do, opens up a variety of possibilities:

- Create shopping lists from a profile of minimum inventory levels.

- Derive a shopping list from a recipe and the known inventory.

- Filter a recipe database down to what's possible using just what's in stock.

- Track expiration dates on your inventory and suggest recipes to use items about to expire.

- List what's expired (which might help you find the problem when the refrigerator starts to stink).

If you found a data source to correlate products to ingredients, you could expand the depth of your database, and then look for products with specific ingredients (for example, ginger or peanuts), which could be useful to avoid food allergies.

Wine cellar

If you keep cases of wine in your basement, or in a wine cellar, knowing what you actually have in inventory — and where it is — can get to be a chore. Many years ago, a friend of ours owned literally thousands of cases, some in his basement and some in a rented wine cellar warehouse. We wrote a custom database application for him that he ran on a "luggable" computer, a predecessor to laptop computers, but the initial data entry was slow and tedious because everything had to be read and entered by hand.

Wine bottles today have UPC codes on them, so, for example, a scan of the UPC 089744422033 returns *Folonari Merlot/Sangiovese*, the correct description of the wine. That solves the basic data entry problem, but if you're really serious about wine collecting, there's a lot more data you'll want to track. Possibilities include:

- Vintage

- Type (red, white, blush, and so on)

- Grape (Merlot, Cabernet Sauvignon, Zinfandel, and so on)

- Region or country of origin

- Vineyard or area

- Rating (yours, Wine Spectator, or other)

- Rating history, reflecting the wine's evolution as it ages

- Tasting notes

- Storage location (for example, bin number)

We keep wine to drink, not as an investment, but if you needed the data you could record both purchase price and current estimated value. Whether or not you do that, there's enough added data for a wine inventory you'd want to keep that exporting data from the Anything Inventory software isn't practical because you'll lose the additional data on each re-export. Modifying the software to add the fields is possible (see the section "Add Other Data Items"), but it might simply be more practical to add barcode scanning to a standalone database such as Microsoft Access. The section "Integrate the Software into Other Applications" offers some ideas on how to use parts of the Anything Inventory software that way.

Insurance inventory

Many people suggest you make a video inventory of what's in your house to use as proof of ownership if your home is burglarized, destroyed in a flood, fire, or earthquake, or some other calamity strikes. Articles by Amazon.com (`www.amazon.com/exec/obidos/tg/feature/-/214541/104-5062761-3181532`) and Imation (`didyouknow.imation.com/articles-video-art6.html`) are typical.

What's unfortunate about a pure video inventory is that you have to scan through the tape to find what you want. An inventory listing is a good companion to the video, particularly if you add to the database a field showing how long into the video the item appears.

Most items don't retain their UPC barcode once you remove the packaging, however, so you'll want to look over the items you're going to inventory to see if there are enough of them with any sort of barcode at all. Most likely, there would be a barcode with model and/or serial numbers, but you'll have to enter the description yourself since there's no database on the Internet you could check against.

Warranty tracking

If you're like us and most everyone else we know, you shove receipts in a drawer or file, and are hard-pressed to remember what has a current warranty when something breaks.

If you add a few fields to the inventory to record where you bought the item and when the warranty expires, your inventory gives you the information you need. Scan the box when you bring the item home, enter the other data, and you're set. If you were to add a filing reference so you could actually find the filed receipt, you'd really be on top of things.

No, we're not that organized either.

Software inventory and licensing

It's unfortunate that bluster and legal threats from the Business Software Alliance (BSA) cause people in complete compliance with software license agreements to have to invest significant time and expense in preparing formal audits and inventories of the software loaded on their PCs. Your only hope of responding to an audit demand with a reasonable chance of success is to maintain an inventory of what's on each machine, cross-referencing the machine to the specific license.

You could maintain that inventory by hand, or track it with barcodes. All boxed software will be barcoded when you buy it; you could print your own barcodes for software you buy and download, filing the download receipt with an attached barcode sticker. Add individual barcode stickers for each PC and the entire operation becomes straightforward enough that you're likely to maintain your inventory accurately.

Many Web sites offer free barcode generators, including one from Barcodes, Inc. (www .barcodesinc.com/generator) and a more comprehensive one from IDAutomation.com Inc. (www.idautomation.com/java/linearservlet.html). Print the barcode onto label stock and you can paste it anywhere. You'll then either have to modify the Anything Inventory to store random barcode information and to track multiple barcoded fields, or integrate the barcode scanning and lookup into an existing database application (see the section "Integrate the Software into Other Applications").

Small rental operation

Suppose you operate a lending library for books, or a small DVD rental operation. You'll want to be able to track what's in stock; what's checked out, when, and by whom; and when items are returned. You'll want a more sophisticated database than our Anything Inventory software, but the barcode lookup functions are essential to readily scanning and identifying your stock. Once again, take at look at the section "Integrate the Software into Other Applications" for some ideas about how to build your application.

eBay store inventory

Finally, suppose you sell items on eBay. You'll need to know what's in stock when you create or update your postings, an application directly suited to the Anything Inventory software. Scan items in when you receive them from suppliers, look up the inventory quantity when you post (including selling multiple items), and scan items out either when you ship or when you post them for sale, depending on how you operate your store. You'll always know what you've got.

Barcode Software

We wrote the Anything Inventory software using Microsoft Visual C++ version 6, and using the Microsoft Foundation Classes (MFC) supplied with Visual C++. MFC simplifies creating Windows applications, and includes classes useful for string handling, Internet access, and other functions. We wrote and tested the software targeting Windows 2000 and Windows XP, and while it may work on Windows 9X, we didn't take that into consideration and never tested it in that configuration.

The program is a Windows dialog box. We've removed the usual OK and Cancel buttons and added a menu to make it look more like a normal Windows application. The Lookup button is the default button, triggered when the user or barcode scanner inputs the Enter key. The radio button controls under the Lookup button determine the action when Lookup is triggered, which could be Lookup (no change to inventory counts), Add (increase the inventory count by one), or Remove (decrease the inventory count by one). The text of the barcode goes into a standard Windows edit control. The program restores the Windows focus — the active control — to be the edit control any time you click on some other control so the program remains ready to accept barcode scanner input.

The essence of the dialog box's operation is in the CUPCLookupDlg::OnLookup function within file UPCLookupDlg.cpp. OnLookup moves data from the dialog box controls to local variables with the call

```
UpdateData( TRUE );
```

and puts the variable data back into the controls with the call

```
UpdateData( FALSE );
```

Calls to UpdateData need not be in symmetric pairs; for example, OnLookup calls UpdateData to retrieve from the controls near the start of the routine, then calls UpdateData multiple times during execution to revise what's in the controls.

The dialog exchanges three sets of variables with the controls using UpdateData:

- The barcode itself, kept in CString m_csUPC
- The item description corresponding to the barcode, kept in CString m_UPCDescription
- The radio button state, kept in decoded form in int m_ProcessingMode

Barcode objects

The fundamental object the software manipulates, an item represented by a barcode, is implemented by the BarcodeObject class. The class data members you'd expect include:

- The barcode itself, represented as a string. You don't want to represent it as a number because some barcodes (including EAN-13 ISBN codes) contain non-numeric characters.
- The type of barcode the item is, which could be INVALID, UPC_A, UPC_E, or EAN_13. INVALID indicates there's no useful barcode stored in the object. UPC_A and EAN_13 are as you'd expect and are implemented. UPC_E is defined, but not implemented in the code.
- The item description, also stored as a string.

The other data members are:

- The ISBN, as a string. It's convenient to have the ISBN isolated to use in lookups against Amazon.com.
- Whether the barcode has been looked up on the Internet, as a boolean.
- Whether the barcode was known on the Internet when it was checked, as a boolean.
- The Web site against which the barcode was looked up, as a pointer to a BarcodeReferenceWebsite object.
- The catalog of Web sites known to the program, used to figure out how to look up the barcode. The member is a pointer to a WebsiteCatalog object.

There's also a data member, called a SiteID, that's used when the inventory is serialized to and from a disk file.

Utility methods for the class read and write some of the data members, including the barcode, description, type, and ISBN; and support serialization.

The remaining methods implement barcode lookup, including querying the Internet interface. The ISBN string is passed to the Internet site object if the barcode is EAN-13; otherwise, the barcode string itself is used. A checksum is added to the 9-digit ISBN string to form a complete 10-digit code.

Inventory object

The inventory is a set of objects, each of which includes barcode objects, but it also has to record information about each object not strictly relevant to the barcode itself. In addition to the corresponding `BarcodeObject`, the `InventoryObject` class includes the number of the item in inventory and times noting when the object was created, modified, checked in, and checked out.

Public methods in the `InventoryObject` class exist to check in and out an object, get and set key attributes, and interface to the underlying `BarcodeObject`. The `WriteInvRecord` method outputs one line to a CSV file being written by the File ⇨ Export Inventory command. If you're planning to change the export format or organization, that's the place to start.

Inventory

The `Inventory` class maintains an array of `InventoryObject` elements in its primary data member. The other data members record the path to the disk file holding the serialized version of the inventory, track if the file is open or the inventory modified, and record the current and maximum length of the `InventoryObject` array. The class grows the array if it fills.

Public methods add and remove items in the inventory, handle I/O to the inventory and export files, and load download files from the UPC Database site. The `Inventory` object maintains the array in order, sorted by the barcode string, and uses a binary search to search the array when you scan a barcode.

The `Inventory` class loops over the inventory array to implement the export command, filtering out objects for which the creation time is the same as the last modification time and which were never looked up over the Internet. That filter eliminates inventory objects created when you load a file downloaded from the UPC Database site that aren't items you've subsequently scanned, which keeps unused items from needlessly inflating the size of your export file.

Internet access

Three classes, used by the classes above, cooperate to implement Internet access and Web data retrieval:

- `InternetReader` — The software uses *web page scraping* to interrogate sites and retrieve data, meaning that it sends a URL to the server, receives back the resulting page, and extracts the necessary data from the page text. Methods to support that functionality are implemented in the `InternetReader` class.

  Web scraping begins by sending a URL to a Web site to request the page containing the data you want. For example, a typical URL you'd send to the UPC Database server is:

  `http://www.upcdatabase.com/item.pl?upc=047875324275`

  Because the barcode needed to complete the URL is stored as a string (with spaces trimmed off either end), a standard format operation serves to insert the barcode into the URL using a format string like this:

  `http://www.upcdatabase.com/item.pl?upc=%s`

We chose to use a format operation rather than a string append because it provides more flexibility should there be data required in the URL following the barcode.

All the interesting information returned by the Web site for web scraping is outside the HTML tags, so we wrote the `GetBufferFromSite` method to strip those tags from the returned buffer. If we send the URL above to the UPC Database, part of the returned Web page are the following lines:

```
Description Doom3 Pre-Order with Figurine
Size/Weight (none)
Manufacturer Activison (047875)
```

The software uses three methods to implement the scraping operation: `GetBufferFromSite` loads the tag-stripped page into the InternetReader buffer data member, `FindPosition` searches for a key string preceding the result and marks the point in the buffer after the string, and `GetRestOfLine` returns the remainder of the text line following the key string. In our example, because the key string is `Description`, `GetRestOfLine` returns the string `Doom3 Pre-Order with Figurine`.

- `BarcodeReferenceWebsite` — A `BarcodeReferenceWebsite` object represents a Web site used to look up barcodes. The important data members include ones defining the type of barcode the site looks up, the format string to produce a lookup URL given the barcode (or ISBN), the format string to produce a site update URL, and the string to search for during the web scraping operation. The update operation isn't implemented, although some of the framework is there, so its input parameters aren't yet precisely defined.

  One `BarcodeReferenceWebsite` object defines a site to retrieve data given a specific barcode type. Use a second object tied to the same site if the site can process multiple barcode types.

- `WebsiteCatalog` — The software presently interrogates the UPC Database site for UPC-A types, and Amazon.com for EAN-13 ISBN codes. The `WebsiteCatalog` object holds an array of `BarcodeReferenceWebsite` objects, and provides methods to both add a site to the catalog and look up a `BarcodeObject`.

Extending the software

There are many things you can do to enhance the Anything Inventory software, such as:

- Use the registry to change built-in values.
- Add other data items.
- Add local inventory edit capability.
- Implement Web site edit methods.
- Display a simple real-time inventory report.
- Permit user control of the CSV file export contents and/or format.

- Change the database format to use XML.

- Support UPC-E and/or the full EAN-13 barcode formats.

- Integrate the software into other applications.

- Port the software to run under other operating systems.

Here are some ideas on how to implement these changes. Our list of changes is of course not all you can do with the program (for example, you could link to online images such as at the Los Angeles County Library), but it should get you going with the source code.

Use the registry to change built-in values

The URLs used to search the UPC Database and Amazon.com are constants in the `OnInitDialog` method, which you'll find implemented in file `UPCLookupDlg.cpp`. If you look at the code in the GeekWaterWatcher software (Chapter 5), you'll see that code uses static methods of the `RegistryInfo` class (defined in the RegistryInfo.h file) that let you route string and integer methods through the registry so you can modify the defaults. Similar processing is done in the void `OnExit` method of the `CUPCLookupDlg` class in the Anything Inventory software, but the `RegistryInfo` class is somewhat easier to use.

Whichever implementation you choose, you could use those methods in the Anything Inventory software to make it possible to readily change the URLs and related strings should those sites change how they operate. For example, here in annotated form is one of the relevant statements in `OnInitDialog`:

```
m_webCatalog.AddSite( UPC_A,          // Barcode type
                      101,            // Site ID
                      szUPCURL,       // Lookup URL format string
                      "bogus",        // Update URL format string
                      "Description"   // Scraping search string
                      );
```

In that statement, the lookup URL format string (szUPCURL) is a constant defined at the top of the `UPCLookupDlg.cpp` file, while the update URL format string and the scraping search string are directly written in as constants. You could (partially) rewrite the statement this way:

```
m_webCatalog.AddSite(
    UPC_A,
    101,
    RegistryInfo::GetString( "UPCDatabaseLookup", szUPCURL ),
    "bogus",
    "Description" );
```

Having done that, the statement looks for the UPC Database lookup URL format string in the registry, using the default in `szUPCURL` only if the registry entry isn't defined. The registry value, if defined, should be a string with one `%s` format element, and should be stored under the key `HKEY_CURRENT_USER\Software\Barry and Marcia Press -- Geek House\GeekWaterWatcher\Settings`, in the value `UPCDatabaseLookup`. If you want to modify the path to the key somewhat, look for this statement in `InitInstance` within the file `UPCLookup.cpp`:

```
SetRegistryKey( "Barry and Marcia Press -- Geek House" );
```

The MFC framework inserts the application name; you can change `Settings` by modifying the `RegistryInfo` class and the `OnExit` processing.

Add other data items

You may choose to record data with your inventory beyond what we've implemented. For example, if you added a notes field, you could keep track of to whom you loan a book or DVD.

You'll do several things to implement additional data items:

- Add the data item to the class.
- Add reading and writing the data item to the `InventoryObject::Serialize` method. You'll want to increment the `SCHEMA` constant at the top of the file, too, to ensure you don't accidentally read old format `UPC` files.
- Add writing the data item to the File Export Inventory command, modifying the `InventoryObject::WriteInvRecord` method.
- Create a user interface for the data item. You could do this with a new button in the main dialog box window, and apply the button to the last item scanned, or — a much better approach — you could implement the real-time inventory report below and add a command editing the note to apply to whatever record is selected in the display.

Add local inventory edit capability

There are no direct edit functions in the Anything Inventory software, meaning you can't directly change the item descriptions or counts, or remove unwanted items. You can use programs like Microsoft Excel or Microsoft Access to modify the information once they load the export `CSV` file, but there's no function to re-read the exported file if you update it, so a future export won't have those changes.

Architecturally, there are at least two ways to implement local inventory editing: You could implement a command to read the export `CSV` file format, so you could use external programs to do the actual editing, or you could implement commands to directly edit the inventory within the Anything Inventory software.

- **External editing** — To implement this approach, use the existing `File Load CSV` command implementation as a model, changing what data items you load and what you do with them to match the format of the exported CSV file instead of the UPC Database download CSV file. You can use the Visual C++ Class Wizard to modify the menu and add the routine to process the menu command; the real work, however, is done for `File Load CSV` in the `LoadCSV` method of the `Inventory` class.

- **Internal editing** — If you choose to add commands so the software does editing directly, we suggest you first add real-time inventory reporting (as below) so you have a user interface from which you can pick the inventory item to edit. However you select the item to edit, we suggest you then implement a dialog box displaying the barcode, description, and inventory count. We'd make the barcode itself display-only (that is, non-editable) — if the barcode is wrong, we suggest deleting the item from inventory and adding the correct one.

Implement Web site edit methods

None of the freely available Web sites on the Internet, and specifically not the UPC Database, list every barcode you might encounter. The UPC Database is an open database, however, in the sense that it provides a Web interface by which users can update the database to provide descriptions for new items. The user interface could be as simple as a popup dialog box that appears if the item is not found on the site, letting you enter the description and transmit it to the site.

Implementing the Web site interaction is more complicated, in that the W3 HTML specification (www.w3.org/TR/html4) recommends using a POST transaction for database updates. The UPC Database follows that recommendation. The WinInet classes and methods InternetReader uses have additional functionality to support the POST transaction, but the support isn't yet in InternetReader.

Overall, the processing to implement POST is:

- The verb in the CHttpConnection::OpenRequest call must change to HTTP_VERB_POST.

- The body of the request should be formatted to look like the form response according to the specifications of the Web site. In the case of the UPC Database, the form is set up using this HTML code:

```
<form method=post action=modify.pl>
UPC: 047875324275<p>
Old Description: Doom3 Pre-Order with Figurine<p>
Old Size: <p>
<input type=hidden name=upc value="047875324275">
Description: <input type=text name=new_desc size=50
maxlength=100 value="Doom3 Pre-Order with Figurine"><p>
Size/Weight: <input type=text name=new_size size=15
maxlength=15 value=""><p>

<input type=submit value=" Save Changes ">
<input type=reset><p>
</form>
```

You'll send back at least the name and new_desc fields to return the UPC-A code and the description; you might choose to implement sending new_size too.

- Use the CHttpFile::SendRequest method to add the POST data to the request and send it to the server.

- Use methods similar to what's in InternetReader to get the response code.

Display a simple real-time inventory report

The only inventory reporting in the version of the Anything Inventory software we've provided is the output in the dialog box you get in response to a lookup, add, or remove operation, which shows the barcode, description, and current inventory count after the operation completes. A more comprehensive inventory report would be useful so you could see what you've done previously, or so you could see the current inventory status.

A log of what you've done to the inventory might be a sequence of lines looking like this:

```
Add: 047875324275, Doom3 Pre-Order with Figurine (1)
Remove: 063649001134, Barracuda ATA HD (0)
```

You can format strings like that readily—see CUPCLookupDlg::OnLookup for an example of code doing a similar operation—and add them to a simple list box tied to a CListBox variable. If you add them to the end of the list box, and don't sort the list box, you'll have a running log.

Current inventory status is more complicated. We'd still use a list box, but we'd use a multi-column one tied to a CListView variable with columns for barcode, description, count, and some or all of the four times tracked in the software. The column sorting features of the CListView would permit analysis of the inventory by any of the columns, and implementing the same functionality that reverses the sort order on a second click in the column (as in Windows Explorer's details view mode) would enhance the analysis capability significantly. A helper class to read and write column widths to the registry would let user column width settings be persistent across invocations of the program.

You can go as crazy as you want with the CListView—for example, you could monitor right-clicks on lines in the control to pop up a menu of commands, such as commands to edit the item, force a new description lookup on the Internet, delete the item, or most anything else that uses the item's data elements as input. You could implement a command that lets you tie an image file to the item (store the complete path, including the network server path instead of a drive letter if the file is remote, to make sure working directories don't matter). That capability would be useful to connect the inventory to photographs you took during a house inventory sweep.

Permit user control of the CSV file export

The format we implemented for the File Export Inventory, although we included a header line at the top of the file to simplify using the format, may not be what you want. Some of the enhancements you could add include:

- **Selectable columns**—A simple dialog box with check boxes to enable or disable writing each of the columns we now export would let you tailor the output to just the data you want to see, which would reduce the export file size and might simplify the processing you do in the external application.

- **Selectable, orderable columns**—In addition to choosing what columns you want to output, you could set the ordering of the columns along the lines. That might be useful if you need to export to software with different requirements, or if you want to sort the file by one of the columns now output later in the line using a sort utility that doesn't understand CSV formats and therefore must treat each line as an undifferentiated text string (such as the Windows XP sort utility).

- **Different export order or filter criteria**—The File Export Inventory command outputs items sorted by barcode, and filters the inventory to just those which have been modified since creation or looked up on the Internet. You might want the items sorted differently, or want different filter rules. The Inventory::ExportInv method writes the file, supported by `InventoryObject::WriteInvRecord`. An alternative sort, preceding the overall loop, would go in `Inventory::ExportInv`, as would changes to the filter.

The simplest enhancement of the filter would let you choose from several pre-programmed filters (such as "everything modified in the last week"); a more sophisticated version would let you program the filter from a script or a filter configuration dialog.

Change the database format to use XML

The .UPC files currently use the serialization capabilities of the Microsoft Foundation Classes. The resulting file format, however, isn't directly useful to any other software, which is why there has to be an export command. If you changed the File Save and File Open handling to use the eXtensible Markup Language (XML), the resulting files could be read by many other programs, and could be used directly by supporting Web pages.

Our approach to doing that upgrade would be to incorporate the open source Xerces XML parser from the Apache XML project (`xml.apache.org/xerces-c/index.html`). Some other useful projects might include XiMoL, a non-validating XML reader/writer library written in C++ (`sourceforge.net/projects/ximol`), and Babel Blaster, a file format converter supporting CSV, flat files, and XML (`sourceforge.net/projects/babelblaster`).

While you're at it, it would be worth investigating if you can make the database disk-based so you don't need to keep the entire data set in memory.

Support UPC-E and/or the full EAN-13 barcode formats

The Anything Inventory software doesn't implement UPC-E barcodes, or the full EAN-13 barcode. Implementing them requires not only adding to the code, but finding an Internet source you can use to do lookups. The UPC Database handles some UPC-E codes, so that interface might be useful — you could try some sample codes on the site to investigate. We haven't found a free Web site supporting EAN-13.

Of course, you could start a site similar to the UPC Database and create an open EAN-13 database yourself.

You could also extend the software to handle random barcodes of all types, which would let you scan model and serial numbers from items that have them, which would be useful for insurance inventory scans when you don't have the actual UPC-A barcode.

Integrate the software into other applications

Microsoft Access and Excel use a dialect of Basic to program in unique functionality. The Anything Inventory software is in C++, though, so you'll need to link Basic to C++ to call into portions of the software. You'll need to take several steps to convert parts of the software for use from Basic:

- **Make a DLL** — Dynamic Link Libraries (DLLs) contain code you can load and execute from within other programs, and are the framework both Access and Excel use to link to external code. You'll have to package the necessary classes of the Anything Inventory software into a DLL.

- **Resolve data type differences** — Basic represents strings differently than does C++. You'll need to convert strings on entry and exit between the types.

- **Adapt entry point naming conventions** — You'll have to make sure you create appropriately named functions with the right calling conventions to make them accessible from Basic. See Microsoft's page at `support.microsoft.com/default.aspx ?scid=kb;en-us;109338` for more information.

Port the software to run under other operating systems

The software runs under Windows 2000 and Windows XP, and will be non-trivial to port to Linux and X-Window because we used the Microsoft Foundation Classes. Nevertheless, there are several approaches you can take:

- IBM has an article on how to approach porting MFC applications to Linux on their Web site; see *Porting MFC applications to Linux: A step-by-step guide to using wxWindows* at `www-106.ibm.com/developerworks/linux/library/l-mfc/?open&l =920,t=gr`.

- There's an equivalent to the MFC CString class at The Code Project at `www .codeproject.com/string/stdstring.asp`.

- The algorithms themselves are suitable for any operating system, so if you want to build a new X-Window application from the ground up, you could take the architecture and algorithms and build them into your framework.

Another adaptation you might want to consider is porting the software to run under Windows CE, which would make it run on a variety of handheld computers. The job shouldn't be as hard as a Linux port, because the MFC architecture runs on Windows CE. Combine that modified version of the software with a barcode scanner you can plug into the handheld computer and a wireless Internet link and you've got your inventory in portable form so you can walk around your home, a warehouse, or an office.

Summary

Barcodes give you an easy way to input identification data into your PC, and the standardization offered by the ubiquitous UPC-A and EAN-13 barcodes has led to public databases you can use to identify a wide variety of products. Some straightforward software classes are sufficient to scan items, look them up in a local or Internet database, and maintain a simple inventory. You can use the software directly for many purposes, and can extend it readily to build a wide variety of applications.

Kitchen PC

We're of the opinion that the words *geek* and *kitchen* can and should coexist in sentences with meanings that don't inevitably lead to ordering take out. Cooking well is really just a matter of interest — we know the average geek is smart enough — so if great food's not sufficient incentive, how about a nice bit of electronics and software?

Project Description

The Kitchen PC is, as you'd expect, a PC built into a countertop or cabinet. Locating a PC in your kitchen is worthwhile because once you have processing, storage, and a display where you're cooking, there's almost no end to what you might find for that PC to do:

➤ Internet access gives you the ability to look up new recipes, ingredients, preparation tips, and more. For example, do you know what a kiwano is? (We refer to them as alien seed pods...)

➤ Integrating the last chapter's barcode reader and database lets you maintain a running kitchen inventory, one you can use to help generate a grocery list and to track how you're doing on a diet.

➤ Recipes stored in a database would let menu planning software add items to the grocery list based on chosen dishes and existing inventory.

➤ Tying digital scales to the PC helps you scale amounts.

➤ A video feed — from cable, satellite, or antenna, or from your network using the networked TV in Chapter 3 — lets your PC double as a television.

System Diagram

Figure 7-1 outlines the elements of what you might do with a Kitchen PC, and highlights that, although the PC is the core of the system, it's a relatively small part of the overall project. You should also conclude from the scope of the figure — reaching from every corner of your kitchen out through the Internet — that the overall system is unbounded in scope, a project you need never declare finished.

I will exchange the labels on my folder of top-secret plans and my folder of family recipes. Imagine the hero's surprise when he decodes the stolen plans and finds instructions for Grandma's Potato Salad.

Peter Anspach,
The Evil Overlord List

in this chapter

☑ Information in the kitchen

☑ Sensors, displays, processing, and data

☑ Building the Kitchen PC

☑ Software to deliver information

☑ Fitting a Kitchen PC to your own needs

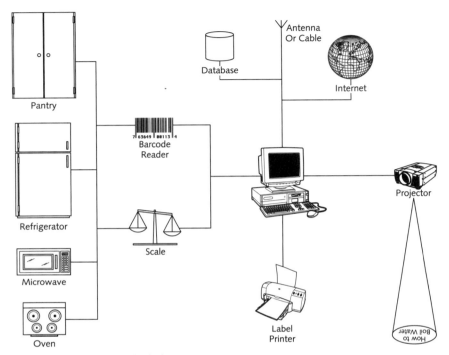

FIGURE 7-1: Kitchen PC block diagram

Every element of Figure 7-1 has its own individual problems and opportunities. For example:

- **Pantry and refrigerator** — An inventory of what you have on hand gives you the opportunity to plan menus based on what's available and to derive shopping lists showing what you need based on a given menu. The problem maintaining an inventory is to keep it accurate, both when you bring new items in and when you consume ones on hand. The barcode reader has to be handy for both purposes, but so do the software and any other elements. You can understand how big a challenge that is by thinking about how likely it is that anyone would be willing to wake up a PC, launch some software, find the barcode reader or keyboard, and log pulling an apple out of the refrigerator. Probably not going to happen that way.

- **Microwave, oven, and cooktop** — Both cooking directions and temperature probes are great opportunities for having your Kitchen PC work with the ovens and range. The problems are both convenience — having the right information where you want it when you want it — and control. It's only recently that any microwave or conventional ovens have been designed for external computer control. Modifying a conventional microwave oven for computer control creates the risk you'll create microwave radiation leaks — we don't recommend doing this unless you're trained in *all* the relevant technologies — while modifying a conventional oven requires you understand everything involved in safely and reliably interfacing to high-power electronics. Neither are skills the average geek has, and the consequences if you screw up are severe.

Stick with a temperature probe and maybe a local display.

- **Display** — Having the right information where you're working, and in a form you can use, is one of the key requirements for a Kitchen PC. A Microsoft concept demonstration kitchen explores this idea effectively by combining a projector in the ceiling aimed at the work counter with a voice command and response system. You may not want to take on the voice (and underlying artificial intelligence) part of that idea, but some carpentry and attention to cooling the projector would let anyone have the countertop display.

- **PC** — Even the PC itself presents both opportunities and challenges. If you have room to spare, you can build in an entire entertainment center for those times you need to avoid watching the pot of boiling water. Few kitchens have cabinet space to waste, though, so the chances are you'll have to build a very small PC or else remote the PC to somewhere else.

- **Connectivity and data** — Information is what makes the Kitchen PC useful, so you'll want both local databases and ties to the outside world. The Anything Inventory project in Chapter 6 provides a barcode database; television and Internet connections are the links to the outside world.

Parts and Designs

The most important component you'll design your Kitchen PC around is your kitchen itself. How big the kitchen is, how it's organized, and how you work in your kitchen should be the starting points for your design.

The first question you should ask yourself is *where are the work areas in your kitchen?* The ovens form one, including the range top, as do the refrigerator, pantry, any other food storage cupboards, and cutting/mixing areas. (Yes, there's a lot of work you do at the sink, but not a lot of information you need at the time.) A survey of our kitchen results in three areas, the refrigerator and pantry together are one, the ovens and range another, and the counter under the spice racks a third. There's a long counter on one side of the kitchen separating it from the rest of the house, but although it's a good place for the PC itself, little actual cooking or preparation happens there.

Once you identify the work areas, ask *what happens at each work area, and what sort of interaction do you want with your Kitchen PC at that location?* This is the beginning of setting the requirements for your Kitchen PC design. For example:

- **Food storage areas** — What happens at these locations is that items get put into and taken out of inventory. You'll therefore need to log the additions to and removals from inventory, but that's not the only opportunity. Access to your recipe database will help you know what to get from storage, and a small video or LCD screen will help you verify the barcode scan results as you put groceries away.

- **Cooking areas** — You use inventory items in the cooking areas, and use information to know what to do. Access to the recipe database helps you know what to do and when; access to the Internet could help you research some of the finer points of the preparation, understand specific terms in the recipe, and research dishes you might serve with the recipe.

  The information you use in the cooking area can be very specific if you'll dedicate the time to gathering and storing the necessary information. For example, a barcode scanner next to your oven or microwave could prompt the PC (which knows you're using the one in the cooking area if you have several) to display the proper settings to bake or microwave the item you scanned.

- **Work areas** — You do much the same thing in work areas as in the cooking areas, plus stage ingredients both for storage and for use, mix drinks, and plan menus. The capabilities in both the food storage areas and cooking areas are useful in the work areas.

You should take the definition you develop and create requirements for each work area, then synthesize combined requirements for the overall Kitchen PC. Once you have that synthesis, you can allocate requirements to each component of your Kitchen PC. For example, you'll be able to decide the specific capabilities and hardware you need, such as wireless or wired barcode scanners, displays, storage, printing, communications, and more.

PC

The most significant requirements on the PC itself are probably size and cooling, and connecting enough peripherals. Small size helps the PC fit into cabinets, but putting the PC in a closed cabinet puts it in a heat pocket where the inlet cooling air will be at temperatures higher than the usual ambient air used to cool the system. You have to address those issues, but have a wide range of options for how you do that — for example:

- **Thin client** — Some years ago Sun, Oracle, and others made a fuss about what they called *thin client computing*, with the idea being that you'd run all applications on a remote server, or download them from the server to execute on the local machine but keep all programs and storage remote. Either way, you'd need little more than a processor, memory, and display locally, not the rich set of equipment that forms a PC. This is probably the smallest option for a Kitchen PC, but it requires you implement the remote server to support it. Many of the companies that used to build thin clients have gone out of business, but if you're running Linux you could put just enough hardware behind an LCD display to run the XWindows server, and then host all the rest of your applications on a backend Linux server.

  Even if you're willing and able to write all the necessary software to make this approach work, and so minimize the PC hardware, you still need to figure out how to connect the secondary displays, if any, peripherals, sensors, and networks. Just the connectors and adapter cards required can be more than what's available on a thin client PC.

- **Laptop or tablet PC** — The compact packaging and integrated display in a laptop or tablet PC works well in any restricted-size application, including the Kitchen PC, and the pen interface on a tablet PC could eliminate the need for a keyboard. Neither form factor will be usable mounted under a cabinet, however, which implies the PC would have to sit on a counter. Power and data connections become a problem in that context, and the limited interfaces on both form factors may not provide what's necessary without a docking station or port replicator. Either accessory will add cost, take more space, and still not solve the problems you encounter placing the PC on a counter.

■ **Shoebox or desktop PC** — A small form factor PC could be the ideal package for a Kitchen PC, because it combines some of the flexibility of a full desktop configuration with the small size that will help you integrate the unit into a cabinet. A desktop is fine too, if you have the space — perhaps inside an island in the middle of a large kitchen.

Most kitchen cabinets are closed wooden structures, such as the basic cabinet in Figure 7-2. Wood is a relatively good insulator, so all the heat generated by a PC and vented into the air within the cabinet can't flow out of the cabinet. Instead, exhaust air from the PC recycles in the heat cells to become inlet air, raising inlet and exhaust temperatures in a cycle that soon spirals out of control and puts the PC well beyond its operating limits.

FIGURE 7-2: Basic cabinet

There are two approaches you can use that will let a PC survive in a closed space. One is to reduce the PC's power consumption, so less energy has to be dissipated; the other is to vent cool air into and hot air out of the space. We haven't measured the heat you can dissipate from a wooden cabinet and still remain within acceptable limits, but it's likely that number is lower than required to power a useful PC. Reducing the power consumption will lower the venting requirement, though, so it's still a useful approach. There are three overall ways to minimize the power consumption:

- **Slow the machine and use a power-efficient processor** — Both the clock rate and the underlying design and fabrication technology of the processor have direct impacts on the power consumed by the processor. High processor clock rates not only consume more power directly, they also tend to be accompanied by faster front side buses which increase the power consumed by the chipset and the memories. Using the slowest machine possible, and using a machine incorporating mobile or other low-power technology, will reduce the power consumption.

- **Remove excess hardware** — All hardware generates heat when there's power applied, so making sure the machine has only the hardware required will eliminate unnecessary heat produced from otherwise unused hardware. The list of hardware you can likely remove includes excess memory, all disks besides the primary one, high-performance video cards, floppy disks, and optical drives.

- **Employ aggressive power management** — Desktop systems rarely apply the Advanced Configuration and Power Interface (ACPI) technology as aggressively as laptops, using the S1 suspend state instead of S3, for example, and rarely throttling the processor based on thermal limits, but it can be. ACPI helps laptops by extending battery life; doing so in your Kitchen PC helps by reducing power dissipation.

Venting cool air into and hot air out of the cabinet will be far more effective a heat management approach. Assuming you put the PC in the bottom of the cabinet (the heat source in the figure), Figure 7-3 shows the two fundamental approaches to venting the cabinet. Both build on the normal bottom-to-top convective air flow generated by the hot air; one vents the air to the side, while the other vents into the attic. Both could use a grid of small, hidden holes to bring in cool air from the bottom.

Neither approach is problem free. Venting to the side not only requires a side opening into the room, it requires you make holes in the side of the cabinet. Making holes on the side of the cabinet that actually look acceptable to you (and, perhaps more importantly, to the next buyer of the place) could be hard. Venting to the top avoids the cosmetic issues, but requires you maintain relatively unimpeded airflow all the way up the cabinet and into the attic. You could simply drill holes in the shelves and the top; the bigger problem is the potential loss of shelf space, since if you then cover the holes they stop functioning. Alternatively, you could build a rectangular duct running up the back or side of the cabinet, minimizing the space loss and preventing accidental obstruction of the airflow path.

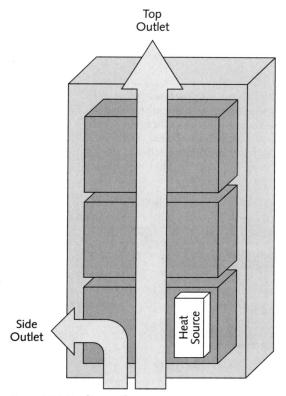

Top
Outlet

Side
Outlet

Heat
Source

FIGURE 7-3: Cooling paths

It may also be possible to craft both the inlet and outlet on the bottom of the cabinet.

Whichever approach you use, passive convection may not move enough air. A muffin fan, similar to what you'd use in a PC case, may suffice for the side outlet and cabinet bottom approaches, but may encounter too much airflow impedance trying to push or pull air to the attic. The top outlet may also suffer from air being drawn from higher up in the cabinet, another advantage of the duct approach. Both top outlet problems — impedance and leakage — suggest you may need a stronger fan than a simple muffin.

Or not. As long as you're custom building, why not build in a water-based cooling system (for example, www.thinkgeek.com/pcmods/cooling/6044)? You can use water conducted in hoses by a small pump to vent the processor heat; it's possible the rest of the heat dissipated in the system can be handled by convection or a very small muffin fan with bottom vents.

Display

We've pretty much ruled out CRT displays for Kitchen PCs unless you have a really big kitchen with space to spare. Few have a kitchen like that. Fortunately, there are lots of alternatives:

- **LCD** — Flat panels are great in small spaces, and the smallest ones can be built into walls or furniture. The same sort of LCDs you might use in a Car PC (Chapter 10) have VGA interfaces and touch screens, giving you a convenient way to build a small remote you'd use with a barcode scanner. Larger LCDs can hang from under a cabinet (see Figure 7-4) or be built into a counter with a glass cover. You'll probably want to use one with a VGA port to simplify cabling, and with the smaller panels you won't lose any resolution.

FIGURE 7-4: Under-cabinet LCD

- **Projector** — Why look away from where you're working to consult a monitor? Building an LCD into a work counter is an attractive way to avoid that problem, but with the display below the surface you're required to keep the area above the LCD free of papers or other clutter. If you build a projector into the ceiling, however, you avoid that problem, because whatever is on the counter, or the counter itself, becomes the display surface.

In addition to standard LCDs, as in Figure 7-4, or the Car PC LCD panels in Chapter 10, you might look at products specifically built for under-counter application such as the Audiovox VE700 (`www.audiovox.com/webapp/wcs/stores/servlet/ProductDisplay? catalogId=10001&storeId=10001&productId=12990&langId=-1`). That unit is a 7-inch, 16:9 (HDTV) aspect ratio drop-down monitor that includes a TV tuner and audio-video input jacks. A TV-Out capability in the Kitchen PC unit can couple into those jacks, but a standard VGA output won't. The VE700 also includes an AM/FM radio, speakerphone, speakers, and a remote control.

Many video cards, including those from ATI and nVidia, let you rotate the screen image. That's exactly what you need if you hang an LCD under a cabinet to restore the upside-down image.

The ViewSonic PJ501 projector (`www.viewsonic.com/products/projectors/pj501`) is representative of what you might use for a ceiling projector. The unit can be found for under $900, and has a good brightness rating. (Brightness matters, because darkening your kitchen to cook isn't a good plan.) It weighs 5.4 pounds, consumes 210 watts, and offers 1024×768 resolution. Between the lens and zoom capability, you can get nearly a four-foot diagonal image with only four-foot throw.

The key design and construction issues using a projector like the PJ501 are mechanical, thermal, and electrical.

- **Mechanical** — The most obvious mechanical requirements are to support the weight of the projector and aim it downwards onto the counter, obeying any constraints on focusing range and image size. Less obvious mechanical requirements are that you'll want to isolate the projector from any vibration — thumping washers, slamming doors, thundering herds — and minimize the noise from its internal fans. You'll also want to make sure you can get to the unit after construction is done to replace the lamp and access any control panels.

- **Thermal** — You'll have to design enough ventilation to manage over 200 watts and keep the projector cool. Fail to do that and you'll shorten both lamp and projector life. If you suspend the projector below the ceiling but above the cabinets, it will be in open air and the internal fans should provide all the cooling that's required. If you hide the projector above the ceiling, you'll need both access panels and an airflow plan, but you'll be subject to much less noise. Attic air can get very hot in the summer, so you should pull cool air from the kitchen area and vent it elsewhere.

- **Electrical** — The VGA cable from the PC to the projector could easily be 10 feet long or more, which is a long run (DVI cables commonly top out at 10 feet without repeaters; in practice, they're good for 1 to 9 meters depending on the individual product). Every foot of cable adds capacitance that degrades the signal from the PC, which can create ghosts in the video signal. You won't want to give up resolution — which does reduce ghosting — so you'll need to make sure you use very low capacitance VGA cable. Extra-shielded VGA cables such as those from Cables N Mor (`www.cablesnmor.com/vga.html`) will solve the problem.

  You'll also have to provide power to the projector. A utility box with outlets should do; be sure to observe all the necessary electrical codes.

Keyboard, mouse, barcode, and printing

The keyboard and mouse in your design can be the simplest part—this is an ideal application for a wireless keyboard and mouse, such as the Logitech Cordless MX Duo (`www.logitech.com/index.cfm/products/details/US/EN,CRID=2162,CONTENTID=6831`), because once you install the receiver with the PC, you can use the keyboard and mouse anywhere in the kitchen.

A barcode scanner (or four) as described in Chapter 6 is essential in your kitchen if you have any hopes of maintaining an inventory, because typing is simply going to be too slow. Multiple scanners are useful because you store cans, boxes, bottles, and fresh food in different places, and you probably won't want to walk across the kitchen to the one and only scanner. We realize it's a small distance, but when you're busy and in a hurry, it's convenience that counts.

Connecting many RS-232 barcode scanners is awkward—you'll need either add-in cards or USB to RS-232 adapters, because many machines only have one RS-232 port, and some have none. We suggest using USB scanners to begin with, saving the RS-232 ports you have for wireless connections (Chapter 2) to places that are hard to reach with cables from the PC.

Here's two ways to make barcode scanning more convenient:

- **Undercounter scanner**—Grocery stores have fixed scanners you move items past to eliminate the motion of reaching for and then putting down the scanner. You could build a scanner in under a cabinet to do the same thing. If you used the CueCat from Chapter 6, you'd have to position it so the aperture was exposed, since the item has to contact the aperture for reliable scanning. Other scanners with better optics would eliminate that requirement, but will be more expensive.

- **Printed sheet**—Fresh fruits and vegetables, and some other items, don't have barcodes on them, and won't ever have them without some serious genetic engineering. Grocery stores again have the answer for you; they print pages of labeled barcodes they can hang at the registers and scan as required.

Barcode scanning can help you solve the problem of knowing what some frozen leftover is and when it expires. If you generate local barcodes and print them on labels, perhaps using a label printer such as from Seiko (`www.siibusinessproducts.com/products/printers.html`), you can maintain an inventory noting what each container holds and when it should be discarded. The tools at Freebarcodes.com (`www.freebarcodes.com`) can help you create the necessary labels, and can be integrated into many Windows applications.

Sensors

The key sensors for a Kitchen PC are ones to measure weight and temperature.

- **Weight**—A digital scale interfaced to the PC can check your measurements to ensure you read the amounts properly, and can convert unfamiliar units in recipes to the ones reported by the scale. It can also provide an audio feedback when you have the right amount.

The Ohaus Corporation builds the Scout SP-401 (`www.ohaus.com/products/`
`glo/scripts/view/viewproduct.asp?Recno=SP401`) you could use as a
kitchen scale. It's somewhat expensive, at about $200 including the USB interface. The
SP-401 handles up to 400 g with 0.1g resolution; other models have varying capacities
and resolution. Phidgets has a USB scale at about half that price with a capacity of
140 kg (`www.phidgets.com/index.php?module=pncommerce&func=`
`itemview&KID=110607692867.161.248.117&IID=60`), but its current resolution
is only to about 4 oz. Look for a higher-resolution product in 2005.

- **Temperature** — There's no end of things a temperature probe can do for you when connected to your Kitchen PC. You can track meat internal temperature as you roast it to know when it's done, track the oven temperature to know if the temperature distribution is even and if the thermostat is accurate, verify thawing poultry or fish stay in safe temperature ranges. The PC can do more than beep when it hits a set point; it can log the readings as often as you want, and using a modified version of the software in Chapter 4 can send you e-mail or SMS messages when cooking's done or a threshold's passed.

  If you've provided USB ports all over the kitchen (see the next section), the easiest way to connect a temperature probe would be to use the same PhidgetsInterfaceKit 8/8/8 interface as in Chapter 4, using the analog section to tie to a thermistor using the circuits in Chapter 8 (see for example Figure 8-9; you would replace the Javelin Stamp with the PhidgetsInterfaceKit). You'll also want to calibrate the probe more accurately than in Chapter 8, and over a much wider range. That will be much easier than in Chapter 8, because you'll have far more computing resources to work with.

Communications

Metcalfe's Law says the value of a network grows by the square of the size of the network. Our
examples above suggest that a similar claim — value grows by the number of connected
devices — is plausible for your Kitchen PC.

If that's true, then you'll want to spend some serious thought on device and network connections, deciding what connections you need where, and how you'll route and terminate the
cabling.

- **Device connections** — USB is a great choice for connecting a wide variety of devices to your Kitchen PC, because it's widely supported, because it can support the distances involved, and because its tree distribution architecture makes it easy to minimize the number of cables to the actual PC while accommodating many devices.

  For example, you could run a single USB cable from the PC to a *powered* USB hub (never use one that's not powered), and then distribute extension cables from there to everywhere you want a USB outlet. Three meters (less than 10 feet) is the maximum cable run you can safely use by specification, but you can combine cables and hubs up to about 25 meters. We haven't found any equivalents to the usual in-wall connectors for LAN, television, telephone, and the like that handle USB, so you'll have to craft the wiring to fit the situation.

The other alternative for device connections is RS-232. We suggest converting RS-232 interfaces to some other standard to overcome the small number of RS-232 ports on PCs; and because RS-232-to-Ethernet terminal servers such as the Patton 2120 are expensive (about $250), you'll want to either build your own Ethernet converter or use a USB-to-RS-232 converter such as the FTDI US232B USB to Serial Adapter (www.parallax.com/detail.asp?product_id=800-00030).

Chapter 2 shows how to run a wireless RS-232 connection should pulling cables be too hard.

- **Network connections** — You have much more flexibility with network connections than the USB or RS-232 ones, because local network connections can be wired or wireless, and can extend over greater distances. Few of your kitchen devices will have Ethernet interfaces, though, so the network connections are going to be useful primarily to put your Kitchen PC on your LAN. A wireless LAN connection to the Kitchen PC will be the easiest to install (although you should first verify the absence of interference from your microwave oven and wireless phone handsets); and if you use some of the less well standardized versions of IEEE 802.11, you can get 100 Mbps performance (versus the ceiling of 54 Mbps for IEEE 802.11g).

Of course, you only need the higher data rates if you're going to feed video to the PC over your LAN, such as with the networked television server in Chapter 3. Otherwise, even IEEE 802.11b at 10 Mbps is fast enough.

Software

Software is what integrates the Kitchen PC into something useful. We've not found a single application that does everything you'd want, but here are some options for a collection of programs you can use and enhance:

- **Inventory** — Barcode-driven inventory software is one of the two fundamental applications for your Kitchen PC. Our Anything Inventory software (Chapter 6) is a fully functional, although simple, application, and has connections out to the Internet to resolve barcodes to products.

- **Recipes** — Cookbooks are great, but you'll want a database to store the recipes you use over and over, including the unique changes to the original recipe you've made. Later on in this section, we'll describe a Microsoft Access database we built to show some of the possibilities.

- **Timer** — Cooking is a sequence of steps, many of which take specific lengths of time. We found several small programs that operate as kitchen timers, including Tiny Timer (www.tucows.com/preview/355030.html, freeware), and Egg Timer (www.tucows.com/preview/374811.html, $5 shareware). Of the two, we prefer Egg Timer, because Tiny Timer lacks an audible alarm.

However, neither program can stack a series of timed steps; nor do they tie to a recipe database. You could enhance the recipe database we provide to include a series of timer values in each recipe's data, and then add application functions to execute those timers.

Standard Windows applications, such as your Web browser, are useful too — for example, some of the best sources for recipes are sites such as Food Network (`www.foodtv.com`), Epicurious (`www.epicurious.com`), Williams-Sonoma (`www.williams-sonoma.com`), Emeril Lagasse's (`www.emerils.com`), Wolfgang Puck's (`www.wolfgangpuck.com`), and Bobby Flay's (`www.bobbyflay.com`). If you're one who flips among Web sites comparing information, consider the Firefox browser with its tabbed browsing capability (not to mention its much better security versus Internet Explorer).

The networked home television server in Chapter 3 includes client software that puts live television on your Kitchen PC screen without a local tuner. If you can run a television signal to the Kitchen PC and have the space for the tuner electronics, the same SageTV software described in Chapter 3 works wonderfully, or you could use the software suite ATI provides with their All-in-Wonder combined TV and video graphics cards.

The recipe database

We built a Microsoft Access database, and populated it with some of Marcia's recipes, to show what you might do in your Kitchen PC. (See Appendix C for how to get a copy from SourceForge.) Figure 7-5 shows one of the recipes in the database as it prints for reference. All the fields are in the recipe's record with the exception of the ingredients at the bottom, which are in a separate table and linked to the recipe.

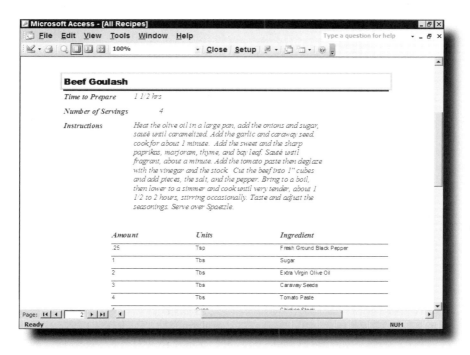

FIGURE 7-5: Recipe printout

Figure 7-6 shows the table structures and relationships for the recipes, including the linkage from each row in the Recipes table to any number of Ingredients rows, and from each Ingredients row to a corresponding Food row.

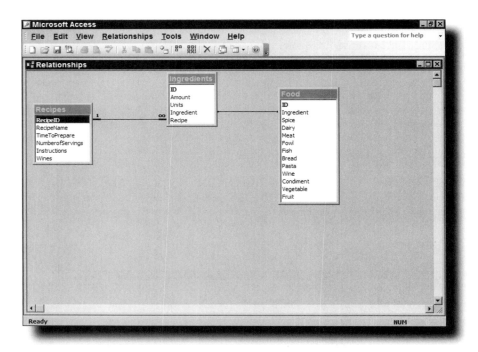

FIGURE 7-6: Table structures and relationships

The idea of the Food table is to categorize each ingredient, which lets you query the database more broadly — for example, you can search for recipes using meat (or not) versus those that call explicitly for beef.

A simple form supports entering and editing recipes, as in Figure 7-7. The form takes care of linking the ingredients table entries to the individual recipes.

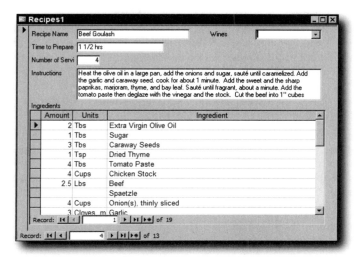

FIGURE 7-7: Recipe entry and edit form

Extending the Kitchen PC

The Kitchen PC is a wide-open platform for you to experiment with and extend. Most of the extensions you'd look at today are based on software, but as we'll show in this section, computer equipment and home appliance manufacturers are starting to see better opportunities in the home and kitchen, and are starting to market more information-enabled products.

Software

The software we discussed above is only the beginning of what you might do. For example:

- **Access** — Within Microsoft Access you have the tools to create your own queries and reports. We've provided some basic ones, but by no means exploited all the possibilities in the database structure. Moreover, you need a little know-how running Access to use the database; you could fix that with a front-end menu.

- **Integrate inventory with the recipe database** — The barcode inventory software in Chapter 6 and the database in this chapter need not be separate; you could instead keep the barcode inventory in the database. That's what we had in mind with the Food table — that its individual rows would really be items from the barcode scanner.

  The easiest way to build this extension is to add a field to the Food table that holds the actual barcode value — the sequence of numbers — and then tell Access how to look up the barcode when the ingredient name in that row is empty. You'd do that by modifying the Anything Inventory software to be an *automation server* in Microsoft's terminology, and then writing code in Access Basic to hook to the automation server.

Automation can be terrifying when you first approach it, because you implement it via Microsoft's Component Object Model (COM) technology, something every bit as simple as, say, nuclear physics or brain surgery. Fortunately, you don't need much to happen across the automation interface, you just need to hand off the barcode value and get back the returned description. There's a nice article on the Code Project Web site that walks you through what you'll need to do on the C++ side (`www.codeproject.com/com/mfc_autom.asp`). Once you've done the C++ work (and perhaps tested it with a simple Visual Basic application), integration into Access Basic should be easy.

- **Leftovers** — Adding leftover expiration dates to the database isn't too hard, either — you'll need a function to create and print a barcode label for each leftover container, and you need to add a leftovers table. We'd store the barcode value, description, and (if available) the original recipe in each row of the table, along with the expiration date. You don't need a quantity field for this, because you'll want an individual label for each container (so, the quantity is always one).

- **Cooking instructions** — If you add the necessary information into the Foods table, you could look up and display microwave and oven cooking information when a barcode scanner activates, reading out the result on an LCD right at the cooking area.

- **Wines** — There's a sketch of an approach for linking wines to recipes in the database, but it's literally only that. You could build something functional.

Equipment

It's undoubtedly being driven by the realization that there are geeks with money, but nevertheless manufacturers are starting to build products that provide and use information more intelligently in the kitchen. For example:

- **Microwave oven** — LG Electronics now makes a microwave oven with a PC network interface (`www.lge.com/products/homenetwork/internetproduct/microwaveoven/microwaveoven.jsp`). A data cable connects the oven to your PC; specialized software (yeah, we know, more proprietary protocols to reverse engineer) lets you download recipes to the oven. They've got an "Internet Refrigerator" too (`www.lge.com/products/homenetwork/internetproduct/refrigerator/introduction.jsp`), but it looks to be little more than an LCD panel (with a processor) on the front.

- **Salton line** — The Salton company has created a line of kitchen appliances (`www.esalton.com/control/catalog/category/~category_id=C10004`) targeting what they call the "connected home." So far, that includes a bread maker (`www.esalton.com/control/product/~category_id=C20002/~product_id=WBYBM2`), a microwave oven (`www.esalton.com/control/product/~category_id=C20002/~product_id=WBYMW2`), and a control/processing/entertainment console to tie it all together. It looks to us like one company's closed-garden view of what you might build yourself as a Kitchen PC, with the advantage of connections to the two appliances.

- **PDA** — There's no reason why you have to revert to paper when you go shopping. If you hook your PDA to your Kitchen PC, you can load in an electronic copy of your shopping list. Build your own application and you can check off what you do and don't buy, simplifying updating your inventory at home. Add a small barcode reader to the PDA to record items while you shop — your Kitchen PC can supply the barcodes to look for — and inventory update is just painless.

Many more options will undoubtedly come to market. If we're all lucky, manufacturers will collaborate to create an open command and control protocol anyone can write to.

Summary

Providing the right information in the right place at the right time is the job of a Kitchen PC. What that means in practice depends on how intense you are about cooking, and about how you work in your kitchen. Building your own Kitchen PC lets you adapt it to your specific kitchen and your way of working.

Automated BBQ Temperature Control

This is, unabashedly, a chapter for your inner carnivore. We did find nearly 300 hits on Google searching for "smoked vegetables", but that was out of curiosity more than anything. We like smoked barbeque a lot — sidebars in this chapter show you our favorite recipes for pulled pork and for beef brisket — but to be right it has to cook on a very low heat for a long time to let the fat render out. We also like the flavor we get by smoking with charcoal logs — an electric smoker just doesn't do the job right.

That combination, long, slow cooking with charcoal, is hard to do well. We keep the smoker at around 225°F, a temperature so low that it's easy for the fire to go out. You can do it if you're willing to tend the fire constantly, but we're not that patient.

Project Description

Instead of tending the fire yourself, a small control system can tend it for you, controlling the air flow to maintain a set temperature. You could enhance our design to warn you to add fuel during a very long smoke cycle.

Figure 8-1 shows the smoker we use. It's a slight enhancement of the common horizontal design, hanging a separate firebox on the left of the main smoker. The separate firebox keeps the direct radiant heat from the coals away from the meat, letting the hot smoky air do the cooking. The placement of the firebox lower than the smoker causes the upwards convection flow of the heated air to draw air into the smoker and then up the flue. The air inlet and flue damper are manually adjustable to control airflow and therefore the rate of combustion, which determines the internal smoker temperature.

Before employing any captured artifacts or machinery, I will carefully read the owner's manual.

Peter Anspach,
The Evil Overlord List

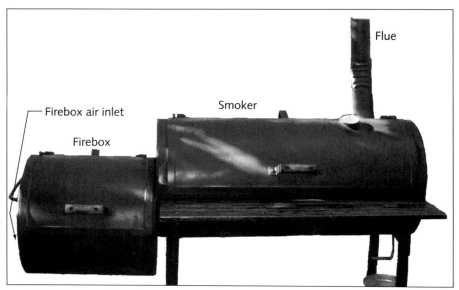

FIGURE **8-1**: Horizontal smoker

Pulled Pork

Make a brine from 1 cup dark molasses, 1 ½ cups Kosher salt, and 2 quarts water. Use bottled water if your tap water tastes bad. Make the brine in a 2 to 2 ½ gallon food storage bag, then put a 6–8 pound Boston butt (it's part of a pork shoulder—ask your butcher) into the brine. Put the bag into a large bowl for support and to guard against leaks, and squeeze the air out of the bag so the brine completely covers the meat. You'll need to get the right size bowl to make this work easily. Let the meat soak in the refrigerator for 8–12 hours.

Remove the butt from the brine, dry it, cover with plastic or foil, and bring to room temperature. Make a rub by first grinding 1 ½ teaspoons whole cumin seed, 1 ½ teaspoons whole fennel seed, and 1 ½ teaspoons whole coriander to a powder. Add 1 tablespoon chili powder, 1 ½ table-spoons onion powder, 1 tablespoon paprika, and 1 tablespoon hot paprika. Sprinkle the rub evenly over the butt, patting it in and working to make sure it all sticks to the meat. We use a spoon to sprinkle the rub on, cover the meat and the rub with plastic wrap, and pat in the rub through the plastic. Turn the assembly over and repeat. Use all the rub for the spiciest results, less for a milder version.

Remove the wrap and smoke the meat at 225°F for 8–12 hours, checking to see if it's done after 8 hours. It's done if it pulls apart easily with a fork. If you run out of time, smoke it at 225°F for 3-4 hours, then cover with foil and bake for 3 hours in an oven preheated to 300°F. Once it's done, let the meat rest and cool for at least an hour covered with foil, then pull apart into bite-sized chunks.

Serve with a mustard sauce made from 3 ounces Dijon mustard, 3 ounces sweet pickle juice, 1 ounce cider vinegar, and Tabasco to taste.

Beef Brisket

Make a rub from 4 tablespoons dark brown sugar, 2 tablespoons chili power, 2 tablespoons paprika, 1–2 tablespoons hot paprika, 2 tablespoons Kosher salt, 2 tablespoons garlic powder, 2 tablespoons onion powder, 1 tablespoon black pepper, 1 tablespoon white pepper, 1 tablespoon cayenne pepper, 1 tablespoon dry mustard, and 1 tablespoon finely ground cumin. Coat a 6–8 pound trimmed beef brisket with the rub, then wrap tightly in plastic and marinate in the refrigerator for at least 8 hours (overnight is best).

Bring meat to room temperature, then unwrap it and smoke at 225°F until it's done, which is when it reaches an internal temperature of at least 175°F. Do not cook too quickly or for too short a time, because the meat needs time at heat for the fat to drip out. Let the brisket rest for 20 minutes before slicing against the grain into thin slices.

If you replace the chili powder, cumin, and mustard with 4 tablespoons dried thyme, 4 tablespoons dried oregano, and a tablespoon of ground coriander, the rub works well on pork ribs or a pork shoulder.

System Diagram

Figure 8-2 shows the smoker system as a block diagram. Air enters the system at the left and exits at the top right. Heat is generated in the firebox and exits everywhere; the amount of heat generated is determined by the amount of charcoal in the firebox and the volume of air moving past the charcoal.

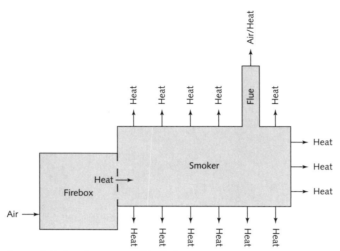

FIGURE 8-2: Smoker system block diagram

Under pure convection, the volume of air moving through the system is itself determined by the heat differential between the air in the system and the outside air, and by the size of the inlet and flue openings. One option to control the internal temperature is, in fact, to physically move one or the other of the dampers in the openings, but because that approach requires knowing the absolute position of the damper as well as being able to move it, we chose another approach — we decided to set the dampers so the system had slightly too little air flow, then use a fan to push air through the too-restrictive opening. That approach gives the control system the ability to reduce and increase heat, and requires only that we control the speed of a fan.

The overall control system has the block diagram shown in Figure 8-3. We used the Javelin Stamp processor to run the software, giving it a thermistor as a sensor and a variable speed fan as an actuator. There's a balance between the damper setting and the size of the fire you build in the firebox. Getting that setting right is a matter of trial and error, but the control software can help by telling you it can't stabilize the system and indicating whether the damper needs to be opened further or closed.

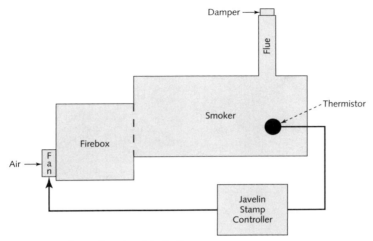

FIGURE 8-3: Control system block diagram

Sensor

The two most common sensor types for applications in this temperature range are thermocouples and thermistors. A *thermocouple* is a junction of two dissimilar metals, a bimetallic junction, which produces a voltage related to the temperature. Connecting wires to the thermocouple leads form additional bimetallic junctions between the metals forming the thermocouple and the copper wires, generating spurious voltages. Correcting out those additional voltages requires knowing the temperature at the additional junctions, increasing the hardware complexity.

A *thermistor* is a thermally variable resistor, a device whose resistance varies with temperature. We designed this project to use a thermistor because it's much simpler to implement in hardware, and because we could get one already packaged to survive barbeque conditions. There are two basic types of thermistor, ones whose resistance goes up with increasing temperature and ones whose resistance goes down with increasing temperature. The former are *positive temperature coefficient* (PTC) thermistors, the latter *negative temperature coefficient* (NTC) ones. Thermistors are relatively sensitive, producing a relatively large resistance change per degree of temperature change. Unfortunately, they're highly nonlinear over their full operating range, obeying the following equation:

$$R = R_0\, e^{\beta \left(\frac{1}{T} - \frac{1}{T_0} \right)}$$

We're interested in temperatures at approximately 225°F, so we measured the resistance of the sensor we used over the range 210–240°F with the results shown in the *Resistance* column of Table 8-1. (We'll come back to the right-hand column shortly.)

Table 8-1   Measured Thermistor Sensor Resistance

Temperature Reading (Degrees F)	Resistance (K Ohms)	Voltage Drop on 10K Ohm Resistor
210	10.50	2.44
211	9.90	2.51
212	9.60	2.55
213	9.40	2.58
214	9.21	2.60
215	9.01	2.63
216	8.84	2.65
217	8.68	2.68
218	8.53	2.70
219	8.43	2.71
220	8.29	2.73
221	8.18	2.75
222	8.05	2.77
223	7.95	2.79
224	7.84	2.80
225	7.70	2.82
226	7.52	2.85
227	7.33	2.89
228	7.25	2.90
229	7.10	2.92
230	6.98	2.94
231	6.77	2.98
232	6.66	3.00
233	6.58	3.02
234	6.51	3.03
235	6.38	3.05
239	5.98	3.13
240	5.76	3.17

Circuits to measure the resistance of a thermistor are shown in Figure 8-4. In both circuits, the thermistor in series with a fixed resistor forms a voltage divider across the regulated 5-volt supply. The circuit on the left measures the variable voltage across the thermistor directly; the one on the right measures across the fixed resistor. The right-hand circuit helps linearize the measurements versus temperature, so it's the one you should use. The right-hand column in Table 8-1 is the voltage measured across a 10K Ohm fixed resistance using the right-hand circuit.

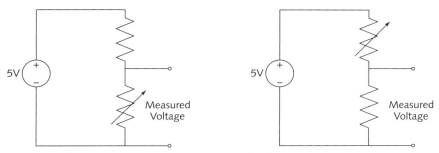

FIGURE 8-4: Thermistor resistance measurement circuits

Figure 8-5 graphs the data from Table 8-1. The dashed, downward-sloping line is the calculated curve fitting the thermistor equation for the unit we used, and has the parameters T_0 = 210°F, R_0 = 10.5K Ohms, and β = 1008.74. The straight downward-sloping line is a linear curve fit to the measured data (the equation parameters are just below the line on the right), while the points overlaying the linear curve fit are the measured data itself. The 10K Ohm resistor isn't too far off the measured resistance at the 225°F target temperature, erring on the low temperature side, and is a readily available value.

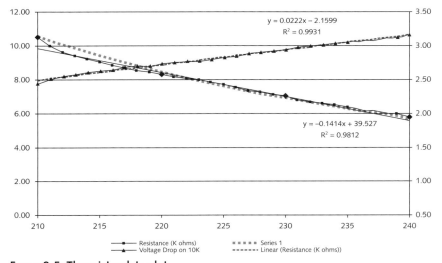

FIGURE 8-5: Thermistor data plot

The rising line and points in Figure 8-5 are the voltages measured using the right-hand circuit in Figure 8-4 using a 10K Ohm fixed resistor. The corresponding linear curve fit equation is shown in the upper right corner.

The plots are relatively linear over the operating region we care about — the measurements across the fixed resistor even more so — so we didn't bother to include any other logic or circuitry to address the nonlinear properties of the thermistor. (We also clamped the measured voltage between 2.5 and 3.2 volts to ensure that our computations stayed in the linear region — see the software section — and did a quick calculation of the load current, less than a third of a milliamp, to be sure it wouldn't overload the Javelin Stamp supply.)

Actuator

Even though we discarded the idea of moving either the flue damper or the firebox damper (Figure 8-6) in favor of using a fan to control the airflow through a restricted port, we still had engineering challenges to solve in creating the actuator our control system requires. Foremost among them were how to mount the fan on the barbeque and how to keep the fan within its maximum heat rating.

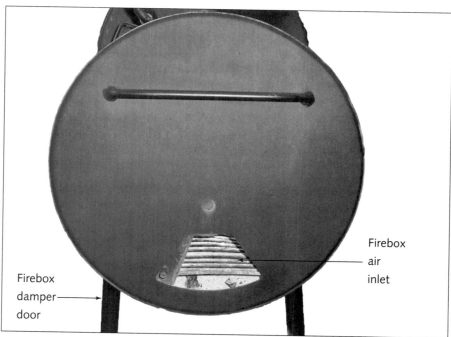

FIGURE 8-6: Firebox inlet

Those two challenges are related, of course, because mounting at the irregularly shaped firebox inlet is harder than mounting on the vertical, cylindrical flue, but the firebox inlet lets the fan operate in ambient temperature air, while the flue requires that the fan operate in the high temperature, smoke, and possibly grease-laden exhaust gases.

We searched the Web for a long time for high-temperature DC fans — we chose a DC fan to make it simple to interface and control with a microprocessor — and simply could not find any that were both sized for the 3-inch flue diameter on our smoker and priced reasonably. A Google search for *fan dc "high temperature"* returned the best results we found, and we then searched both the Thomas Register and the W.W. Grainger site (www.grainger.com) without success. We found a wide variety of fans such as you'd use to cool a computer case, but they all had maximum temperature ratings of 158°F (70°C). Even running as cool a smoker as we planned, we have to handle air temperatures up to 300°F (149°C), so one of these fans mounted on the flue won't last long.

That problem, more than any other factor, drove us to mount the fan at the firebox inlet, where the fan would operate at ambient outside air temperatures and the only temperature problems we'd face would be thermal isolation from the fire itself. The design also has to ensure the airflow remains slow enough that it doesn't blow ashes into the smoker.

The remaining actuator design element is how to drive the fan over a range of speeds. It's simple to output a pulse width modulated (PWM) signal from the Javelin Stamp — there's code built in to do the job — so all that's required is to provide a driver transistor to handle the power levels required by the fan motor. The fans we looked at typically required less than 210 ma at 12 volts. We searched a catalog of transistors readily available at RadioShack and chose the IRF510 MOSFET, rated for up to 60 volts at 3 amps; 20 watts. We wired a diode in parallel with the fan, wired backwards to the current flow, to snub any reverse switching spikes. Figure 8-7 shows the fan drive circuit; the PWM Drive signal connects directly to the output pin on the Javelin Stamp.

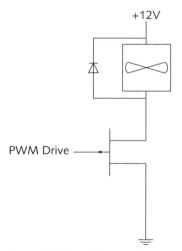

FIGURE 8-7: Fan drive circuit

Parts and Designs

While we were developing this project, we found a complete product that did much the same thing, the BBQ Guru from HomeBBQ.com. It's no longer available on their site (shop .homebbq.com/pd_bbq_guru.cfm), but you can see what it was using the Wayback Machine (web.archive.org/web/20040224101508/http://shop.homebbq.com/ pd_bbq_guru.cfm).

Our initial plan for the project used a PC, simplifying the software by making a highly capable platform available for processing and display. A laptop would be convenient to take outdoors, and could use a plug-in probe and fan. PC-interfaced thermometers are available, so the remaining electronics design work would be what's needed to drive the fan. We thought a while about using an expensive laptop where it was likely to fall or get spilled on, though, and decided a standalone controller with its own embedded processor was a better idea.

Sensor

We wanted a sensor that we could use as either an ambient air temperature probe within the smoker or as a meat probe, looking forward to other projects in which we'd extend the calibrated range of measurements beyond the 210–240°F range. We happen to have a wireless barbeque thermometer with an appropriate probe (see Table 8-2), so we designed our circuits around it. We've also seen probes as part of oven thermometers and other equipment at Bed Bath and Beyond, and at Super Target, so look around.

Table 8-2   Temperature Probe

Sensor	Source
Pal Products Nu-Temp model NU-701 Simple Wireless BBQ Thermometer	Nu-Temp www.nu-temp.com/701.htm
	Probes available at http://www.nu-temp.com/replace.htm

The probe (Figure 8-8) is a negative temperature coefficient (NTC) thermistor encased appropriately for food use and with a high-temperature cable.

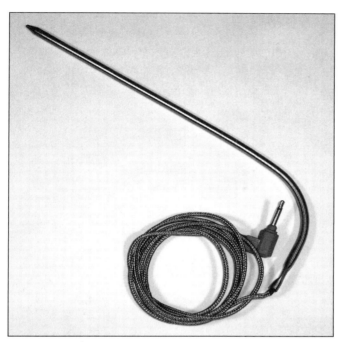

FIGURE 8-8: Probe

Table 8-1 records our measurements using this probe. We used the sigma-delta analog-to-digital converter (ADC) capability of the Javelin Stamp processor to read the probe, connecting them together in the circuit shown in Figure 8-9. The probe itself is in series with a 10K Ohm resistor, as in Figure 8-4; the junction of the two is the measurement point for the ADC. The sigma delta converter works by summing the two voltages fed to the integrating capacitor in Figure 8-9. One voltage is the output of the resistive divider formed by the thermistor and fixed resistor; the other is the direct 0 or 5-volt output of a pin on the Javelin Stamp. The software in the Javelin Stamp modulates the pulses on that output pin to cause the input pin, connected directly to the integrating capacitor, to settle at the 2.5 volt logic threshold.

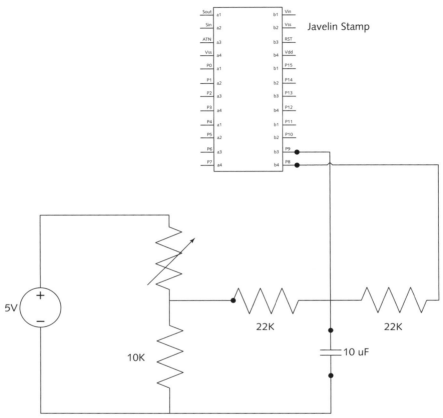

FIGURE 8-9: Temperature probe measurement

The result of the sigma delta ADC software processing is a count from 0 to 255, corresponding to the duty cycle on the output pin. A value of zero corresponds to zero volts from the divider; a value of 255 corresponds to 5 volts.

Actuator

We tried to find a 12-volt DC fan designed for outdoor use, but without success, so ultimately we settled for a simple 120 mm fan originally designed for cooling PC cases. Although most any 120 mm fan would do (smaller fans likely won't move enough air), we really like the RadioShack unit we list in Table 8-2 because of its metal body. The fan blades are still plastic, though, so it can't get too close to the firebox even though it's working at the inlet. No matter what fan you use, they're inexpensive enough that should the fan fail after being used beyond its intended temperature ratings, the replacement cost is small. Put connectors in the wiring between the fan and controller to simplify replacement.

We mounted the fan in a foot-long, square cross section metal pipe we made using four pre-bent galvanized step flashing pieces we found at The Home Depot (Figure 8-10). We used high-temperature aluminum foil tape to hold the sections together and sprayed the assembly with high-temperature paint. The pipe guides the air from the fan to the inlet while spacing the fan back from the hot zone around the inlet. You'll want to keep the pipe close around the fan and near the inlet to make sure all the available air flow goes to the smoker. If you're building a permanent brick barbeque, consider building in an air pipe to conduct the airflow from a fan to the fire pit.

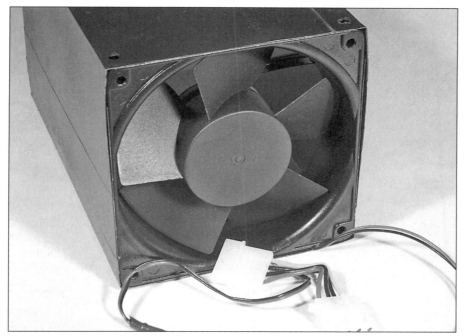

FIGURE 8-10: Fan mounting

We used the power transistor (and heat sink) shown in Table 8-2 to drive the fan, as in Figure 8-7, coupling the gate on the MOSFET to the PWM signal pin on the Javelin Stamp through a 10K Ohm resistor.

We needed a 12-volt supply for the fan. The Javelin Stamp demo board accepts from 6 to 24 volts, so by ensuring we provided enough current from the power adapter, we were able to use a common source. Don't use just any 12-volt AC-to-DC power adapter, because most of the ones you'll find are unregulated and likely put out 13 to 16 volts. We smoked a couple of fans before we thought to actually measure the adapter voltage output. The RadioShack unit in Table 8-3 is regulated to a selectable voltage, making it useful for a variety of projects, and outputs 0.8 amps — enough to power the fan shown (0.32 amps) and the Javelin Stamp (0.3 amps).

Table 8-3   Actuator

Component	Source

RadioShack
Catalog #: 273-238
4" Cooling Fan
	RadioShack
	`www.radioshack.com/product.asp?`
	`catalog%5Fname=CTLG&product%`
	`5Fid=273-238`

RadioShack
Catalog #: 276-2072
IRF510 Power MOSFET Transistor
	RadioShack
	`www.radioshack.com/product.asp?`
	`catalog%5Fname=CTLG&product%`
	`5Fid=276-2072`

RadioShack
Catalog #: 276-1368
Heat Sink
	RadioShack
	`www.radioshack.com/product.asp?`
	`catalog%5Fname=CTLG&category%`
	`5Fname=CTLG%5F011%5F002%5F008%5F000&`
	`product%5Fid=276%2D1368&site=search`

RadioShack
Catalog #: 273-1667
3-12VDC/800mA Regulated
AC-to-DC Adapter
	RadioShack
	`www.radioshack.com/product.asp?`
	`catalog%5Fname=CTLG&product%`
	`5Fid=273-1667`
	
	You'll also need power leads to connect to the project; see these:
	Hobby Power Leads Adaptaplug
	`http://www.radioshack.com/product`
	`.asp?catalog%5Fname=CTLG&product%`
	`5Fid=273-1742`

Processor

We'd far rather program in reasonable, object-oriented languages, so given that the Parallax Javelin Stamp offered both that and the peripheral device support we needed — the sigma delta analog-to-digital converter and the pulse width modulation output — it was a simple choice to make. We hosted the prototype on the Parallax Javelin Stamp Demo Board, identified in Table 8-4 and shown in Figure 8-11. The solderless breadboard area on the right is convenient for prototyping, and the spacing is such that you can plug in the LCD directly across a set of five rows.

Table 8-4   Embedded Processor

Processor	Source
Parallax Javelin Stamp	Parallax `www.parallax.com/javelin/`

FIGURE 8-11: Javelin Stamp

Display

We used the Parallax BPI-216 Serial LCD Module for the display output (see Table 8-5). The LCD connects to power, ground, and any I/O pin on the Javelin Stamp, and not only provides a 2.4 or 9.6 Kbps, one-wire interface to the processor, it also responds to a number of commands to clear, scroll, and address the cursor to locations on the display.

Table 8-5   LCD Display

Display	Source
Parallax BPI-216 Serial LCD Module	Parallax www.parallax.com/detail.asp? product_id=27910

Figure 8-12 shows the LCD displaying output from our software. At the point we took the photo, we'd just started up the fire. The ADC was reading a very low value, below the linear region of the thermistor, and the computations were therefore driving the fan to the full speed state.

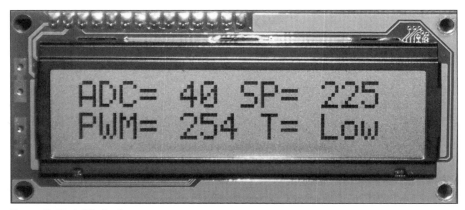

FIGURE 8-12: LCD display

Software

The software for the controller is all in Java for the Javelin Stamp, written to live within that processor's characteristics of no garbage collection (so you don't want to allocate memory or strings as the software runs) and 16-bit integer arithmetic (so you have to pay attention to ranges of values and order of computations).

Sensor

The values from the ADC correlate linearly to the voltage input to the sigma delta converter. Figure 8-13 shows a range of measurements we made, along with a linear trend line and the corresponding equation.

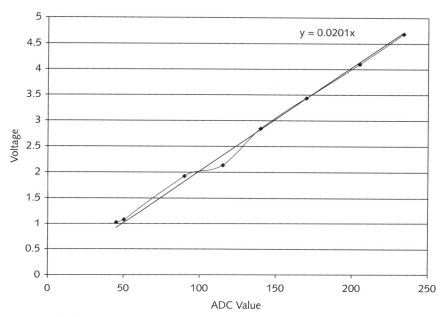

FIGURE **8-13: ADC values versus voltage**

The linear relationship between voltage and temperature (over a limited range) shown in Figure 8-5 combines with the relationship in Figure 8-13 to create a linear relationship directly between ADC value and temperature, as shown in Figure 8-14. The actual constant offset (98.151 in the figure) you'll need varies from one sample of the probe to another; you'll probably want to adjust it (and perhaps the variable coefficient too) to match the probe you use. We saw a variation of 5 to 10 degrees among probes.

The essential details you need from Figure 8-14 for software implementation are these:

- The useful range of ADC values runs from 125 to 159.

- The ADC value range corresponds to a temperature range of 211 to 240°F.

- The equation T = 0.8945 * ADC + 98.151 converts ADC values to temperatures.

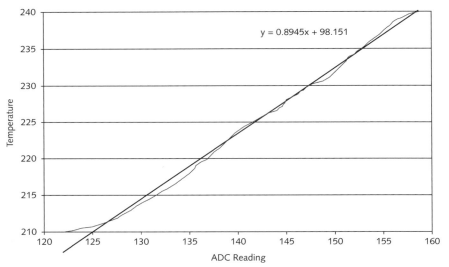

$$y = 0.8945x + 98.151$$

FIGURE 8-14: ADC values versus temperature

The Javelin Stamp only directly implements 16-bit integer arithmetic, however, so the software has to process these equations without floating-point support and without overflowing the 16-bit signed integers. The following code segment converts ADC values to temperatures using the points above:

```
//
//  Constants used to convert ADC readings to other units
//
final static int LOWADC = 125;          // Temp is too non-linear below this
final static int HIGHADC = 159;         // Upper limit of linear readings
final static int TEMPNUM = 178;         // ADC to 100th of deg
final static int TEMPDENOM = 2;         // ADC to (100ths of deg)
final static int TEMPADD = 9815;        // Scaled for 100ths of deg


//--------------------------------------------- ConvertToTemp ----------------
/** ConvertToTemp
 * Converts ADC sample value to temperature in degrees F
 * @nADC - sample value from ADC, range 0 - 255
 * @return - temperature * 100, or +/-1 if out of range
 */
  public int ConvertToTemp( int nADC) {
    int nTemp;

    if (nADC < LOWADC)
      nTemp = -1;
    else if (HIGHADC < nADC)
      nTemp = 1;
    else
```

```
      nTemp = (nADC * TEMPNUM) / TEMPDENOM + TEMPADD;
   return( nTemp );
}
```

The `ConvertToTemp` routine both thresholds the ADC values, returning ±1 for out-of-range values, and computes the temperature for values in range. The computation multiplies by the numerator of the fraction 179/2 first, before the divide, to ensure there's no loss of precision due to integer truncation after the divide. We derived 179/2 in this sequence:

1. The coefficient for the ADC samples is 0.89, derived from the equation T = 0.89*ADC + 98.

2. We converted 0.89 to 89/100 to make the calculation a sequence of integer operations.

3. Multiplying both factors by 2 keeps the ratio constant, but retains the most accuracy in the calculation by using all the bits available for the multiply. You can check this by noting that the maximum ADC sample is 159, so the largest possible multiplier without overflow is 32767/159 = 206.081, which rounds down to 206. The corresponding denominator would be 206/0.89, or 231.46, rounded to 231.

4. We wanted to maintain the integer temperature in hundredths of a degree (that is, multiplied by 100), and chose to incorporate the factor of 100 in the denominator of the factors. Dividing 231 by 100 with integer truncation creates an error of over 13 percent, so instead we chose the denominator to be 200/100 = 2. The corresponding numerator becomes 200 * 0.89 = 178.

5. Finally, the additive constant gets scaled by 100 to match the units we're converting to, becoming 98.151 * 100 = 9815.

The ADC values themselves are sampled by the Javelin Stamp ADC virtual peripheral; the code to set up and sample it in the `TemperatureProbe` class is as follows (the lines above the `sample` method are globals within the class definition):

```
//
// ADC Connections
//
final static int ADC_IN_PIN = CPU.pin9;
final static int ADC_OUT_PIN = CPU.pin8;

//
// ADC device
//
static int ADCValue;
static ADC voltMeter = new ADC( ADC_IN_PIN, ADC_OUT_PIN );

//----------------------------------------------- sample ----------------------
/** sample
 * Read the voltmeter and return the sample value.
 * @returns in int with the value, range 0-255
 */
public int sample() {
  return( ADCValue = voltMeter.value() );
}
```

The ADC updates its measurement every 2.1 milliseconds, far faster than we sample in the controller application.

Actuator

Using PWM fan speed control makes the software to control the fan simple, requiring only that we connect one pin on the Javelin Stamp to the gate on the power transistor, and then drive that pin with a PWM virtual peripheral in the code. Here's the software to run the fan (the globals and method are within the FAN class):

```
//
// Globals
//
final static int PWMPIN = CPU.pin1;
static PWM pwm = new PWM( PWMPIN, 0, 255 );

//----------------------------------------------- update ----------------------
/** update
 * Update the running PWM parameters
 * @nPWM - the new duty cycle setting, 0-255
 */
public void update( int nPWM ) {
  if (0 <= nPWM && nPWM <= 255) {
    pwm.update( nPWM, 255 - nPWM );
  }
}
```

The PWM object runs in the background, delivering a constant pulse train to the fan at the duty cycle specified to the update routine.

There's a minimum pulse train duty cycle that will actually rotate the fan; the fan we used didn't rotate for PWM values below 30 or 35. For that reason, we incorporated this logic into the main loop of the controller to keep the motor either shut off or rotating slowly:

```
// Adjust fan minimum -- it doesn't run at less than around 30 or 35
if (nPWM <= FANZERO)
  nPWM = 0;
else if (nPWM < FANMIN)
  nPWM = FANMIN;
fan.update( nPWM );
```

We set FANZERO to 5, and FANMIN to 35.

Display

We programmed the LCD display (see Figure 8-12) to output the information we found useful debugging and operating the controller. We chose to output the ADC sample values, set point temperature, PWM parameter, and temperature computed from the ADC samples, but it's relatively simple to change what's displayed. All the display code is in a method in the main BBQController class:

```
//-------------------------------------------------- OutputToLCD -----------------
// Show the readings on the LCD as ADC, volts, and degrees
// Line 1: ADC= xx Set= xxx
// Line 2: PWM= xxx T= Low/High/xxx
  final static int BUFLEN = 16;                         // LCD width
  static StringBuffer buf1 = new StringBuffer( BUFLEN );
  static StringBuffer buf2 = new StringBuffer( BUFLEN );

  public static void OutputToLCD( int nADC, int nTemp100, int nSet, int nPWM ) {
    // Line 1
    buf1.clear();
    buf1.append( "ADC= " );
    buf1.append( nADC );
    buf1.append( " SP= " );
    buf1.append( nSet / 100 );
    buf1.append( "     " );

    // Line 2
    buf2.clear();
    buf2.append( "PWM= " );
    buf2.append( nPWM );

    buf2.append( " T= " );
    switch (nTemp100) {
      case -1:
        buf2.append( "Low     " );
        break;

      case 1:
        buf2.append( "High    " );
        break;

      default:
        buf2.append( nTemp100 / 100 );
        buf2.append( "          " );
    }

    // Output
    LCD.WriteLCD( 1, buf1 );
    LCD.WriteLCD( 2, buf2 );
  }
```

The BBQLCD class wraps around the BPI216 class provided by Parallax; the most significant added functionality in BBQLCD is the itoas routine, which takes an integer scaled by a power of ten and decodes it to a StringBuffer.

The display routine, as written, pads the output strings with extra spaces at the end to ensure all previous characters on the display are overwritten. We originally wrote the code to simply clear the LCD and then write the text, but noticed some objectionable flicker we were able to eliminate with this approach. The text moves left and right a little depending on the number of characters in the first set of digits (the ADC and PWM values); if you found that objectionable, you could use direct cursor addressing and output the display items as four different sequences (two on each line) instead of two (one per line).

PID Loop

What connects temperature readings to fan speed settings is a *Proportional-Integral-Derivative (PID)* control loop. The equation underlying the calculation is

$$Co_{pid} = \left(Kp \times E \right) + \left(Ki \times \int Et \right) + \left(Kd \times \frac{\Delta E}{\Delta t} \right)$$

where

Co = controller output (the fan drive)

Kp = proportional drive gain

Ki = integral drive gain

Kd = derivative drive gain

E = error, computed as reading – setpoint

t = time

$\Delta E / \Delta t$ = change in E over time

Our code implementing this equation is as follows. We compute the error as a percentage over the measurement range (scaled by 100) to normalize the computations, and limit the resulting drive to 100 percent.

```
//----------------------------------------------- compute ---------------------
/** compute
 * Do the PID loop calculation, returning a 0-255 value for PWM use
 * @nTemp100 - current temperature * 100
 * @nSetPoint - what the correct temperature should be * 100
 * @return - PWM value
 */
public int compute( int nTemp100, int nSetPoint ) {
  int nErr;               // Error signal
  int nPctErr;            // Percentage Error
  int nProp;              // Proportional drive
  int nInt;               // Integral drive
  int nIntDelta;          // Integral total change value
  int nDeriv;             // Derivative drive
  int nDrive;             // Total drive
  int nPWM;               // PWM result

  // Calculate percentage error
  nErr = nTemp100 - nSetPoint;     // 100ths of a degree
  nPctErr = nErr / (RANGE / 100 / 2);

  // Calculate proportional drive
  nProp = (nPctErr * KP + ONEHALF) / 100;

  // Calculate integral drive
  nIntegralError += nPctErr;
  if (++nIntegralCount >= nIntegralLimit) {
```

```
      nIntDelta = (((nIntegralError + ONEHALF) / nIntegralLimit) * KI) / 100;
      nIntegralTotalError += nIntDelta;
      nIntegralTotalError = Math.max( -100, nIntegralTotalError );
      nIntegralTotalError = Math.min( 100, nIntegralTotalError );
      nIntegralError = 0;
      nIntegralCount = 0;
    }
    nInt = nIntegralTotalError;

    // Calculate derivative drive
    if (bFirst) {
      nDeriv = 0;
      bFirst = false;
    }
    else
      nDeriv = ((nPctErr - nLastDerivativeError) * KD + ONEHALF) / 100;
    nLastDerivativeError = nPctErr;

    // Total Drive
    nDrive = (BIAS + nProp + nInt + nDeriv);
    nDrive = Math.max( -100, Math.min( 100, nDrive ) );
    nPWM = 127 * -nDrive / 100 + 127;

    return( nPWM );
}
```

The code is a relatively direct implementation of the equation, integrating the error over a pre-defined number of periods and controlling the computations to maintain accuracy and avoid overflows.

The first element of the control loop to understand is the proportional drive, which simply computes a drive value as a factor times the error. The more the measured value differs from the set point, the greater the drive. Negative error speeds up the fan, while positive error slows it down.

The problem with using only proportional control is that it produces zero drive for zero error — when the measured temperature is equal to the set point temperature. If the fire can't maintain the set point temperature with zero drive, the system temperature will drift off. You can fix that with a bias drive component (the BIAS term in the code above, along with the bias introduced by making 127 equivalent to zero drive in the conversion from drive to PWM), but it's subject to error. Integral control drives that error out.

Finally, neither proportional nor integral control responds rapidly to more dramatic changes (such as opening the smoker lid) without overcontrolling the system. Derivative control solves that problem by adding drive in response to the change from one sample to the next.

There's a good overview of PID control in the Experiment 6 section of the Industrial Control text offered by Parallax at www.parallax.com/dl/docs/books/edu/ic.pdf. You can order the text as a book from Parallax at www.parallax.com/detail.asp? product_id=28156.

Somewhat harder is tuning the coefficients so the control loop drives the system properly. We've included this code at the bottom of the `compute` method (commented out) to dump the key variables back to a connected PC:

```
System.out.print( "T: " );
System.out.print( nTemp100 );
System.out.print( " S: " );
System.out.print( nSetPoint );
System.out.print( " Err: " );
System.out.print( nErr );
System.out.print( " PctErr: " );
System.out.print( nPctErr );
System.out.print( " P: " );
System.out.print( nProp );
System.out.print( " I: " );
System.out.print( nInt );
System.out.print( " D: " );
System.out.print( nDeriv );
System.out.print( " Drive: " );
System.out.print( nDrive );
System.out.print( " PWM: " );
System.out.println( nPWM );
```

If you plan to use the values with Excel, you might want to revise the code to output in comma separated value (CSV) form.

Extending the Controller

There are many ways you can extend our basic design and software. Here's a few; they're not necessarily ordered in increasing difficulty:

- Build it into a case able to protect it from being dropped or spilled on, and package it with a display window and connectors able to withstand outdoor conditions. RadioShack has a variety of project boxes you could use (www.radioshack.com/category .asp?catalog%5Fname=CTLG&category%5Fname=CTLG%5F011%5F002%5F01 2%5F000&Page=1), and Hobby Engineering has solderable prototyping boards (www.hobbyengineering.com/SectionCP.html).

- It's a nuisance to have to have a power cord to run the controller and fan, and you need less than 10 watts to run the entire assembly. If you integrated a Peltier cell (www.peltier-info.com) into the firebox (which will generate power when one side is hot and the other cold), you could generate the necessary power with nothing but the fire itself.

- We noted that the readings from different samples of the same model temperature probe can vary. You could calibrate your specific probe against an accurate source, such as an infrared temperature gun (for example, the Raytek MiniTemp at www.raytek-northamerica.com/cat.html?cat_id=2.3.6&PubSessID=6d7694588d3d0 eb588117c988675ab0e&PHPSESSID=publicRaytekNorthAmerica), modifying the additive constant and, if necessary, the variable coefficient for more accurate readings.

- The 16-bit arithmetic in the Javelin Stamp made some of the code awkward, and creates some restrictions such as the duration over which you can run the integrator in the PID loop. Parallax has both `Int32` and `IEEE754` floating-point math classes on their Web site you could use to revise the code. The Int32 code is at `www.parallax.com/javelin/applications.asp#AN011`, while the floating-point code is at `www.parallax.com/dl/appnt/jav/class/float32.zip`.

- We fixed the set point as a constant in the code to simplify the design. If you added some switches (or a keypad), you could create a user interface that lets you modify the set point (and perhaps the tuning coefficients), storing the new values in the EEPROM.

- The coefficients in our code are specific for our smoker, and aren't yet optimal. You could tune the coefficients to your equipment; one of the best resources for tuning we found on the Internet is *Tuning Criteria or "How do we know when it's tuned"* by John A. Shaw (`www.jashaw.com/pid/tutorial/pid6.html`). His book on PID control is available at `www.jashaw.com/pidbook`. You might also want to read the *sci.engr.* newsgroup FAQ on PID controller tuning (`www.tcnj.edu/~rgraham/PID-tuning.html` or directly in the newsgroups).

- The range of temperatures over which we use the sensor is very limited to avoid problems with thermistor non-linearity. You could extend the range; one approach would be to create a lookup table based on the fundamental equation for the sensor and some calibration measurements. If you do, you'll still need to bound the interval over which the PID algorithm operates, considering the error to be 100 percent outside that range. You might have to adjust the bias for the significantly different set points this enhancement makes possible, such as cold smoking at 150°F.

Summary

Using the barbeque controller is something of an art, because there's a lot of variation in fire size and heat loss — coefficient tuning simply can't do everything. You'll need to tune the inlet and outlet dampers to make sure the combination of fire size and damper settings keeps the system within the range of controllability of the system, or build a servo system to adjust the dampers automatically when the control loop goes beyond its limits. Categorically, too small a fire won't let the smoker stay hot enough; too big a fire tends to be more controllable because you can simply close the dampers more.

It's worth the effort.

In the Garage and Out the Door

part

IV

Automated Sprinkler Control

How often have you driven past a lawn being watered in a full rainstorm, stepped in a small bog of mud left over from too much watering, or shaken your head in frustration over that one dry spot on the grass you can't keep up with? Doesn't that sound like an opportunity?

Project Description

Unfortunately, the automated sprinkler controllers sold in hardware stores are simply fixed-function microcomputers programmed to turn on relays that activate your sprinkler valves at specified times. Few people install the available rain sensors, which would let the systems avoid the public stupidity of watering while it rains, but even with a rain sensor the systems are too simplistic to detect and eliminate the wet or dry spots. The duration each valve stays on is fixed unless you adjust the program yourself for changing conditions and soil moisture.

Fat chance. If you were going to be that meticulous, you could just turn manual valves on and off yourself.

On the other hand, sensors exist that can tell you how much moisture is in the soil — for example, visit the garden shop at your local hardware store and find the watering meters, the ones that indicate how wet the soil is. The ones we can find are usually cheap and not very durable, but imagine what you could do if you hooked up similar sensors to your PC. Combine the sensors with some relays to control the sprinkler circuits and software to control the system, and you could dynamically control how much water your garden gets.

System Diagram

Figure 9-1 shows how a conventional automated sprinkler control system works. The microprocessor uses a bank of relays to control electrically operated valves, one valve per sprinkler circuit, and one relay per valve. When a relay closes, the corresponding valve opens and water flows. The valves all share a common ground line that, if interrrupted, disables all the valves. Some controllers come with wiring terminals in the ground line designed to support a rain sensor that opens the circuit.

I will never employ any device with a digital countdown. If I find that such a device is absolutely unavoidable, I will set it to activate when the counter reaches 117 and the hero is just putting his plan into operation.

Peter Anspach,
The Evil Overlord List

in this chapter

☑ Conventional sprinkler controllers

☑ Soil moisture sensors

☑ Controlling the sprinkler controller

☑ Software

☑ HomeSeer interface

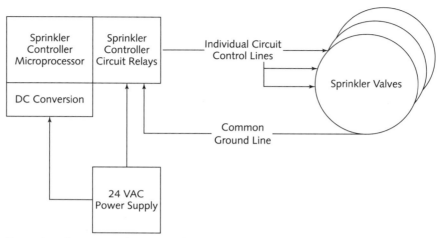

FIGURE 9-1: Conventional automated sprinkler controls

As in most control systems, an automated sprinkler controller has processing and actuators; it lacks the sensors and related processing it needs to be smart. Figure 9-2 shows how we modified the conventional system, adding moisture and weather forecast sensors, more capable processing (a PC), and one or more new actuators.

You could implement the system without a PC, using a standalone processor such as the Javelin Java processor, but we found it convenient to have the greater hardware resources and Internet connectivity of a PC available. The standalone processor can directly support an interface to read the moisture sensors, and you could still use the X-10 actuators we've used with a standalone processor if you interfaced it through its own interface module, such as an X-10 TW523 or CM11A.

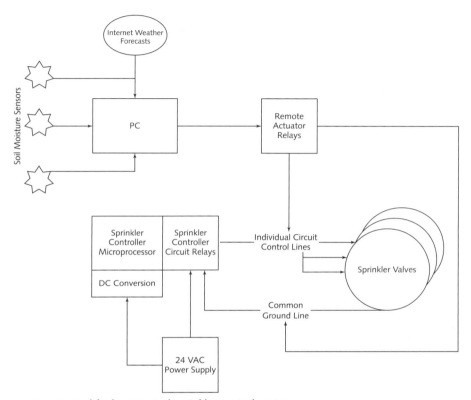

FIGURE 9-2: Modified automated sprinkler control system

Parts and Designs

Letting a processor control sprinkler circuits is simple, requiring only a way to control a relay, so we started our design at the sensor end of the system. We failed to find an affordable, low-maintenance soil moisture sensor for over a year, and were on the verge of starting to modify one of the cheap soil moisture meter probes to create a PC interface. Fortunately, we found both an inexpensive sensor and a sensor subsystem incorporating that sensor.

Sensor and sensor interface

Table 9-1 shows the viable hardware options we discovered for the soil moisture sensor. The Watermark sensor is the basis for the Davis Instruments soil moisture station.

Table 9-1   Soil Moisture Sensor and Interface Options

Sensor or Interface	Source

Irrometer Company, Inc.
Watermark soil moisture sensor
	Irrometer Company, Inc.
	`www.irrometer.com/agcat.htm#`
	`watermark`
	Davis Instruments
	`www.davisnet.com/weather/products/`
	`weather_product.asp?pnum=6440`

Parallax Inc.
Javelin Stamp embedded microprocessor
	Parallax Inc.
	`www.parallax.com/detail.asp?`
	`product_id=27237`

Davis Instruments
Vantage Pro Envoy and
soil moisture station
	Davis Instruments
	`www.davisnet.com/weather/products/`
	`weather_product.asp?pnum=6361`

We measured about 10M ohms resistance across a Watermark sensor when bone dry, settling to 5.6M ohms after more than an hour. You could use the Javelin Stamp analog to digital converter (ADC) class with a voltage divider and regulated voltage source to measure that resistance and operate the sensor.

Alternatively, you can use the complete subsystem offered as the Davis Instruments Vantage Pro Envoy wireless sensor data logger coupled with their soil moisture remote (Figure 9-3). Within Figure 9-3, (a) shows the Watermark sensor, and (b) is the remote wireless station to which you connect up to four Watermark sensors and four temperature probes. The indoor Vantage Pro Envoy receiver is in (c), while (d) shows a close-up of the switches you must configure in the remote wireless station to set the operating frequency.

The Envoy gathers indoor temperature, barometric pressure, and humidity directly, and reads up to four each soil moisture and temperature sensors from a wireless remote you station in the yard. The Envoy provides a serial port interface to your PC (consider a USB-to-serial port adapter such as the Parallax FTDI unit available from Parallax at `www.parallax.com/` `detail.asp?product_id=800-00030`), with a documented interface for both current data and archived samples. We chose to use the subsystem rather than build up our own interface, because the subsystem already had the features we wanted, including sensors besides just soil moisture, and because the wireless link to the remote station simplified connecting the outdoors sensors to the indoors PC.

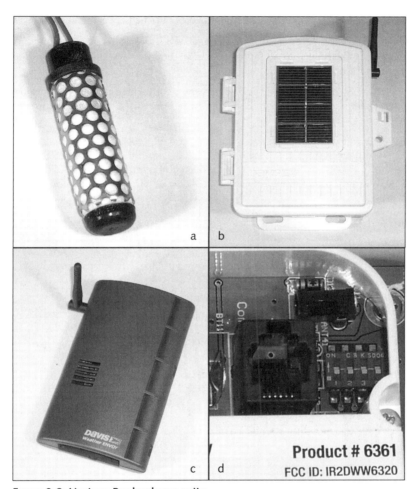

FIGURE 9-3: Vantage Pro hardware suite

We wanted to gather data from the soil moisture sensor to understand how it behaved in our yard while we worked on the rest of the system design and implementation. Davis Instruments documents the interface to the Vantage Pro in a specification at www.davisnet.com/support/weather/software.asp#vantagecomm, so to both gather data and verify we understood the interface we wrote some test software. Figure 9-4 shows a Microsoft Excel plot of the data we gathered, revealing some interesting properties of the sensor:

- Although it's specified as having a data range of 0 (very wet) to 200 (bone dry), the useful range of the sensor appeared to be 0 to 10 or so, because at readings higher than 10 the soil itself was too dry to grow anything.

- The target readings for the sensors in our yard appear to be between 1 and 3.

- The actual range as reported through the Vantage Pro interface is 0 to 200, but if you leave the sensor to dry further after it reaches 200, the interface will eventually report the same value as for no sensor connected.

- It takes only a few minutes for the sensor to respond to being dunked in a container of water, but it's far slower to dry out. The speed of response both ways is fast enough for garden watering applications.

- The movement of water through soil to a sensor placed 6 to 12 inches down is much slower than the sensor response time — we found it takes hours before the sensor reports a change after a good soaking from the sprinklers. You might want to stack two sensors, one to track surface water and another to track water at a depth for the roots of larger shrubs.

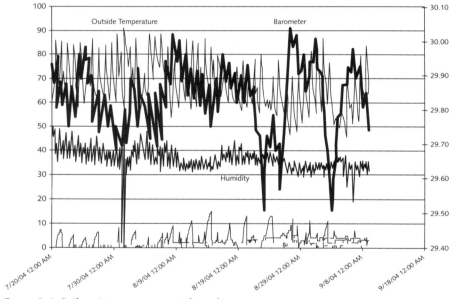

FIGURE 9-4: Soil moisture sensor test data plot

The abrupt drop in the soil moisture values near the middle of the plot are points where the interface reported no sensor data available. That wasn't because the ground suddenly dried out, though, it was because we powered up a second wireless transmitter station and forgot to change its operating frequency. Its transmissions jammed the signal from the operating one, a reminder that — as with any wireless link — you should both verify the link's integrity before trusting it, and build your control systems to respond in a known way if the wireless link fails. In the software we wrote, for example, missing data values result in guaranteed successful comparisons against thresholds, letting you program operating rules that leave the sprinklers on or off as you choose.

Processing

Because our sprinkler control circuits and our existing automated controller all are in the garage, and because we don't want to leave a PC in the hot and cold extremes of the garage, we decided we needed to use actuators remote from the PC running the control software. We don't want to run new control wires from PC to actuators, either, leaving the possibilities of either a wireless link such as you saw in Chapter 2 or X-10 power line controls. If we'd planned to control each sprinkler circuit independently, an embedded microprocessor with a relay bank at the sprinkler control station would have made using a wireless serial link simple. We chose to use X-10 interfaces instead, however, because we planned to control the sprinklers on an overall on/off basis.

The logic behind the decision to control only the entire bank of sprinkler circuits (using one relay in the ground line) was that we didn't want to deploy as many soil moisture sensors as would be required to sample enough areas of the yard to be able to resolve the need for running one circuit versus all the rest. Consequently, our system design works like this:

- We use the conventional automated sprinkler controller to sequence the time of day when each sprinkler circuit will run and for how long.

- We set the conventional controller to run more often than necessary — every day — and rely on the PC control to enable or disable watering for the day based on the soil moisture readings.

- We use a combination of infrequent deep watering and more frequent, light surface watering. The deep watering is under control of the PC, while the surface watering is always enabled and just enough to get shallow-rooted plants through the heat of the day.

- Because we use the PC controls only to modulate the deep watering cycles, we keep the sprinklers enabled except for the time spans when deep watering is scheduled. That approach makes it possible to run the sprinklers manually at any time, too, so we don't have to go running to the PC when we need to test sprinklers for coverage or other faults.

Using X-10 power line communications to control the actuators drove another design choice, too — we separated monitoring the sensors and computing whether watering was required from controlling the actuators. We wrote new software (Figure 9-5) for monitoring and controlling, described later in this chapter, and used the same HomeSeer software we use for other home automation responsibilities for actuator control.

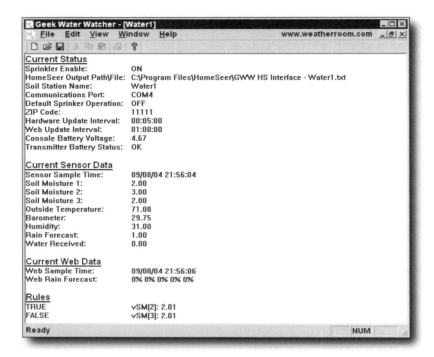

FIGURE 9-5: Control software

The other major component of our processing was the decision to link the monitoring and computing software to an Internet weather forecast source. The Vantage Pro equipment we used provides a weather forecasting function, and we built decoding into the software to detect when the hardware was forecasting rain. We noticed that the forecast changes relatively frequently, however, and that it didn't correspond to actual events as often as we wanted. Supplementing the hardware forecast with samples from an Internet source (based on ZIP code) creates the option to use either forecast, both, or none.

Table 9-2 lists the HomeSeer software and Internet weather forecast sources. We used an XML feed from the Web (as opposed to the Web page scraping we used in Chapter 6) for the forecast data to simplify locating and parsing the data, and found usable feeds at both weatherroom.com and weather.com. We initially planned to use the weather.com feed (because it explicitly includes a probability of precipitation estimate), but found them impossible to work with. Not only does their license agreement require consent to terms in a developers' guide you can't get before you consent, they were completely unresponsive to e-mails asking for clarification of how to comply with the licensing terms in the context of our software. The weatherroom.com license was far more lenient, but their forecast data provides only qualitative descriptions of the chance of precipitation. We made some arbitrary assignments of probabilities to those terms in our software to fill the gap.

Table 9-2   Processing Sources and Components

Data Source or Component	Source
HomeSeer Automation software	HomeSeer Technologies LLC `www.homeseer.com`

Internet XML weather feed	weather.com
	`www.weather.com/services/`
	`xmloap.html`

Internet XML weather feed	weatherroom.com `www.weatherroom.com/add.html`

Simple as the communication needs to be—HomeSeer merely needs to be told when the sprinklers are enabled or disabled—the interface between our software and HomeSeer required some thought. There were two key design issues:

- There is some time required to read the serial port on the Vantage Pro, and a potentially much longer time required to read in the XML weather forecast feed. HomeSeer's architecture requires plug-ins, its most tightly coupled programming interface, to respond faster than those delays would permit, requiring use of a multi-threaded plug-in, making the programming more complex.

- HomeSeer presents an interface to its plug-ins designed for use with Microsoft's Visual Basic. The C++ equivalent interface is fairly complex due to Microsoft's design of the Visual Basic interface conventions, and not explicitly documented by HomeSeer.

Rather than deal with the complexity of a plug-in, therefore, we decided to use an old Unix-style approach and communicate the interface data through a file. The software we wrote is therefore a standalone C++ application. Its design, implementation, and use is described in the section "Software" later in this chapter. HomeSeer monitors the interface file using a recurring event (we set it to run every minute, but you could poll less often). The event runs the following HomeSeer script, giving it a device and file path as parameters:

```
'
' HomeSeer script to monitor a file output by the GeekWaterWatcher application
' and set an HS device based on the content of the file
'
' Copyright (C) 2004 by Barry and Marcia Press.
' Licensed under the GNU Public License.
' See license.txt
'
' Function is to turn the device off if and only if OFF is in the file,
' else turn on.
'
' The script requires the scrrun.dll. However, that DLL presents security issues
' relating to unauthorized access to the local file system via vbscript
' or jscript, so you should carefully consider its use on a PC with web access.
```

```
`

sub main()
end sub

sub poll(dev,fname)

    Dim fso, fil, s
    Set fso = CreateObject("Scripting.FileSystemObject")
    Const ForReading = 1

    if fso.FileExists(fname) then
            Set fil = fso.OpenTextFile(fname, ForReading)
            s = fil.ReadLine
            fil.Close
            if (Left(s,3) = "OFF") then
                    hs.SetDeviceStatus dev, 3           ' Turn it off
            else
                    hs.SetDeviceStatus dev, 2           ' Turn it on
            end if
    else
            hs.SetDeviceStatus dev, 2                   ' Turn it on
    end if

end sub
```

You set the device to receive the enable/disable status and the fully qualified interface file path plus file name as parameters to the script in HomeSeer, as shown in Figure 9-6. The parameters in parentheses are the name of the routine within the script, the device to be turned on or off, and the name of the interface file to poll, just as defined in the script code above.

The script turns the given device off if and only if the file exists and has OFF as its first three characters; otherwise, it turns the device on. Turning the device on if anything goes wrong helps the system recover from problems in a way that keeps your plants from drying out. If you lived in a wet zone where too much water was more of a problem, you could change the script around to fail off rather than on.

Figure 9-7 shows how you set up HomeSeer to run the script with a recurring event. The event isn't tied to any trigger; instead, it's set to poll the file (through the script) periodically. We've set it to poll every minute in Figure 9-7, but the timing could be more relaxed if you chose.

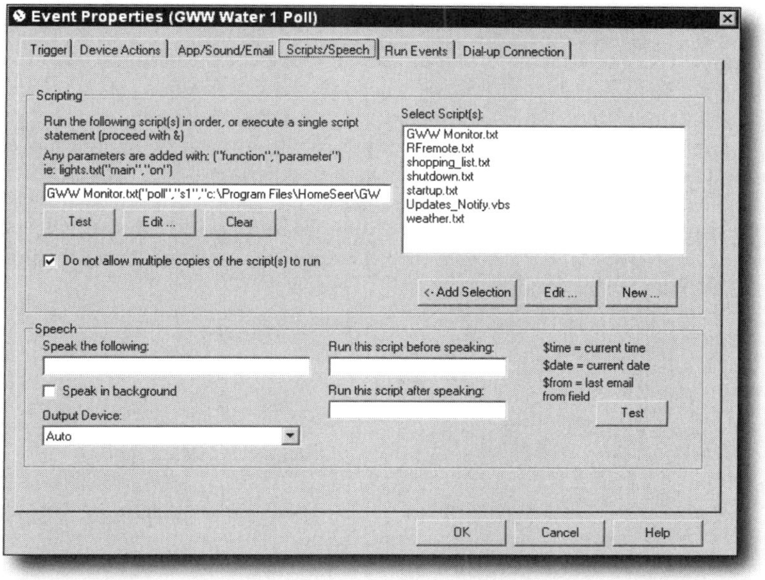

FIGURE 9-6: HomeSeer recurring event script configuration

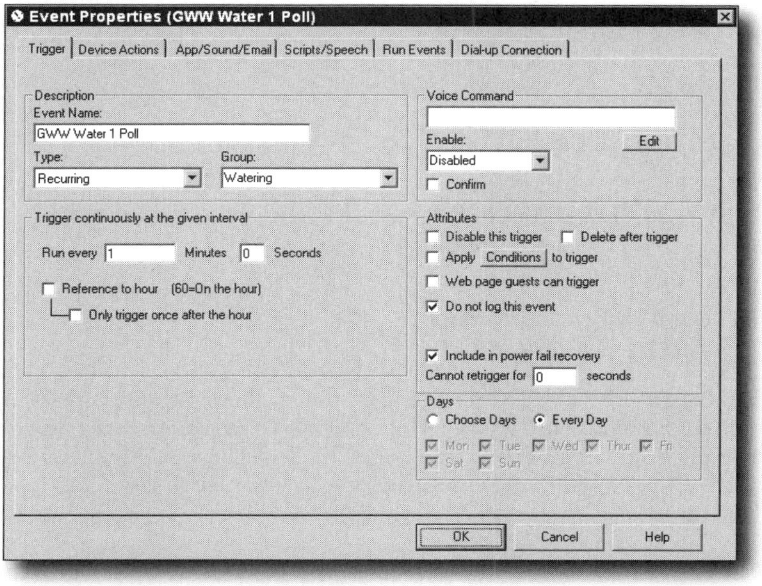

FIGURE 9-7: Recurring event configuration

Actuators

If you're not using X-10 modules to control the sprinkler valves, you're going to want to open and close a relay directly from a microprocessor. The sprinkler valves require AC voltage to drive them, and at voltages that are high compared to what most semiconductors are rated for. Relays typically draw more current than a microprocessor output can take directly, too, so you'll need a switching transistor to handle the load. Figure 9-8 shows the generic circuit you need assuming an open collector output on the microprocessor. The diode connected across the relay coil prevents the field collapse across the windings from generating too high a reverse voltage that would destroy the transistor. Be sure to use both a transistor and diode rated for the relay surge currents and applied voltages.

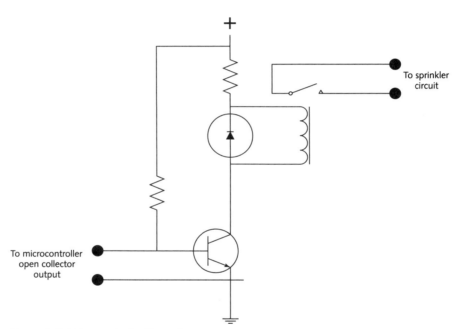

FIGURE 9-8: Relay control with a microprocessor

X-10 power line controls offer several choices for actuators, as shown by the examples in Table 9-3. You'd choose the Rain8 acutator if you planned to control each sprinkler circuit individually, putting one relay in the individual circuit wiring. The X-10 Universal Module is a less expensive alternative if you're going to control all circuits simutaneously, as we did, since in that case you'll only need one relay to interrupt the common return lines.

Table 9-3   X-10 Sprinkler Circuit Actuators

Actuator	Source
WGL Rain8 X-10 Sprinkler Controller	WGL and Associates `www.wgldesigns.com/rain8.html`
X-10 PF284 Powerflash Module	X-10 `www.x10.com/security/x10_pf284.htm`

X-10
UM506 Universal Module
	X-10
	`www.x10.com/automation/`
	`x10_um506.htm`

You can detect and counter failures in the power line transmission to the actuator by paralleling the UM506 with a PF284. A few lines added to the polling script can check if the read-back from the PF284 doesn't match what the actuator state should be, and simply send the right command again if the actuator state is wrong.

Software

The software to operate the automated sprinkler controls became a more complicated engineering effort than the hardware development, even though we stopped short of writing software to completely replace the conventional sprinkler automated controller.

Our approach (Figure 9-9) is to use the PC-based processing to modulate the operation of the conventional controller—we set the conventional watering program to run a long cycle every day, and use the PC to enable or disable the cycle depending on whether the yard actually needs water. Our software makes the enable/disable decisions based on real-time data from the available sensors and a set of rules you program into it, while the HomeSeer X-10 control software commands the Universal Module appropriately based on the enable/disable output of our software.

Ignoring the Microsoft Foundation Classes application framework we used for the software, based on the Microsoft document/view architecture (`msdn.microsoft.com/library/default.asp?url=/library/en-us/vccore/html/_core_document.2f.view_architecture_topics.asp`), there are five parts to the sprinkler control software:

- Sensor interface and data collection
- Web interface and XML processing
- Rule processing and output
- User interface
- Data logging

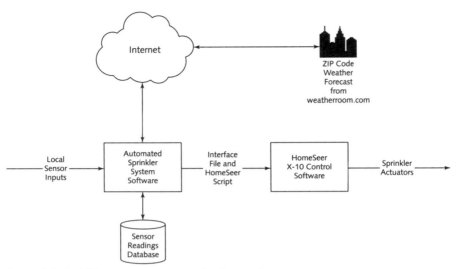

FIGURE 9-9: Sprinkler automation control software elements

The following sections describe the design and implementation of each one, and wrap up with coverage of the registry options you can use to configure the software without modifying the code. There's a lot of code in the software; it would be worth your time to read it for understanding after working through what's here in the text.

Sensor interface and data collection

The lowest level processing in the software reads data from a serial port connected to the Davis Instruments Vantage Pro Envoy. The VP_SerialPort class does the actual port I/O, while the VP_Loop class provides access to the data returned from the hardware. (The Vantage Pro Envoy can also archive and report historical data in its memory, but we've not used that capability in our software.) The VP_SoilInterface class manages receiving the data and storing it into the program's internal RuleData data structure. If you were using an alternative data source, you'd start by replacing VP_SoilInterface and the lower level classes with the equivalent functionality tailored for your hardware.

Serial port processing in the VP_SerialPort class uses overlapped I/O, although it does so to enforce timeouts and not because the processing is overlapped with program operation. Timeouts are largely defined as a base time plus a time per character being transferred, but they're very loose. We used some registry data to create a list of serial ports on the PC, but that may not work on all systems, and is likely not to work on Win9X-based PCs.

Our code opens and closes the serial port each time it reads data, which makes it possible for two independent windows (i.e., open a new window in the application via File ➪ New) to use the same serial port. That would be useful if you had multiple soil moisture sensors installed and wanted to use them to control the status of different watering zones independently — each window would control a specific zone, with specific rules looking only at the sensors for that zone. You can also connect multiple Vantage Pro units to the PC, each on its own serial port, and use separate windows within the application to process the readings from each unit. The only thing the software really isn't set up to do is to use the readings from multiple ports in a single window within the application.

If you wanted to do the serial I/O in parallel, which would eliminate the "Checking" notice you see in the window during updates, we'd suggest using a thread that handled the data gathering at a higher level. We've built the RuleData class to support doing that enhancement — every read or write access is framed with a critical section, and copies use one critical section to lock the entire transfer.

The LOOP data structure received from the Vantage Pro hardware is defined in the Davis Instruments Vantage Pro Serial Communications Reference (www.davisnet.com/ support/weather/software.asp#vantagecomm). There are many more data elements in the data structure than we used in the software, including the ability to trigger "alarms" when conditions such as falling barometer or battery failure occur. If you want to use some of those elements, consider first how you'll extend the abstracted data interface (the RuleData class).

Another property of the Vantage Pro interface is that it specifies limit data values that indicate when no data is available (such as when a specific sensor isn't installed in the system). We've wrapped detecting those values in an interface that throws an exception when no data is available, and use catching the exception to set a boolean kept in parallel with each data element that indicates whether the element is valid. A naming convention tracks the correspondences, with the access function *name*Status() returning a boolean value indicating whether or not the data value is available through the function *name*().

The RuleData and RuleDataArray classes contain all the data you'll find in the rules the program operates on, including booleans for noting whether data is present. The classes provide serialization support using the document/view architecture model. RuleDataArray is literally an array of RuleData elements, and is based on the CObArray MFC class.

Web interface and XML processing

We used our InternetReader class to access Web pages, much as in Chapter 6, but modified the version in this software with an option not to strip markup tags from the text of the returned page. That change lets the software return extended markup language (XML) data we can then parse into readily walked trees of data. Thus, the query to weatherroom.com of

```
http://www.weatherroom.com/xml/ext/90210
```

returns the XML result

```
<?xml version="1.0" encoding="utf-8" ?>
<WeatherFeed xmlns:xsd="http://www.w3.org/2001/XMLSchema"
xmlns:xsi="http://www.w3.org/2001/XMLSchema-instance"
xmlns="http://www.weatherroom.com">
<Current>
<internal />
```

```
<Location>Beverly Hills, CA, United States</Location>
<RecordedAt>Santa Monica, Santa Monica Municipal Airport, CA, United
States</RecordedAt>
<Updated>251 PM PDT SAT SEP 11 2004</Updated>
<Image>http://www.weatherroom.com/images/fcicons/sunny.gif</Image>
<Link>http://www.weatherroom.com/forecast/90210.html</Link>
<Conditions>Mostly Clear</Conditions>
<Visibility>10 Mi</Visibility>
<Temp>80°F</Temp>
<Humidity>60%</Humidity>
<Wind>WSW 8 MPH</Wind>
<Barometer>29.9 in.</Barometer>
<Dewpoint>65°F</Dewpoint>
<HeatIndex>82°F</HeatIndex>
<WindChill>80°F</WindChill>
<Sunrise>6:34 AM PDT</Sunrise>
<Sunset>7:06 PM PDT</Sunset>
<MoonPhase>Waning Crescent Moon</MoonPhase>
</Current>
<Forecast>
<Config />
<Date>SAT SEP 11 2004</Date>
<Time>230 PM PDT SAT</Time>
<Tonight>
<Conditions>Clouds</Conditions>
<High>°F</High>
<Low>65°F</Low>
<POP />
</Tonight>
<Sunday>
<Conditions>Mostly Sunny</Conditions>
<High>87°F</High>
<Low>65°F</Low>
<POP />
</Sunday>
<Monday>
<Conditions>Mostly Sunny</Conditions>
<High>85°F</High>
<Low>63°F</Low>
<POP />
</Monday>
<Tuesday>
<Conditions>Clouds</Conditions>
<High>77°F</High>
<Low>77°F</Low>
<POP />
</Tuesday>
<Wednesday>
<Conditions>Clouds</Conditions>
<High>77°F</High>
<Low>77°F</Low>
<POP />
```

```
</Wednesday>
</Forecast>
<PoweredBy>www.weatherroom.com</PoweredBy>
<Copyright>Canadian forecasts are obtained from and are copyright of Environment
Canada. If you use Canadian weather information you must give Environment Canada
due credit in accordance with their terms
(http://weatheroffice.ec.gc.ca/mainmenu/faq_e.html#general2). All other data is
derived from the NWS and public domain sources. This feed is copyright 2004
weatherroom.com. It may be used freely provided that you include a link to
www.weatherroom.com or to the appropriate forecast page.</Copyright>
</WeatherFeed>
```

The interesting part of that return for the sprinker control software is the `<Forecast>` branch, and within there the fourth child through the end, which collectively represent the next five daily forecasts. The `<Conditions>` element is the text description of the forecast (a list of all possible conditions is at `www.weatherroom.com/conditions.txt`), while the `<POP>` (Probability of Precipitation) element will contain a percentage value if non-empty.

You need an XML parser to turn the text into a data structure, and there's no really good reason to write your own, because there's no shortage of existing XML parsers. (For example, try searching Sourceforge for *xml parser*, requiring both words in the search.) Few of the existing ones both work with MFC, as used in our software, and let you feed the parser text from a memory buffer. We experimented with several, and found TinyXML by Lee Thomason (`www.grinninglizard.com/tinyxml/index.html`) to be easiest to incorporate into our software and use to parse the weatherroom.com feed. Source code for TinyXML is available on Sourceforge (`sourceforge.net/projects/tinyxml`), and literally the only changes we had to make were to fix up the files to use the *stdafx.h* convention expected by Visual C++. The license for TinyXML is very generous, being simply what's in the sidebar *TinyXML License*.

TinyXML License

This software is provided "as-is," without any express or implied warranty. In no event will the authors be held liable for any damages arising from the use of this software.

Permission is granted to anyone to use this software for any purpose, including commercial applications, and to alter it and redistribute it freely, subject to the following restrictions:

1. The origin of this software must not be misrepresented; you must not claim that you wrote the original software. If you use this software in a product, an acknowledgment in the product documentation would be appreciated but is not required.

2. Altered source versions must be plainly marked as such, and must not be misrepresented as being the original software.

3. This notice may not be removed or altered from any source distribution.

The C++ code to retrieve and parse the XML structure is in the class WebForecast, and relatively simple in concept. Once the code retrieves the XML data and loads it into TinyXML, the fragment

```
pXElt = Xdoc.RootElement()->FirstChildElement( "Forecast" )
            ->FirstChild()
            ->NextSibling()->NextSibling()->NextSiblingElement();
```

returns a pointer to the first day's forecast element, from which the fragment

```
sscanf( GetXMLElementText( pXElt, "POP" ), "%d", &nData );
```

returns the <POP> value, if any; and the function call

```
GetXMLElementText( pXElt, "Conditions" )
```

returns the forecast string.

`WebForecast` doesn't use these fragments directly, because the returned XML structure may not correspond to the expected pattern. If it doesn't, one of the calls will fail and return a NULL pointer, causing subsequent references to fault. We've encapsulated the XML navigation in a *try-catch* sequence to catch these faults and handle the consequences.

What we didn't do, however, was provide a data-driven way to parse the XML. There's no schema defined for weatherroom.com (and TinyXML doesn't handle Document Type Definitions [DTDs] or other schema definitions anyhow), so that wasn't a good approach. We considered a dynamic path definition we could store as strings in the registry, such as:

```
Forecast: Root.Forecast.4
Probability: POP.text.int
Step: NextSiblingElement
```

The idea is that there would be keywords, such as *Root*, *text*, *int*, and *NextSiblingElement*; and numbers, which imply take the *nth* child. Anything else, such as *Forecast* or *POP*, is a literal tag for a child element. If weather.com had been a viable alternative for an XML feed, we'd have implemented that approach to make switching sites easier.

Another enhancement to the implementation you might care to make is to store copies of the parsed forecast at the application level, where it would be available to all view windows and therefore fetch forecast data less often. As things are, the timer controlling when the software fetches a new forecast is kept locally to the document tied to each view window, and therefore separate forecasts are retrieved for each one. Server requests don't return instantaneously, either, so while you were at it you might want to do the Web operations in a thread.

There's no option to enable or disable Internet access, but it would be simple to add a menu option, as in Chapter 6, and then examine the corresponding boolean flag in the UpdateWebData method within WebForecast.

Rule processing and output

The point of the software is to evaluate a series of rules against a data set (specifically, the most recent instance of the RuleData class). We consider a rule to be true if and only if for every data item present in the data set (not just defined in the structure, but with an actual sampled data value), the relation

```
Minimum ≤ Current value ≤ Maximum
```

is true. If any data item fails the test — has an out-of-range value — the rule fails. We drop relation tests for data items missing from the data set; that is, we consider the test to pass.

For example, suppose you have a relationship that says

```
2.01 ≤ Soil Moisture 1
```

The test says the reading from the first soil moisture sensor has to be at least 2.01. Values of 2.0 and less will fail. (In practice, the soil moisture sensor readings are integers, so the test is the same as saying 2 < Soil Moisture 1, but we've only implemented closed intervals in the relations.)

Given that concept, a rule data structure needs only two RuleData elements, one for the minimums and one for the maximums. The boolean flags denoting whether or not a value is present are particularly useful too, because they conveniently record whether the value is used in the rule. A RuleArray is similar to a RuleDataArray, except that it encapsulates an array of Rules rather than one of RuleData elements.

The code evaluates an array of rules in the context of a RuleData structure carrying the current sample data following this algorithm:

1. Set the initial evaluation state to the default state.

2. Set the current rule to the first rule in the array.

3. Evaluate each relation in the current rule.

4. If all relations evaluate to true, the rule evaluates to true. If so, set the evaluation state to the inverse of the default state and terminate.

5. Set the current rule to the next rule in the array. If there are no more, terminate.

If the initial state is OFF, the rules act as OR elements, any of them being true turning the result on. If the initial state is ON, the rules act as AND NOT elements, any of them being true turning the result off. Within a rule, every relation has to be true (an AND condition) for the result to be true.

The document class method CGeekWaterWatcherDoc::ProcessRules() gets called when the sample data or the rule data change. ProcessRules() in turn calls the routine that writes out the HomeSeer interface file, ensuring the interface file is always up to date. The interface file also gets written when the view window closes, ensuring the sprinkler status is on if the rules aren't running.

User interface

Figure 9-10 shows the main window for the program. The user interface is a Multiple Document Interface (MDI) application, so although we've shown the open view window maximized to fill the application frame window, you can have several such view windows open, and can cascade or tile them within the application. The output is all text, consisting of a sequence of lines output by the application as part of the work of the GeekWaterWatcherView class.

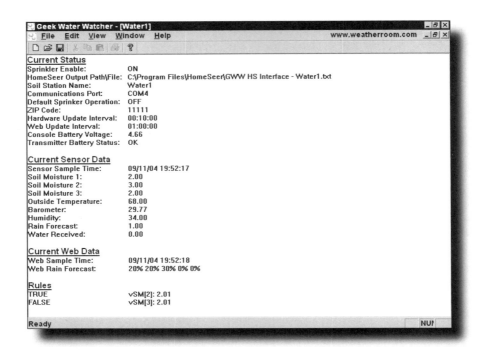

FIGURE 9-10: Main window

Each line in the display is managed by an element of the `LabelsAndValues` class. The program calls the `AddLine()` method to pass the next line in sequence (and optionally a font), or calls `SetLine()` to rewrite an existing line. `Reset()` empties the display. Each line consists of one or more columns of text separated by tabs; the window processing sets the tab stops automatically so the left edge of each column lines up.

Rules are represented in the display by their current evaluation status (before application to the sprinkler status) and a text representation of the rule. In that text representation, each comparison (half of a relation) is represented by a symbol for minimum (v) or maximum (^), an abbreviation for the value (e.g., SM for soil moisture), and the value stored in the rule. In Figure 9-10, therefore, there are two rules. One says the minimum on soil moisture sensor 2 is 2.01, while the other says the same thing for soil moisture sensor 3. Based on the current data shown in the window, the first rule evaluates to true while the second one evaluates to false.

We used simple Windows timers to sequence hardware updates, and poll for Web updates within the processing for hardware updates on the assumption that Web updates will occur less frequently. (In practice, therefore, Web updates occur at multiples of hardware update intervals. Add a separate timer if you prefer.) We used the document pointer to form the Windows timer ID so we can maintain multiple timers in the case of multiple windows.

Data logging

We used standard MFC document serialization to read and write the contents of the document to a file. The specific elements written to the file are shown in Table 9-4.

Table 9-4   Document File Contents

Element	Content
m_csStationName	Name assigned to the soil station, displayed in the window title
m_ctsHardwareUpdateInterval	Seconds between hardware updates
m_ctHardwareLastUpdateTime	Time when last hardware update was performed
m_ctsWebUpdateInterval	Seconds between Web updates
m_ctWebLastUpdateTime	Time when last Web update was performed
m_csZIPCode	String containing ZIP code used in Web updates
m_bDefaultHSStatus	Default rule evaluation status
m_csHSPath	Path and file name for HomeSeer output file
m_rdDataArray	Array of RuleData elements recording all samples
m_ruleArray	Array of Rule elements defining rule set

The File Export Log command sequences through all recorded samples and writes a comma separated value (CSV) log suitable for import into Microsoft Excel or other programs.

Registry values

We routed many of the constants in the program through the registry to make parts of the program configurable without having to modify the code. Those settings are in the registry key HKEY_CURRENT_USER\Software\Barry and Marcia Press -- Geek House\ GeekWaterWatcher\Settings; be sure to back up your registry before making changes.

Table 9-5 shows the items you can modify. We implemented the registry lookup using the RegistryInfo class, calls to which take default values, and return either the default or a registry value if it's present. If you wanted the default serial port to be COM3, for example, you'd set the registry key HKEY_CURRENT_USER\Software\Barry and Marcia Press -- Geek House\GeekWaterWatcher\Settings\DefaultCommPort to have the string value COM3.

Table 9-5   Registry Configuration Settings

Registry Setting	Default Value	Purpose
BarometerOutputFormat	"Barometer:\t%.2f"	View pane output format
CommInputBuffer	4096	Default VP communication input buffer size
CommOutputBuffer	1024	Default VP communication output buffer size
DefaultAutoSave	1	If AutoSave is enabled
DefaultCommPort	"COM1"	Serial port proposed as default if nothing more intelligent known
DefaultCommTimeout	1000	Default timeout writing a string to VP (1 ms per character also added)
DefaultHardwareUpdateInterval	3600	Time between hardware updates
DefaultHomeSeerStatus	1	Default rule evaluation - 1 means sprinklers on, 0 means off.
DefaultWebUpdateInterval	3600	Time between Web forecast polls
DefaultZIPCode	" "	ZIP code proposed by default
HeadlineFontFace	"Arial"	Headline font face used in the view panes
HeadlineFontHeight	0	Headline font height used in the view panes
HumidityOutputFormat	"Humidity:\t%.2f"	View pane output format
LOOPRecordTimeout	4000	Default VP LOOP Record string input timeout (plus characters)
MinimumHWUpdateInterval	10	Won't update from HW faster than this number of seconds
OutsideTemperatureOutputFormat	"Outside Temperature:\t%.2f"	View pane output format
Preliminary URL	" "	URL to fetch and ignore before actual WeatherURL
RainForecastOutputFormat	"Rain Forecast:\t%.2f"	View pane output format
SoilMoistureOutputFormat	"Soil Moisture %d:\t%.2f"	View pane output format
SoilTemperatureOutputFormat	"Soil Temperature %d:\t%.2f"	View pane output format

Registry Setting	Default Value	Purpose
TimeIntervalOutputFormat	"%H:%M:%S"	View pane output format
TimestampOutputFormat	"%c"	View pane output format
ViewPaneTabGap	10	Gap following text before tab stop in view panes
WaterReceivedOutputFormat	"Water Received: \t%.2f"	View pane output format
WeatherForecastURL	"http://www.weatherroom.com/weather?forecast=zandh&pands=%s"	Where to get viewable forecast
WeatherURL	"http://www.weatherroom.com/xml/ext/%s"	Where to get XML forecast
WebUpdateInterval	3600	Web update interval, min 300, seconds

HomeSeer programming

We used virtual device S1 in our HomeSeer script call to record the sprinkler enable status. You could just as well directly control the actual Universal Module address; we chose to separate the two so we could control the times when the module is open to being disabled, and enable it at all other times. We created events that sample the virtual device status just before we've programmed our deep water cycle to start, turning the real device on or off appropriately, and force the same device back on a few hours later. It stays on until the same sample time the next day.

Enhancements

We've noted several enhancements you might make throughout the chapter. The following are relatively straightforward additions to the software:

- The weatherroom.com site provides a five-day forecast, but we only hooked up the first value into the rules. You might want to use some or all of the other four, requiring that you expand the rule editing dialog box and supporting code.

- If the console or transmitter battery has failed, the program could (via a MAPI interface or another device and a HomeSeer script) send e-mail to your usual mailbox to warn you of the problem. You could examine the status each time the program accesses the hardware.

- Similarly, you might add an e-mail alert if one of the sensors gets too dry. We put one of our sensors in a planter not serviced by sprinklers, not to use it to drive a rule, but to have a digital readout of the planter status. Because responding to that sensor requires manual action, it's convenient to have an alert.

- There are commands we've put in the software that don't correspond to buttons on the toolbar. You could add the buttons. Additionally, you could implement visual marking, and copy operations to the clipboard.

- You might not want the program to always be open on-screen. It will minimize now, but even so takes space in the taskbar. Instead, you could modify it so on minimize it only has an icon in the tray.

If you're more ambitious, here's a list of more challenging enhancements:

- You could implement all the functionality of a standard automated sprinkler control, using the Rain8 circuit board for direct control. That would let you eliminate the standard controller altogether and any limitations on what you can program into the cycles since you'd be writing the software yourself.

- It's possible you'd want to include readings from additional sensor types into your rules, or want to use actual in-ground soil temperature probes to calibrate the moisture sensors. The moisture probe readings are sensitive to the soil temperature, so you'll get a more accurate reading if you compensate against soil temperature. We use one of the soil moisture probes, but used above ground in the shade to read outside temperature. The software incorporates that adaptation, so if you're really using soil temperature probes for their intended purpose, you'll need to do some rework in the data acquisition classes.

- If you take our suggestion of writing a complete software suite to implement the sprinkler controller function entirely within your PC, you could abandon the notion of fixed water cycles and time of day to water. Instead, you could combine the historical data record with a control algorithm to compute how long to water and when. We suggest you also give the algorithm minimum and maximum time limits per cycle, minimum inter-cycle times, and guidance on when watering is permissible based on your own schedule. That's a complex proposition; a simpler enhancement would be to simply avoid banned watering times.

Summary

As simple and pervasive as the usual hardware store automatic sprinkler controller is, there's a lot of complexity to be conquered adapting its fixed watering programs to adjust for varying weather conditions. The system we implemented in this chapter takes a moderate approach to the problem, giving you a relatively wide selection of data elements to use in creating rules that dynamically adjust watering based on need.

Using the changed water cycle possible with this controller, we've reduced our total water consumption by 25 percent. That's worth some work.

Car PC

This project is to build a PC into a car, integrating a cell phone for Internet access, and integrating applications such as MP3 player, DVD player, and navigator. Yes, you can take it with you. It may not be cheap — running hundreds to thousands of dollars, depending on what you want to do, but you can do it.

Project Description

We have a broad view of what's in the geek's leisure traveling car. Don't think two-seater roadster — such as a Miata or S2000 — in which minimalism is everything. Think about at least a four-passenger car when you envision building this project, because in a tiny roadster you may well lose the ability to put even a backpack in the trunk, and possibly lose the place for the all-important road trip passenger. This layout is for a vehicle where you have power, lots of space, and a lot of time on your hands to play with the results. A motor home could be ideal.

That said, this chapter is more of a guide to what you can do and how, not a design for a specific assembly. We chose that approach because there are so many variations of what people will want to include and of how the system has to be packaged into a car. That and, well, because our road trip car *is* an S2000.

In addition to the technology you'll need to successfully host a PC in a car in the first place, this chapter looks at how to integrate the following:

➤ Displays, voice, and inputs

➤ Navigation

➤ Mobile Internet connectivity

➤ Sound

➤ Video

➤ Engine diagnostics

➤ Wireless LAN

When my Legions of Terror park their vehicle to do reconnaissance on foot, they will be instructed to employ The Club.

Peter Anspach,
The Evil Overlord List

in this chapter

☑ It's not just a project, it's an adventure

☑ Server and communications

☑ Power

☑ Audio and video

☑ Sensors

☑ Software

System Diagram

This project is interesting both for the number of subsystems the PC can work with — at least communications, audio, video, navigation, and engine diagnostics — and the options you have for building the PC and the interfaces. Figure 10-1 shows the overall concept for the Car PC; we expect any given version will implement a subset of the ideas in Figure 10-1, and may add others. The server and communications group includes not only the PC itself, but the audio and video sources, the navigation source, and the radios. The power group provides both 12 VDC and 120 VAC (or 240, depending on where you live). The audio video group implements the display outputs for computer interface, navigation, and video, and the audio outputs for music and computer voice interface. The sensor group watches the environment, providing driver or navigator inputs, listening for radar scans, and monitoring the engine status. You could add a forward-looking infrared video camera if you drive at night a lot.

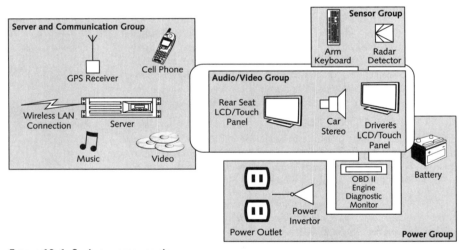

FIGURE 10-1: System components

The interfaces to the devices in Figure 10-1 are each very different — power, analog audio, video, and networking, for example — so you'll likely use independent connections for each of them. The resulting large volume of cabling requires that you think about cabling and grounding very carefully. An installation with loose wires running everywhere not only won't look very good, it won't be reliable in the long run, either.

Parts and Designs

The segmentation in Figure 10-1 divides the Car PC system into tightly coupled groups, with looser, less dependent interfaces between the groups. Software for the system runs only on the server, but it's what makes all the elements play together.

Server and communications group

Figure 10-2 is a larger view of what comprises the server and communications group. The server itself provides computing and storage; the GPS receiver, cell phone, and wireless LAN provide communications; and audio/video content stored on the disk provides material for later playback.

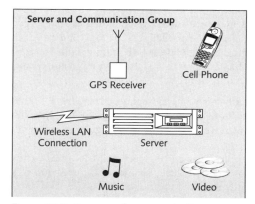

FIGURE 10-2: Server and communications group

You have two basic options for how you implement the server:

- **Build it in** — You can package a small motherboard and the necessary peripherals into a rugged case and mount it permanently in your car. Doing so lets you put it out of the way, perhaps in the trunk or under a seat, and ensures that the power and wiring are both out of the way and perfectly integrated with your vehicle.

- **Build in interfaces and use a laptop** — Alternatively, you can exploit the fact that laptop PCs are small and rugged, and that they already incorporate a keyboard, display, and speakers. You'll likely want to keep the laptop in the passenger compartment with you, since otherwise you'll lose the ability to use those peripherals, but keeping it in the passenger compartment requires that a lot of cabling connect to the laptop.

A laptop goes with you and brings its own battery power, but a Car PC server specialized for the purpose faces problems different from a server under a desk or in a rack:

- **Shock and vibration** — The bumps and vibration you feel when driving, filtered by the springs and padding in the car seats, are significantly less than what a PC chassis sees when rigidly mounted to the car.

- **Limited space** — The usual desktop tower or mini-tower won't fit under the seat in most cars, and would use up far too much room if mounted in the trunk. The configuration of what's in the server is less likely to change versus what's at your desk, though, so you can make some compromises to reduce the package size. (Of course, if you really *are* installing the system in a motor home, a desktop tower would have some charm, because you'd have the space to build in an entire home entertainment capability *in addition* to the Car PC functionality.)

- **Temperature extremes and limited cooling** — Cars must operate in temperature ranges from well below 0 to 120°F and above, and must survive temperature extremes beyond those limits. The passenger compartment will (eventually) come to within more benign ranges when the car is in operation, but there's no cooling or heating while the car is off. If the PC is to be useful on demand, then it must survive and operate in any temperatures it encounters without fail and without damage.

- **Bad power** — Aside from vehicle power being 12 VDC, it almost defies belief how bad the power is in a car. There's noise from the ignition, a wide variation in the supply voltage, and loss of power only slightly more often than we get from our local regulated utility.

Figure 10-3 and Table 10-1 show the Opus Solutions chassis, specifically designed to host a car PC. It holds a Mini-ITX form factor motherboard with a two-slot PCI riser card to keep the size down, and incorporates a power supply designed to bridge between 12 VDC automotive power and the computing electronics. Brackets on the bottom of the chassis let you anchor it securely to the vehicle body, while the compact, well-braced mechanical construction minimizes low-frequency mechanical resonances and improves durability.

Table 10-1   Car PC Chassis

Component	Source
OPUS Solutions chassis www.opussolutions.com/modules.php?name=News&file=article&topic_id=3&sid=21	MP3Car www.mp3car.com/store/product_info.php?cPath=28&products_id=57

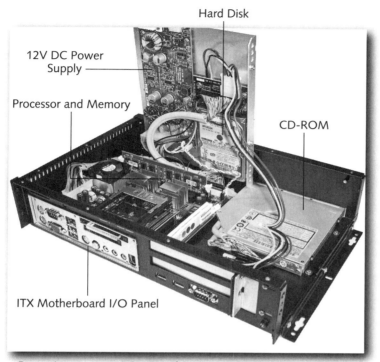

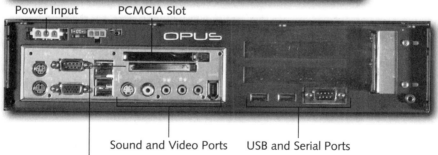

FIGURE 10-3: OPUS Solutions Car PC chassis

You could build a shock tray to isolate the PC from those mechanical loads; this chassis is simply sturdy enough to withstand them. We don't believe you have to worry about damaging a securely mounted disk drive—for example, Seagate specifies its Barracuda 7200.7 series drives (Ultra ATA/100 interface, up to 120 GB capacity) for 63 Gs operating shock over 2 ms and 350 Gs non-operating shock over 2 ms. We suggest mounting the drive flat, not vertical, to minimize positioning errors caused by jolts to the head positioners.

Via originated the Mini-ITX form factor (`www.via.com.tw/en/downloads/whitepapers/initiatives/spearhead/ini_mini-itx.pdf`). Motherboards are now available from Via with their processors, or from other manufacturers (for example, Axiomtek, Commell, DFI, Eyetech, IBASE, Insight, Lex, Lippert, Samsung, and Unicorn) with processors, including the Intel Pentium 4 and others. Form factor is not as well standardized as ATX and others, and the manufacturers are typically not the proven large houses you expect to hear of building PCs, so you need to be careful that the actual chassis, motherboard, cards, and peripherals you get really do fit together and are electrically compatible.

It's common for a Mini-ITX motherboard to use a chipset integrating many functions directly, including networking, graphics, and sound; some include PCI, USB, FireWire (IEEE 1394), and TV out too.

The limited expansion possible with a small chassis and a Mini-ITX motherboard requires you to design the interfaces to each of the functions in your Car PC before choosing the specific components, because the server group must support the kind and number of interfaces required to connect to each subsystem in the car. If a specific interface your car subsystems will require isn't supported by the Car PC, you'll have to add some electronics to make up the shortfall. For example:

- **USB**—The components we suggest use powered USB ports for the GPS receiver and cell phone Internet access. If you have only two USB ports on the server, you'll fill them with this equipment; if you have fewer, you'll need to wire in and mount a powered hub.

- **Serial ports**—You're likely to need a serial port for the touch panel interface (if it doesn't use USB), two if you have two touch panel displays, and yet another serial port for the on-board diagnostics (OBD II) port. You're not likely to find a small motherboard with two or three serial ports, so you'll have to add them with a PCI card or USB adapter.

- **PCI**—The choices for hooking up your wireless LAN, which you'll use to load content on the server while parked in the garage or driveway, are PCI and USB. We suggest a PCI card so you have the data rate to support the faster IEEE 802.11g standard and don't have to craft an external mounting for the unit. You have two PCI slots on a horizontal riser in the Opus chassis, so you could use one for the wireless LAN and still have a spare.

Table 10-2 lists the communications suite, including GPS, mobile Internet access, and wireless LAN. You'll need some miscellaneous parts and brackets to extend the antenna from the wireless LAN card to outside the trunk (having the antenna in a metal box greatly reduces the range), but they're very much dependent on the specifics of your card and car.

Table 10-2   Communications Suite

Component	Source

Cell Phone
Sanyo RL-7300
	Sprint PCS
	`www.sprintpcs.com/explore/`
	`PhonesAccessories/PhoneDetails.jsp?`
	`navLocator=%7Cshop%7Cphones`
	`Accessories%7CallPhones%7C&select`
	`SkuId=sanyoscp7300&FOLDER%3C%`
	`3Efolder_id=1476015`

Cell Phone Modem Interface Cable	Boxwave
	`www.boxwave.com/products/minisync/`
	`minisync-retractable-cable-sanyo-`
	`scp-7300_301.htm`

GPS Receiver
DeLorme Earthmate
	DeLorme
	`www.delorme.com/earthmate/`
	`configlaptop_info.asp`

Wireless LAN	IEEE 802.11g PCI Adapter
	D-Link
	`www.dlink.com/products/?sec=0&pid=308`
	
	Linksys
	`www.linksys.com/products/product.`
	`asp?grid=33&scid=36&prid=635`
	
	Netgear
	`www.netgear.com/products/details/`
	`WG311.php`

The cell phone networks give you a way to maintain Internet access in motion; digital cell phone networks will give you decent data rates, too. The Sanyo RL-7300 we list is available from Sprint, and works with their PCS network. The phone looks like a modem once you connect it to the PC with the Boxwave USB cable and install the necessary drivers (`www.boxwave.com/products/minisync/sanyo/sanyo_usb_driver.zip`). You then create a Windows dial-up connection using the phone number #777 (yes, it looks odd; it works for the Sanyo), activate the connection, and you're on the Internet anywhere you have digital coverage. The phone charges through the Boxwave cable too, so you don't have to worry about running out of power.

The GPS receiver needs a clear shot—that is, not through metal—to the sky for it to work, so you have to think about how to position the receiver. That's probably even harder in a motor home; you might consider mounting the receiver on the roof in a non-metallic, waterproof enclosure. The Wide Area Augmentation System (WAAS) enhancement to GPS (North America only) transmits through a geosynchronous satellite over Brazil, so you'll want to make sure the GPS receiver can see the southern sky to get the best position accuracy possible.

Power group

Figure 10-4 expands the view of the power group. Collectively, the power group exists to supply and manage power to the devices in your system, which turns out to have three elements:

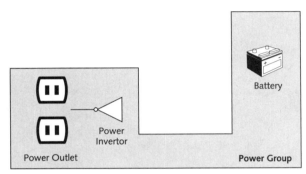

FIGURE 10-4: Power group

- **Provide 12 VDC power** — The cleanest approach to powering on-board electronics is to drive them from the 12 VDC vehicle source directly. That requires different power supplies than usually found in consumer electronics, but eliminates the inefficiency and cost of a double conversion from 12 VDC to 120 VAC and then back down to the necessary DC voltages inside the electronic assemblies.

- **Provide 120 VAC power** — If you can't adapt to 12 VDC power, you'll need to source 120 VAC (or 240 VAC, depending on where you are and the characteristics of the units). Power conversion units, called *inverters*, are commonly available from 100 to 400 watts.

- **Supervise PC operation** — DOS didn't care much, because it didn't often cache important data, but you shouldn't just cut power randomly using operating systems such as Linux and Windows. You'll need to wire the server directly to the battery — a relatively permanent source of power — and use the on/off status from the switched power to control PC operation.

The 12 VDC supply in a car isn't fixed at 12 volts. Instead, you'll see a range from 10 (battery essentially discharged, and possibly during engine crank) to 15 volts (past full charge; typically the maximum input for radios), and any 12 VDC power supply you connect should be capable of accepting that full range. You may find the supply you have can't hold up its outputs during engine crank; if so, you can use a diode and auxiliary battery (the diode prevents current from flowing back into the car from the auxiliary battery) between the car power source and your power supply.

The current you'll draw from the 12-volt source depends on the efficiency of your power supply or inverter. Assuming it's 85 percent efficient, a 400-watt total load will draw 400/12/0.85 = 39.2 (or about 40) amps. You must use wire and automotive spade connectors rated for the current draw, with some surge reserve, and must fuse the circuits appropriately. Table 10-3 shows the wire gauge to use for different current draws.

Table 10-3   Wire Size versus Maximum Current Draw

Wire Size (Gauge)	Maximum Current Draw (Amps)
18	8
16	10
14	20
12	25
10	40
8	60

The spade connectors are important because, although they're easy to connect and disconnect, they're vibration resistant and won't drop off at an unfortunate time. It's common to use red for unswitched +12 volts and black for ground. You could use other colors for switched +12 volt lines. When you're running grounds that collect multiple circuits, be sure to add the total draw for each circuit to calculate the current for the ground wire.

A power inverter drives any electronics that can't operate directly from 12 VDC. There are directions on how to make your own on the Internet (www.aaroncake.net/circuits/inverter.htm; be careful with high voltage), but typically there's no downside to buying what you need. The Xantrex catalog (www.xantrex.com/web/id/6/inter.asp) has a wide selection, and there are many manufacturers to choose from (for example, search www.shopper.com for *power inverter*, or Google for *"power inverter" DC AC*). Power inverters that plug into a cigarette lighter-type socket can't get very much power that way; if you're going to need more than 100 or 150 watts, hardwire the inverter into the car's electrical system with the right wire, connectors, and fuses.

Wiring into the electrical system isn't a matter of picking a random wire and splicing. You should run the primary power feed directly back to the fuse box, tapping into a spare fuse of adequate capacity. If you don't have any, consider adding a new auxiliary fuse panel. The circuit from the fuse will always be powered so long as the battery is connected; use a power supervisor such as the one shown in Figure 10-5 to manage when equipment is on or off.

The power supervisor draws little to no power from the ignition switch connection; it's just using it to determine whether the engine is on or not. Be sure to examine the fuse block carefully — the electrical shop manual for your car would be ideal — because some cars have connection lugs for both battery and ignition power ready for your use.

The power supervisor will sequence the PC off whenever the ignition power signal goes off by simulating pushing the power button on a PC case through the ACPI power switch connector. You need to set up the Windows ACPI power management configuration (or its Linux equivalent) to shut down the PC when the power button is pushed, but that's all that's necessary.

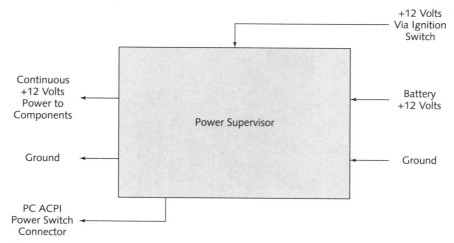

FIGURE 10-5: Power supervisor block diagram

If you're using a 12-volt supply in the PC case, and powering everything outside the PC via USB, all the power supervision you need is likely built into the power supply itself. For example, the Opus case's DC-DC Power supply includes a supervisor to monitor automobile battery voltage to protect against deep discharge and control the ACPI signals. The supervisor can't itself know how long the PC takes to shut down after the switch signal, however, so it simply uses a timer and, after the timer expires, shuts down power to the PC leaving only the required ACPI standby power lines active. You can program the power supply to shut down the PC after a delay of up to one hour. The input power is filtered for transients and other problems so the PC does not reboot during engine start or cranking. You can also adapt an existing low-power 120 VAC case to use 12 VDC using replacement power supplies such as the one from MPEGBox (www.mpegbox.com/MPBS1_Spec.pdf).

If you're using an inverter to produce 120 VAC power for use with a conventional PC power supply, you'll need a separate power controller. The Micro Shutdown Controller (Figure 10-6) sold by MP3Car (www.mp3car.com/store/product_info.php?products_id=58) works for this purpose, and includes not only a header connector for the computer connections, but also a fuse and spade connectors for the automotive wiring.

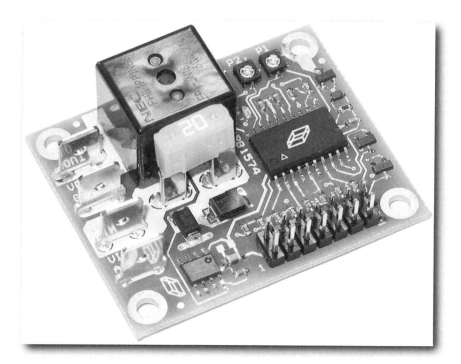

FIGURE 10-6: Micro Shutdown Controller

Something else to consider when wiring your system, mundane as it may sound, is grounding. Not only do you need to use big enough wire, good connectors, and tie to a robust connection with the frame (or run the ground wire directly back to the battery cables), you also need to consider the relationship between grounds for all the interconnected equipment in your system. The problem you're trying to avoid is that, depending on the relative resistance and current flow between each component and the common ground reference (say, at the battery ground terminal), the voltage drop to the ground point from the components can vary. The difference in ground reference voltage can cause noise when you connect two components — especially audio — at different ground potential together and form what's called a *ground loop*. The easiest solution is to make sure all ground connections tie together at a single point, rather than to random points on the chassis, but the best solution is to isolate equipment with fiber optics. That's often easy to do for audio, because the S/PDIF (Sony/Philips Digital Interface) specification has been widely adopted and may be present on both your PC and your car stereo head unit.

Laptops have their own batteries, but most don't have the endurance for more than a relatively short trip — especially if you're keeping the display on all the time. If you're using a laptop, you'll want to get a power converter. You can get them from iGo (www.igo.com) and many other sources. You can then configure your laptop so the display stays on at all times when working from external power and you'll never be interrupted by a screen saver, standby, or hibernate.

Audio/video group

You'll want to spend some time thinking about how you'll use your Car PC before you settle on the design for the audio and video interfaces, because they're part of the user interface as well as the output devices for sound and video. Here are some points to consider:

- **Wiring** — Connecting the PC audio outputs to the car's stereo is much better than adding a second set of speakers and amplifiers, so much so that you're better off upgrading those components if necessary versus adding the second set. You can hardwire the connection, which requires running properly grounded, shielded cables from the PC location through the passenger compartment to the head unit, or you can install a small FM transmitter to link the PC wirelessly to the head unit.

- **Display** — Assuming you have a display at all, you won't want its resolution to be less than 640 × 480, and you'll need 800 × 600 to run Windows XP. Cathode ray tubes (CRTs) are impractical for a car — desktop CRT monitors simply won't stand up to the shock, vibration, and temperature extremes. LCD panels are readily available at those resolutions; look for ones between 7 and 9 inches, diagonal measure.

- **Display integration** — If you want multiple displays but not multiple PCs, such as for playing DVDs on the back seat display while you navigate from the front display, you'll have to consider how the displays integrate with the operating system and your control software. Windows combines multiple displays into a single desktop surface, but most software is relatively brain-dead about working with desktops spanning multiple displays.

- **Controls integration** — You shouldn't try to use either a keyboard or a mouse while driving, nor a handheld remote control. The section on sensors describes how to integrate a keyboard and mouse; nevertheless, a touch panel is better, the built-in stereo controls are even better, and (done well) voice command is probably best. The section on software discusses approaches to build voice command software under Windows.

Assuming you set up the boot sequence operation so the right programs start and there's no user interaction, you don't need a video display for a Car PC that's only serving music through the car's stereo. If your stereo's head unit has a CD changer port, you can control the PC through that (see Chapter 11 for some ideas), and can feed the head unit track information. Rather than build your own Car PC, you can buy a complete music server system — storage, playback, interface, and controls — from PhatNoise (www.phatnoise.com/products/digitalmediaplayers/index.php). You could base a version you build on an iPod you interface through the CD changer port (see Chapter 11).

Alternatively, if you don't connect through a CD changer port, you can broadcast the audio to the head unit on an FM frequency (for example, use the kit at www.ramseyelectronics.com/cgi-bin/commerce.exe?preadd=action&key=FM10C), and if your head unit understands Radio Data System (RDS) encoding, you can add track playback information using kits such as the very basic unit from Broadcast Warehouse (www.broadcastwarehouse.com/p/BW/RDS-Encoders/R.D.S.-Kit?pid=6), the computer-interfaced encoder from Pira.cz (www.pira.cz/rds), a more capable one from PCS Electronics (www.pcs-electronics.com/en/products.php?sub=RDS_encod), or the integrated transmitter and encoder design at MyRDS (`www.myrds.fr.fm`). Printed wiring boards and pre-programmed microcontrollers are available there. There's an introduction to RDS on the net, too (`www.ee.ucl.ac.uk/~hamed/docs/final%20report.pdf`).

If you're going to play back video, or if you're going to run any programs on the PC that require display, you'll need an LCD panel. Windows XP requires at least 800×600 resolution; although MP3 players in cars started out using Linux, the guys at MP3Car.com report that Windows XP has become more common. Our speculation is that may have happened because a significant number of the people building car PCs seem to be car modders rather than programmers, and so are more comfortable with Windows and simplified programming tools such as Visual Basic. Whatever the cause, however, you'll have to fit the hardware platform to the operating system you use.

Physically larger LCD panels will be easier to read, but because there's only so much space in a car, and because large flat spaces are uncommon in car dashboards, the larger the panel is the harder it will be to integrate into the car. Small panels, such as the Lilliput 7- or 8-inch VGA-compatible touch screens (`www.mp3car.com/store/product_info.php?cPath=25&products_id=33` and `www.mp3car.com/store/product_info.php?cPath=25&products_id=42`, respectively) are common. Be prepared to pay $275 and up for a touch screen LCD; and if you can, evaluate the panel's readability in both sunlight and darkness before you buy it. Try to find a panel with brightness controls so you can dim it down for night driving.

How you encode and store music and video will determine both how much storage you need and what storage technology you use. Table 10-4 shows how much disk storage you need for different MP3 compression data rates for 1 to 10 hours of music. The storage is listed in MB of disk storage as you buy it, so it's 1,000,000 bytes (versus the 1,048,576 bytes per MB used by Windows). We've configured our MP3 compression software — we tend to use MusicMatch (`www.musicmatch.com`) — to use 256 Kbps as the default rate, because we can hear the difference in our cars at lower rates, and can't hear an improvement in the cars at higher rates. You might want to use higher rates if you can hear the difference on your home stereo, because disk storage is so cheap that it's ridiculous to compress to two different rates.

Table 10-4   MP3 Compression Data Rate versus Storage Capacity

Data Rate (Kbps)	Storage Capacity Required for N Hours (GB)									
	1	2	4	8	16	32	64	128	256	512
128	0.06	0.12	0.24	0.47	0.94	1.89	3.77	7.55	15.10	30.20
192	0.09	0.18	0.35	0.71	1.42	2.83	5.66	11.32	22.65	45.30
256	0.12	0.24	0.47	0.94	1.89	3.77	7.55	15.10	30.20	60.40
384	0.18	0.35	0.71	1.42	2.83	5.66	11.32	22.65	45.30	90.60

Storing DVD video on the server disk is wonderfully convenient, and supported by all the DVD players we've ever used (for example, InterVideo WinDVD, www.intervideo.com/jsp/WinDVD_Profile.jsp), but it will take much more storage if you plan to store very many titles at all. The Star Wars DVD (Episode IV, A New Hope, in widescreen) occupies 8,133,427,200 bytes on DVD (7.57 GB in Windows), so you should assume you'll need *at least* 80 GB, and probably more, to store 10 DVDs on the server. Fortunately, disks are cheap. There are programs that will conveniently move the video content onto your hard drive (for example, www.dvddecrypter.com), but those programs don't make the files any smaller. You *can* further compress a DVD, such as to the DivX format (www.divx.com) with tools such as GordianKnot (gordianknot.sourceforge.net) and Auto Gordian Knot (www.autogk.net), although it takes some care to get the software cleanly set up on your PC. In no case do we suggest you use any of these capabilities to make illegal copies of CDs or DVDs.

Sensor group

Sensors give your Car PC information about the environment. There's almost no limit to what sensors you can hook up. Many of them would even be useful:

- **Engine monitoring** — The On-Board Diagnostics II (OBD II) specification provides a reasonably standardized interface to the engine computer in your car. (We only say reasonably standardized in that individual manufacturers define their own diagnostic codes in addition to the standard ones.) We wrote about how to attach a data logger chip to the OBD II port in *PC Toys* (Wiley, 2003); you can also attach a direct port-to-PC cable to get diagnostic data in real time.

- **Keyboard** — It's pricey, but L3 Systems makes a QWERTY keyboard (l3shop.com/Merchant2/merchant.mvc?Screen=PROD&Store_Code=LSOS&Product_Code=SA0023&Category_Code=2) you can strap to your forearm. That's not a great idea for the driver, but it could be convenient for a passenger, although touch typing becomes out of the question.

- **Radar detector** — Although radar detectors such as the Valentine One (www.valentine1.com) and Escort 8500 (www.escortradar.com) don't provide ports to interface to PCs, you could mount photocells next to their indicators, wire in a small microphone with a filter for the frequency of their alert, or tap the internal display circuitry to detect voltages sent to the indicator LEDs. Any of those signals could be processed in the PC — for example, to map radar trap locations (combine the data with the GPS location) — or mute the stereo to make sure you hear the alert.

- **Security** — Wiring your PC to monitor the door switches or indoor lights lets it know if a door was opened while you were away, and if you wired in a siren is the start of an automotive security system. The PC has to remain on or be turned on by the monitoring hardware for this to work, so you'll either need some more complex electronics or have to solve the power consumption problem when the car's turned off.

- **Soft gauges** — The OBD II port makes data besides diagnostics available in real time, such as vehicle speed, battery voltage, and others. Inputs you want that aren't available from the OBD II port (oil pressure and temperature, perhaps) are accessible by attaching sensors to the car and monitoring their readings from the PC using USB analog and digital interfaces such as the Phidget 8/8/8 described in Chapter 4.

- **Touch screen and buttons** — The Lilliput LCD panels (for example, www.mp3car .com/store/product_info.php?cPath=25&products_id=33) include both a touch screen and buttons at the bottom of the panel. The touch screen simulates a mouse to the PC, and you can program the buttons to activate functions in your software. If its cost isn't a problem (think $1,500 and up), an interesting alternative to a built-in touch screen LCD would be the Wacom Cintiq (www.wacom.com/lcdtablets/index .cfm), which is a drawing tablet with a built-in LCD (see Figure 10-7). You use the drawing pen as a mouse, too, so it's a combination of input and output device that sits in your navigator's lap. Best of all, it uses standard video interfaces, requires no integration into the vehicle dashboard, and can be safely locked away when you're not using it.

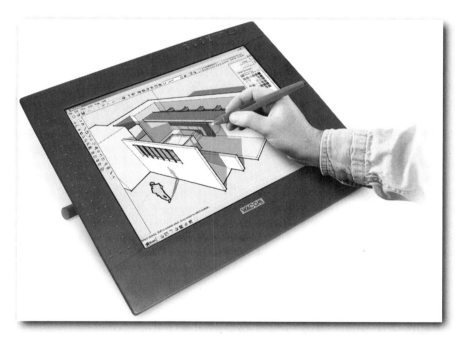

FIGURE 10-7: Wacom Cintiq (photo courtesy Wacom)

- **Video cameras** — Larger motor homes often have video cameras on the back. Couple in a video capture card — internal or USB — and an inexpensive webcam from Logitech (www.logitech.com/index.cfm/products/productlist/US/EN,crid=2203) or X-10 (www.x10.com/products/cat_cameras.htm) and you have the same capability.

There are a variety of sources for OBD II interfaces. The cables are more expensive than you might expect, because there's some electronics involved to translate from the OBD II port to a PC serial or USB port. obddiagnostics.com (www.obddiagnostics.com/index.html) supplies plans to build your own interface if you'd prefer.

Table 10-5 lists some sources. All the interfaces in the table include software; obddiagnostics .com has links to software from a variety of sources in addition to the software available on the site, and provides the information you'll need to write your own at obddiagnostics.com/ obdinfo/info.html.

Table 10-5   OBD II Sources

Component	Source
OBD II Interface	Alex C. Peper www.obd-2.com/index.html
OBD II Interface	AutoEnginuity, L.L.C. www.autoenginuity.com/products-scantoolpc.html
OBD II Interface	AutoTap www.autotap.com/autotap_for_windows.html
OBD II Interface	B. Roadman www.obddiagnostics.com/order.html
OBD II Interface	Digimoto www.digimoto.com

Some of the OBD II software included with the interfaces in Table 10-5 will display gauges for monitored values (for example, see www.obd-2.com/dashg.htm).

Products to help you know about speed traps are available (for example, www.originbluei.com), and there seems to be an enormous selection of similar products in the U.K. (Google for *radar trap database*), driven perhaps by outrage over the cameras placed throughout the country. An open U.S. database of radar traps exists (www.speedtrap.org), but it's not terribly location specific — GPS coordinates can be posted but rarely are — and it's unknown how comprehensive the database is. Products that integrate real-time radar detection, GPS, and a database do not seem to have reached the market.

Software

No one piece of software does everything you might want in a Car PC — the developer would have to be wildly creative to have *a priori* thought of everything anyone might want a Car PC to do. Unless you're building a Car PC to do a small number of very specific tasks, you'll want the software to be a collection of programs tied together by a configurable, flexible menu and program launcher. Done that way, each function in your Car PC — such as DVD playback, navigation, and others — can have unique software, software that you can update or replace at will.

Whatever software architecture you use, however, the way the system interacts with the driver is crucial. The fact that we've seen people on freeways in Los Angeles and elsewhere driving the speed limit (and more) while reading, putting on makeup, and worse doesn't change the fact that it's irresponsible to take as much attention off the road (and your hands off the wheel) as is required to operate a keyboard or mouse. If the software is well designed with large easily read buttons, touch screens solve much of the problem by creating an interface similar to that used successfully for controls in cars for decades.

Voice command and response

Voice command and response is even better than touch screens and buttons when implemented well, because it can eliminate all need to take your eyes off the road. If you're programming under Windows for your Car PC, you can use the considerable resources Microsoft makes available in your software for voice command and response, including the following:

- **Speech SDK** — If you're programming in C++ or Visual Basic (VB), you can access the Microsoft speech libraries through the Speech Software Development Kit (SDK, www.microsoft.com/downloads/details.aspx?FamilyID=5e86ec97-40a7-453f-b0ee-6583171b4530&DisplayLang=en). As stated in the Speech SDK documentation:

  Microsoft Speech SDK is a software development kit for building speech engines and applications for Microsoft Windows. Designed primarily for the desktop speech developer, the SDK contains the Microsoft® Win32-compatible speech application programming interface (SAPI), the Microsoft continuous speech recognition engine and Microsoft concatenated speech synthesis (or text-to-speech) engine, a collection of speech-oriented development tools for compiling source code and executing commands, sample application and tutorials that demonstrate the use of Speech with other engine technologies, sample speech recognition and speech synthesis engines for testing with speech-enabled applications, and documentation on the most important SDK features.

  You can define the specific lexicon and grammar the system recognizes, and can change them from one application to the next. The speech libraries do require you use the Microsoft Component Object Model (COM), which in C++ is — to be charitable — complex, but there are sample applications you can grab code from. A discussion of using the speech tools with the Microsoft Foundation Classes (MFC) is included in the SDK documentation titled "Using MFC to Automate SAPI." You'll want to read it before starting to build speech into a C++ program. There are VB samples too, and much of the COM complexity is hidden by the underlying VB platform.

- **Technical articles** — The Microsoft site hosts a number of articles on how to build a good speech interface (msdn.microsoft.com/library/en-us/dnnetspeech/html/TechOvrvw.asp). The articles are written from the perspective of developing a speech-enabled Web application, but many of the concepts apply well to automotive and embedded applications too, including the articles "Voice User Interface Design: Tips and Techniques," "Voice User Interface Design: Purpose and Process," and "Heuristics: Lessons in the Art of Automated Conversation."

Software components

Not only does using a launcher application to integrate your system let you add any functionality you want, it also enables you to use whatever application you choose for a specific task. For example:

- **DVD player** — The FrodoPlayer software can play audio, video, CD, and DVD content (it links to Windows Media Player internally), but nevertheless may not be the software you want, or may not be the user interface you want. You can use an external application if you prefer, be it WinDVD, Windows Media Player, or some other software. You can interface PC remote controls (for example, www.streamzap.com), too, since whoever's watching a DVD really shouldn't be driving.

- **Navigation and GPS** — A program called Destinator 3 (www.destinator1.com) has a following for Car PCs, particularly because maps are available outside North America. The software sold by the manufacturer, HSTC, is for PocketPC, but you can find software on MP3Car (www.mp3car.com/vbulletin/showthread.php?t=36487) that enables you to use the maps on a PC.

  DeLorme also does mapping and navigation software, and packages it with their very small Earthmate USB GPS receiver (www.delorme.com/earthmate/configlaptop_info.asp). The software implements voice command and response, so you need not keep consulting the map display (see Figure 10-8). There's much more information on the Earthmate and the Street Atlas software in Chapter 10 of *PC Toys*.

  A third choice for GPS and navigation software — more expensive when combined with the GPS receiver than the equivalent DeLorme package — is iGuidance, from iNav (www.inavcorp.com/products/iguidance2_combo.html).

- **Monitoring, diagnostics, and gauges** — Each of the OBD II interfaces listed in Table 10-5 includes software. If you're more inclined to write your own software, there's a lot of information to get you started on the OBD Programmer's Page (obddiagnostics.com/obdinfo/info.html). There are also several projects on SourceForge (see Table 10-6) you could use or modify.

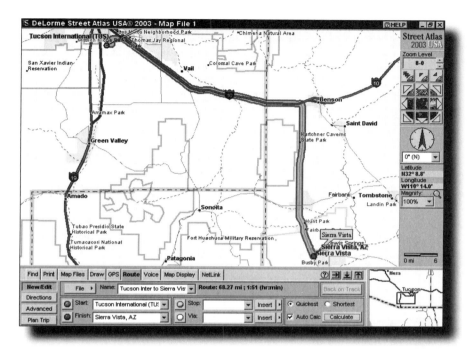

FIGURE 10-8: Street Atlas map display

Table 10-6   Open Source OBD II Software

Project	SourceForge Link
GM OBD-II Java Interface	sourceforge.net/projects/obdmp
Java OBDII Project	sourceforge.net/projects/jobdii
OSAT - Open Source Automotive Tuning	sourceforge.net/projects/osat-1-obd2
ScanTool.net: OBD-II software front end	sourceforge.net/projects/scantool
Vehicle Diagnostics Suite	sourceforge.net/projects/freediag

- **Wardriving**—Defined as driving around locating and logging wireless access points, wardriving *per se* is not breaking into WiFi networks. There's a lot of confusion about that in print, confusion that's led to a paper in the Virginia Journal of Law & Technology (available from the Social Science Research Network Electronic Library, ssrn.com/abstract=585867). It's unquestionably true that people do hack into wireless networks; here we're addressing finding access points. You should find out if the access points are intended for public use before accessing the corresponding network.

Assuming you've put a wireless LAN interface card into your Car PC, along with an extension to the antenna to place it outside any interfering metal shielding, and assuming you have a GPS connected to a serial port on your system (USB units require adapting software such as is available from DeLorme for their Earthmate), the NetStumbler software (stumbler.net) does the rest of the work required to identify, characterize, and log wireless access points.

Figure 10-9 is a NetStumbler screen shot. The upper window shows signal strength for our wireless LAN (we've altered the display of our service set identifier—SSID—for security), while the lower one shows a LAN accessible at times from our location. The display shows the channels the access points are on, the SSID, and the signal strength over time. The signal strength numbers are negative; our signal-to-noise ratio, for example, hovers around -55 dBm, and is therefore significantly stronger than the other access point signal strength of about -80 dBm. The other access point is also completely unsecured—it is not encrypted, indicated by the absence of the lock symbol, and uses the default SSID for the equipment (ACTIONTEC).

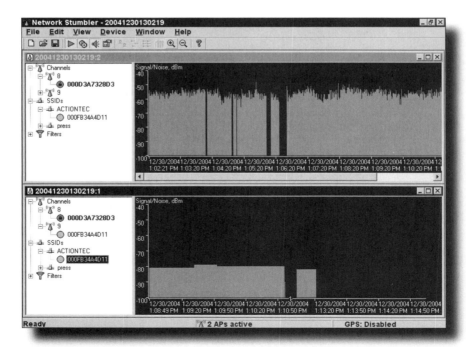

FIGURE 10-9: NetStumbler display

It's entirely likely the owner of the access point in the lower window simply plugged it in and turned it on, giving no thought to securing the network. That's very common because so many naïve users set up wireless networks, and it's one of the reasons you have to verify that public access is permissible before using a network.

Launcher

One of the more popular Car PC front ends and launchers is FrodoPlayer (`www.frodoplayer .com`; discussions are on that site and on MP3Car at `www.mp3car.com/vbulletin/ forumdisplay.php?f=47`). The program is specifically designed for car PCs, and uses large buttons on the user interface to adapt to touch screen operation.

Figure 10-10 shows the initial FrodoPlayer screen using the default skin (you can create your own or download ones from the Internet), with the main function buttons on the left. The initial screen presumes you'll be playing music, and so devotes most of the screen to giving you direct access to audio files on the server disk. The BACK and FWD buttons advance among sources, including all audio files, all video files, the loaded CD, pre-defined playlists, pre-defined favorites, a file system browser, and a list of folders. The FIND, VOL+, VOL-, and MUTE buttons do exactly what you'd expect in that context, as do the usual player buttons in the lower right. The V button cycles the small window to its right among the song data, album cover art, a screen magnifier, and a music-driven visualization similar to what WinAmp, Windows Media Player, and others offer. The F button changes the view to full-screen — the same view as for playing DVDs — displaying whatever had been in the small visualization window normally. You can also toggle what's in the visualization window (small or full screen) by holding your finger in the window for a few seconds.

FIGURE 10-10: FrodoPlayer initial screen

The MENU, MIN, and TASK buttons on the left provide connections to external software. MIN is the Windows Minimize Window function, causing FrodoPlayer to remove itself from the screen, while TASK displays a large-icon version of the Windows Alt-Tab program selection menu (see Figure 10-11). Touching one of the icons brings up that program, and leaves FrodoPlayer in a small form (see Figure 10-12) in the top-left corner of the screen (the menu will disappear after a short interval if you don't pick anything). A single touch on the leftmost icon further reduces the FrodoPlayer window to just that icon; a double touch restores the FrodoPlayer window to full screen.

FIGURE 10-11: Program selection menu

FIGURE 10-12: Small form FrodoPlayer window

The MENU button leads to the screen in Figure 10-13, from where you both launch other functions and software (APPS, DVD, FM RADIO, XM RADIO, GPS, SYNC, FRODOCAM, and FRODO PICS) and configure FrodoPlayer (SETTINGS 1 and SETTINGS 2).

Most of the configuration setup is under SETTINGS 1, including display details, the content database characteristics and locations, skins (separate ones are available for daytime and nighttime), external application configuration, and voice response (FrodoPlayer uses the Microsoft Speech SDK).

FIGURE 10-13: Configuration screen

You can interface essentially any external software; the external software functions FrodoPlayer can coordinate with include the following:

- **FM Radio** — The Radiator software (flesko.cz/radiator.htm) controls FM tuner hardware in your PC, giving you capabilities much like the personal video recorder SageTV (Chapter 3) creates for television. The Web site lists the many compatible cards, including two USB units you could use if you're out of slots in the server chassis.

- **XM Radio** — FrodoPlayer has internal software to drive an XM Radio receiver over a serial port, but you can configure it to use external software instead.

- **GPS** — FrodoPlayer is set to tie to two of the GPS and mapping software combinations above — Destinator using the PC software on MP3Car and iGuidance — plus a program called Routis that seems to no longer be available. It will also link to any other external application, such as Street Atlas or Microsoft's Streets and Trips.

- **DVD** — FrodoPlayer wraps DVD player functionality from Windows Media Player, but as with XM Radio, you can set it to use an external application, such as InterVideo's WinDVD.

- **Arbitrary** — You can set the application launch screen to tie any external application on your server to one of ten buttons. External applications can also be launched from the main menu screen if you create the buttons in your custom skin (see www.mp3car.com/vbulletin/showthread.php?t=37518).

Creating new skins for FrodoPlayer consists of building the graphics for the screen, then defining an `ini` file so the player knows where the buttons are on-screen. There are nine `ini` files: for the main screen (`skin.ini`), DVD playback (`dvd.ini`), on-screen keyboard (`keyboard.ini`), the applications and configuration menu screen (`menu.ini`), the mini-display (`mini2.ini`), playlist build (`plsbuild.ini`), FM radio (`radio.ini`), file search (`searchby.ini`), and XM radio (`xm.ini`). Button positions are defined in the `ini` files as percentages of the overall screen dimensions, given as the top-left corner along with the width and height. Set the top-left corner for any button you don't have in a specific skin (but accepted in the `ini` file) to greater than 100 percent in both dimensions. Do not set the height or width to zero. For example:

```
left=110
top=110
width=1
height=1
```

There's no documentation on the layout of the graphics and `ini` files in one place. Your best approach is to copy the default skin directory structure (it's in `...\FrodoPlayer\Skins\ 800x480`), scan the existing default `ini` files to understand what buttons and controls each supports, design your images, then modify the `ini` files to match. A simple application, FrodoSkinner, is available to help create `ini` files using images (`www.headlife.com/ Program/FrodoSkinner/v1.1/FrodoPlayerv1.1.zip`), but as of version 1.1 it only has support for building the main screen.

Extending the Car PC

The entire Car PC project is really about how you'll extend and adapt the idea to fit what you want and what works in your car. That said, here are a few ways you could both refine what the existing components do and extend the concept to an entirely new arena.

- **GPS WAAS data availability** — The DeLorme Earthmate USB GPS provides both the usual GPS data stream and enhancements using the WAAS signal. No third-party software appears to support the Earthmate USB interface, which means you have to use the USB-to-serial port converter software provided by DeLorme if you're using applications such as NetStumbler or Streets and Trips. The notes with the converter software, however, state that you may lose the WAAS accuracy improvements if you install the converter. If you're a skilled driver developer, you could reverse engineer the USB data stream with WAAS enabled, then implement your own serial converter driver that preserves full accuracy.

- **Multiple GPS** — The serial port GPS interface, despite using a standard format data stream (usually NMEA 183), is only accessible to one application at a time. That's inconvenient, because there are concurrent applications that can make use of the GPS data. For example, in addition to a navigation application, you could write an application that monitors and logs trip start and end times and locations, plus mileage, creating an automobile usage log useful for expense reports and tax returns.

The key to running multiple applications would be a driver that splits the standard GPS data stream to multiple consuming applications. You could let the GPS appear on multiple COM*x* ports to provide an interface, and copy the incoming data stream to all the ports. The complication, aside from writing the driver in the first place, would be providing the necessary control outputs to the GPS (for example, estimated location and time). One approach would be to designate one of the ports as the "real" port, the one that really controls the unit. Control outputs from any other ports would have to simulate the right response from the GPS, if any, and otherwise ignore the command.

- **Simplified skinning** — The FrodoSkinner application is a great idea, but unfortunately incomplete. The ideal application would scan a set of FrodoPlayer ini files to determine what buttons and controls each one supports, and support defining buttons for all the files. The application could also exchange graphics into and out of Photoshop (or any another graphics application) to modify the image. If it could send layers into Photoshop, it could provide outlines for where the button definitions are presently, guiding how to modify the underlying graphic.

- **Wearable computing** — The Segway not withstanding, there's no reason why the Car PC concept has to be so large that it requires a vehicle to move around. Using hardware such as the Xybernaut MA V wearable computer (www.xybernaut.com/Solutions/product/mav_product.htm), you can take the Car PC with you. It's easy to see how a map in a heads-up display could assist map-based sports, including hiking or geocaching.

Summary

The limitations of mobile computing tend to be either lack of storage, such as in MP3 players before they incorporated microdrives, or lack of usable input/output facilities, which limits both the viable applications and the network bandwidth the device can usefully consume (something of great concern to companies that bought 3G spectrum in the very expensive auctions). A Car PC has none of those limitations — you can build in as much storage as you like and as big a display as you like. The limitations relative to your desktop computer need only be that it's hard to do fine precision work when the car's moving. Other than that, what you can do with your Car PC is limited only by your imagination.

Hacking on Your Own

The creation of every project in this book followed the same sequence of steps:

1. Have an idea.
2. Structure the approach.
3. Find the parts.
4. Build and test the project.

For some, having the idea in the first place is the biggest challenge in creating their own projects. For others, structuring the approach and finding parts is the hard part. This chapter suggests more projects, and approaches to building them, and looks at some of the ways you might solve the problems in their design.

The ideas and approaches in this chapter are:

➤ Remote control finder

➤ Laser light show

➤ USB interface to whatever

➤ Speakers, cell phone link, or car radio link for your iPod

Where Do These Ideas Come From?

Project ideas are everywhere. Finding them isn't a matter of pounding your head until ideas fall out, it's a matter of thinking about things you experience with a view toward automation. If you look at the projects in this book, or at the ideas in this chapter, you'll see that daily activities can be made more convenient or more entertaining with better information or with automation. There's little in this book you couldn't do by hand; what the projects do is make things easier or more fun.

If I am recruiting to find someone to run my computer systems, and my choice is between the brilliant programmer who's head of the world's largest international technology conglomerate and an obnoxious 15-year-old dork who's trying to impress his dream girl, I'll take the brat and let the hero get stuck with the genius.

Peter Anspach,
The Evil Overlord List

in this chapter

☑ Creating your own ideas

☑ Figuring out how to build your own designs

☑ More ideas

Look at the laser light show idea below as an example. You've likely been to concerts or planetarium shows with lasers bouncing to the music or writing designs and messages on walls. There's no mystery to how the systems work—it's just laser beams being deflected over time by mirrors, where the mirrors are moved in sync with an input signal. You can buy complete kits to do the same thing yourself, or you could build your own.

The Car PC (Chapter 10 in this book) comes from the same sort of observation: You can buy a new head unit for the stereo in your PC, and clip in a standalone navigator, or you can integrate a lot of applications into a PC and then link them into the existing systems.

The subsections below are ideas for projects. All of them address tasks people do every day; applying PCs, software, and some specialized interfaces makes those tasks easier or does them in better or different ways. Some of the projects are easy; some are relatively advanced.

Remote control finder

We, like many people we know, often have to search for a remote control, wireless phone, cell phone, or other candy bar–size chunk of electronics. Depending on how deep it's buried in the furniture (or how far away it's been carried, see Figure 11-1), that can take a long time because there are no clues where to look.

FIGURE 11-1: The usual suspects

That's a small, neatly defined problem: Eliminate having to look for remote controls. Here're two ways to solve the problem. The first approach extends to finding other items; the second does not:

- **Pager** — If you devise a way to cause the remote to identify itself, you can find it. Any signal you can detect would work, including light, sound, or magnetism.

- **Universal** — If you don't need a remote, you don't have to find it. Replacing some or all of the remotes could eliminate the problem.

There are multiple ways to implement each approach, too. We'll look at some of them in a later section.

Laser light show

Moving mirrors are the essence of the electronics controlling a laser light show. You apply coordinated XY signals to perpendicular mirrors and the beam moves in response. The information you drive the display with depends on what you want. If you simply want visual accompaniment to music, you could drive the mirrors with the left and right music channels. If you want a large graphical display, you could drive the mirrors from a PC, letting you show time, weather, stock tickers, caller ID, or most any other information you can draw with lines.

Apart from its novelty (and therefore entertainment value), a laser display is — with some specific limits — a relatively inexpensive way to create a wall or building-size message. With sophisticated enough software, you can project any information on the wall, an alternative to systems that overlay data onto the television.

USB interface to whatever

The lack of a computer interface need not stop you from reading or controlling devices with your PC, because chips are now available that encapsulate the USB interface into a simple electronic building block.

For example, there are low-frequency atomic clock reference signals worldwide:

- DCF 77 Mainflingen/Germany (77.5 kHz)
- MSF Rugby/U.K. (60 kHz)
- WWVB Fort Collins/US (60 kHz)
- JJY Japan (40 and 60 kHz)
- HBG Prangins/Switzerland (75 kHz)

Want a PC clock tied to one of them, or a worldwide module you can take with your laptop? Interface a receiver chipset to USB.

Still looking at timekeeping, do you want a striking, large format clock? Build a propeller clock — a round clock that displays time by controlling lights on a quickly rotating arm (www.luberth.com/analog.htm) — setting it up from your PC via USB. Add to the software and you can display messages, too.

Or, suppose you're watching your weight, and want to automatically record every reading from the scale. You could use the Phidgets scale (`www.phidgets.com/index.php?module=pncommerce&func=itemview&IID=60`), or if you're more adventurous you could tie a pressure sensor to a USB port yourself. Either way, your computer can watch and note when there's a reading.

iPod accessories

Handheld music players, mostly those playing MP3 files, have been around for years. The market exploded with Apple's introduction of the iPod, a device that now accounts for about a quarter of Apple's total business.

Cool packaging aside, the iPod is far more than a simple fixed-function device; it's a complete handheld computer — indeed, you can load Linux on it if you want (`www.ipodlinux.org/index.php/Main_Page`). The Linux implementation replaces the native iPod software (but you can reload the Apple baseline), and includes support for the following:

- Frame buffer (display)
- Audio device (8-96 kHz 16-bit little-endian)
- Firewire
- Directional buttons, scroll wheel, and hold switch via tty interface
- Remote control
- Piezo
- Hard disk drive
- FAT, UMSDOS, and HFS+ filesystem

As of late 2004, Linux support for power management, battery status, and flash was still missing. USB doesn't seem to be on the list, either; nor does the mini-iPod itself — be sure to check the Web site to see whether your specific iPod is supported.

Those capabilities make the iPod a great platform for both new projects and accessories. In the new projects category, for example, consider that — once USB is implemented — you could combine an iPod and the Phidget interface we used for the home security system as an alternate platform for the barbecue temperature controller in Chapter 8.

There's ample room for creative iPod accessories, too — for example, you could integrate an iPod with powered speakers and a large control panel to form a dock that turns the iPod into a stereo system, but still lets you pick it up and travel. A variant of the same work would let you create a wireless remote control for your iPod, letting you control the program from a distance. You could build your own FM transmitter to broadcast what the iPod plays, and perhaps extend its range to cover your entire house. Or, with some nontrivial software and the right cables, you could arrange to keep your address book synchronized between your iPod and your cell phone.

How Do You Figure Out the Approach?

The approach you take to build a project is going to be a balance between what the project does, what you're capable of designing and building yourself, and what you can find as components. The more you want a project to do, the more you and the components you find have to deliver. The more you can design and build, the less capable (and possibly less expensive) the components you use have to be.

Because of that, defining the best approach for *you*, which may not be the best approach for us or for anyone else, starts with specifying what you want the project to do, along with all the supporting requirements. Here, for example, is the initial set of requirements for the Kitchen PC database in Chapter 7:

1. Store recipes, with fields for amount of ingredient, name of ingredient, name of recipe, number of people, time to prepare, and (free text) preparation instructions. There should be a category of ingredients for wines, and there should be a separate field for a list of recommended wines with the recipe.

2. The number of ingredients should not be limited, and it should be possible for an ingredient to be a whole, complete other recipe you reference by name.

3. Ingredients should themselves have categories, such as spice, dairy, meat, fowl, etc. The categories should themselves be database elements, not fixed.

4. There should be a way to print a recipe scaled for a different number of people.

5. The database should also store an inventory (as per the barcodes) of the ingredients.

6. It should be possible to search for recipes based on what's in inventory and on a specific set of ingredients you want to use.

7. It should be possible to print a shopping list for what's not in inventory to make one or, ideally, several recipes.

8. The inventory should be updateable via the barcode scanner from within the application.

9. Printout capability should include the list of recipes, individual recipes, inventory, and shopping lists.

   Most of these requirements made it into the final implementation; some (based simply on the time available to do the work) did not. In addition to these functional requirements, we had one other supporting requirement: The database should be built on a commonly available relational database application, not be a from-scratch software development.

All those requirements, together, led to the Microsoft Access database in the chapter, along with enhancements to the barcode lookup software we provided for Chapter 6. If you built the database from scratch, your skills and preferences might dictate other approaches. For example:

- If you're only using the database as a recipe collection, you could eliminate much of the complexity having to do with maintaining an inventory of available ingredients.

- If you keep an extensive wine cellar, you might enhance the inventory to include the same sort of wine capabilities we listed in the "Wine Cellar" section of Chapter 6.

- If you run Linux on the PC that will host the database, you won't be using Microsoft Access. You can find alternative relational database software on the net (e.g., `linuxdatabases.info/info/rdbmssql.html`, `sourceforge.net/projects/firebird`, or `databases.foundries.sourceforge.net`).

- You might have chosen to omit the barcode lookup if the programming involved was beyond your skills, or if you simply don't plan to use the capability.

Defining what you want and being realistic about what you're capable of is the key to a successful project.

Remote control finder

The remote control finder idea directly illustrates the difference your skills can make in the approach you choose. Here's how the two approaches described above break down:

- **Pager** — Requiring the pager to emit a sound or light in response to a signal — be that trigger signal sound, radio, or light — requires that you build a transmitter and receiver, that the receiver (including the response transmitter and power supply) be small enough to fit neatly with the remote, and (unless you want them *all* to respond) that the trigger signal be decoded at the remote receiver to determine whether it should respond.

  Assuming you don't want to simply buy one of the available products (`smarthome.com/3285.html`, `www.brookstone.com/shop/product.asp?product_code=360792&search_type=search&search_words=key%20finder`, `www.findonefindall.com`, and more), implementing this approach puts a premium on your electronics design and packaging skills; very little if any PC hardware or software work is required. We tried one from Sharper Image, and didn't have much success, so there's probably room for improvement in a design you do yourself.

- **Universal** — Instead of finding the specific remote you need, suppose you programmed your PC to emulate them all, and then had one device that could tell the PC to issue the command you want. You can readily get an infrared USB transmitter for your PC (e.g., `www.usbuirt.com`), so the work comes down to how to signal the PC plus the requisite software. There are a lot of PC remotes you could use, such as the Streamzap (`www.streamzap.com`) or the ones from ATI (`www.ati.com/products/remotewonder/index.html`) or X-10 (`smarthome.com/4006.html`). Alternatively, you could program a handheld PC to either directly emit the necessary infrared signals or to wirelessly network to a desktop PC with the infrared emitter.

  Whichever variant you choose, and assuming you don't simply download prewritten software for your handheld, the universal remote approach puts the emphasis on your software development abilities. You'll need software to read and learn from the existing remotes, so you know the command codes, software to work with the handheld unit you use for control, and software to emit the proper sequences in response to your direction.

Laser light show

Any approach you take for a laser light show will require good mechanical construction skills, because you're going to be making mirrors move quickly and repeatably. It also requires common sense, because sloppy practices around lasers can blind you. Be careful.

The laser — a handheld laser pointer, perhaps, if not a higher power unit (for example, www.sciencekit.com/category.asp_Q_c_E_429679) — provides you a point source, which you direct with moving mirrors. It's common to use two orthogonal mirrors, one to move the beam in the X direction and the other to move it in the Y direction. The most important design decision is how you'll move the beam — if you let the mirrors run free, tracing out a raster much like the cathode ray tube in an older television or monitor (not an LCD or plasma panel), you can control the display by switching the beam on and off. If you directly control mirrors to determine the beam position, you create a vector display, and need only turn the beam off for dark sections of the vectors.

Those two alternatives lead to two very different architectures for the mirror assembly. The approach you choose should reflect both the application you have for the project and your relative mechanical, electrical, and software skills:

- **Raster scan** — You're likely to find parts you can use for this approach in an old laser printer. The horizontal deflection mirror can be multiple facets on a rotating cylinder, as in Figure 11-2. The angle of the mirror relative to the laser beam changes as each facet rotates past the beam, sweeping out the arc shown in the figure. The process repeats for each facet (eight in the figure); turning off the beam in time for the facet corners ensures that the beam remains confined to the intended width. The critical design characteristics for this mirror are that it spins at a known, constant speed, and that the processor knows precisely the timing for each facet versus the laser beam position. The processor controls the beam timing to create dot positions along the line, and chooses whether a dot is on or not based on the font and what's being displayed.

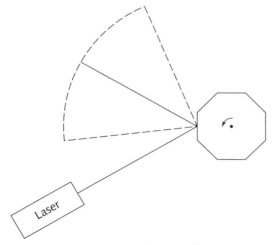

FIGURE 11-2: Raster scan X (horizontal) mirror

Moving from one line down to the next, and returning to the top from the last line, requires the vertical deflection mirror to hold its position while the laser traces each line, then quickly step down to the next line. A continuously rotating mirror won't work for that, as it would cause the line to slope, but either a fast stepper motor or an accurately positioned voice coil would work.

- **Vector display** — A pair of orthogonal mirrors attached to fast actuators (such as speaker voice coils), or a single mirror driven in two axes by fast actuators, can position the beam arbitrarily. The processor synchronizes the on-off beam status to the position to control whether a line segment is drawn or not.

Figure 11-3 is a block diagram for a vector display system. We've shown D/A converters driving the actuators, which we assume are voice coils, but you'd use servos for closed-loop positioning accuracy. You'll also need amplifiers between the D/A converters and the voice coils, which we simply assumed were part of the actuators.

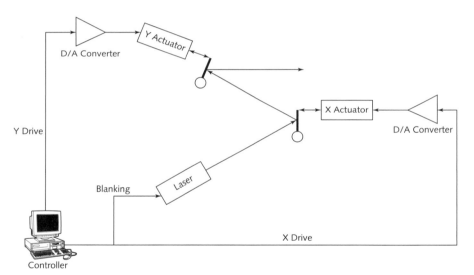

FIGURE 11-3: Vector display block diagram

We also labeled the computer in the lower left as a controller, not a PC, to suggest that a PC running Windows or Linux may not have the fast, consistent interrupt response times necessary to drive the system. Whether that's true or not depends on the refresh rate you want — the more complete cycles of a complex display you want per second, and therefore the total number of vectors you can display per second, the faster the drive has to be. At some point, you'll exceed the real-time response capabilities of either Windows or Linux.

Finally, you have some options for how you create the analog outputs you use to drive the actuators. If you're using a PC directly, you could use the left and right stereo outputs from the sound card; if you're using a small real-time controller, you'll probably want to use D/A converters directly.

The software for either approach has some complexities, too. You may want to pre-process the display content to simplify the real-time processing, laying out the dot patterns or vertex locations and beam status for the raster and vector displays, respectively. Software for the vector display will also have to create arcs as sequences of XY drive values at specific times, and can control relative brightness by retracing some vectors more than others.

There are good descriptions of how to build voice coil–driven mirrors on the Internet (`spt06.chez.tiscali.fr/00/scan2.htm`, `spt06.chez.tiscali.fr/00/scan3.htm`, and `www.amelink.net/laserpage/project1.html`).

USB interface to whatever

Future Technology Devices International (FTDI) makes a line of USB chips that simplify adding USB to your equipment (`www.ftdichip.com/FTProducts.htm`). The chips provide a standard serial or byte parallel interface, making connection to something like a Javelin Stamp trivial. Chips (and a development tool) are available from Parallax (`www.parallax.com/html_pages/products/ftdi/ftdi_chips.asp`). Hobby Engineering sells a module with the FTDI chip, USB connector, surrounding circuitry, and parallel connections (`info.hobbyengineering.com/specs/USBMOD4.pdf`), and also has one for serial interfaces (`info.hobbyengineering.com/specs/USBMOD3.pdf`).

USB makes a nice interface for an atomic clock–based time source. You can receive the WWVB atomic clock reference signals with modules such as the Galleon EM2S (`www.ntp-time-server.com/wwvb-receiver/wwvb-receiver.htm`; implementation at `www.buzzard.org.uk/jonathan/radioclock.html`). You can use the companion MCM-RS232 Microcontroller Decoder Module to produce a serial output for the USB interface, or you could frame the received stream directly and process the data in the PC. The Sanyo LA1650/C (`www.sanyo.com/semiconductors/news/Vol81.pdf`) does the same thing, as does the Nippon Precision Circuits SM9501A/B.

Alternatively, you could simply tear apart one of the many inexpensive clocks now available, or (the *really* advanced project if your electronics and digital signal processing skills are up to it) you could directly sample the signal through an RF amplifier, and then demodulate and decode it entirely in software. There's information on that approach on the Internet, too (`www.qsl.net/k0lr/SW-RX/sw-rx.htm`).

A USB interface makes for an interesting clock output from your PC, too. Figure 11-4 shows the propeller clock concept (see also `www.luberth.com/analog.htm`). An arm with a series of LEDs — as long as you like — rotates around an axis; a processor uses the LEDs to create a clock face in the air by carefully sequencing the LEDs on and off at the right time. The arm has to be balanced around the axis (hence the lower extension), but could be a clear disk or virtually any other design if you preferred.

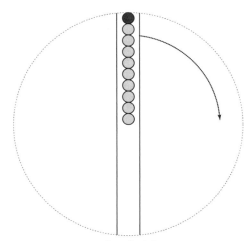

FIGURE 11-4: Propeller clock layout

The clock has to rotate fast enough to give the illusion that the lit points are simply hung in space, but that creates some interesting timing constraints. For example, suppose the outermost LED creates a continuous arc from the 12 position to the current location of a (unseen) second hand. At 10 rotations per second (RPS), only 1.667 ms separates one position from the next. That 1.667 ms interval is also the duration the inner LEDs should be on for minimum-width hour and second hands. That's tighter timing than you'd want a PC to do, and it doesn't really make sense to tie up a PC just to run a clock.

There are at least two other ways to build the clock:

- **Direct logic** — You could use a complex programmable logic device (CPLD) or direct logic using counters, along with a crystal oscillator, to sequence the LEDs on and off at the right time. A USB-connected (or wireless!) PC could update the logic once a minute to change the display and resynchronize the clock. Resynchronization is necessary because an inexpensive crystal oscillator (for example, www.vectron.com/products/xo/vcc1.pdf) may only be accurate to 100 parts per million, which translates to over 8 seconds error per day, and nearly an hour per year. Depending on how you designed the logic, the PC could download a pattern for every one-second position of the arm, letting you display raster fonts as well as a clock face. If you limited the display to 8 LEDs, a simply byte-wide static memory would store the data.

- **Microprocessor driven** — A FIFO memory clocked at the tick rate (that is, the revolutions per second times 60 seconds per revolution) can sequence out the display raster data, be it fonts or a clock face, and remove the requirement for critical timing by a processor. A small microprocessor on the clock could then handle the processor interface, receiving messages, timing reference, and other commands. Indoors temperatures are relatively stable, too, so in conjunction with the time reference from the PC, the microprocessor could determine an adjustment factor to make the crystal clock accurate — inserting or deleting a few clock interrupt counts per hour should be all that's necessary.

Perhaps the most difficult part of the design is how to convey power and data to the rotating component. You could use brushes on the arm and slip rings near the axis, or use that approach just for power and send data wirelessly (since you don't need to pass much data). A combination of batteries and wireless probably isn't the answer, though, because the assembly will draw too much power to have any useful battery life. If you're successful at making the crystal oscillator sufficiently accurate, you won't need the time reference from the PC, and could simply pass power, stopping the rotation to hook up the USB port and send commands.

iPod accessories

For all the resources the iPod offers, connecting anything to the iPod besides a PC or Mac stumped us for some time, because it's an undocumented, closed system, with a unique connector for all its interfaces. Internet searching became the primary skill to enable iPod projects for us, because all the interface problems disappeared once we found the iPodLinux Project Web site (www.ipodlinux.org/index.php/Main_Page). Buried down near the bottom of the main page is a link to the Technical Details page (www.ipodlinux.org/index.php/Technical_Details), where you'll find links to pages describing nearly everything you'd want to know, including the following:

- Differences between versions of the iPod

- Pinouts and the manufacturer of the iPod dock connector

- The serial communications protocol used to query and control the iPod

- Internal formats of the files on the iPod disk that store what music the unit contains and the play history

- Photos of the internals of iPods

Armed with that information, building an iPod-based stereo system becomes a matter of choosing the right components (well-powered speakers, an embedded processor, and a touch panel display), packaging them up, and writing some embedded software. For example:

- **Processor** — The Javelin Stamp would make a perfect embedded processor given its built-in serial ports and digital outputs to drive the display.

- **Display and touch panel** — The Amulet display would work well and is easy to interface (www.parallax.com/detail.asp?product_id=30053 or www.mouser.com/catalog/620/5.pdf), but is expensive. Mouser has some inexpensive Microtips displays with touch panels (in the catalog at the same URL), but you'll need to investigate the interface to make sure you order an appropriate one.

  We suggest a touch screen interface just because it's so much more convenient than a keyboard or actual buttons. You'll want to look for a bright LCD that lets you dim and turn off the backlight so you can use the system under any lighting conditions.

- **Speakers** — Your choice of speakers is an intensely personal thing. The easiest and least expensive approach is to use a great pair of powered speakers intended for use with a computer, but there's no reason you couldn't use a full-scale stereo pre-amp, amp, and speakers.

Or, you could simplify the project greatly and just use the iPod interface itself, providing only the powered speakers with a docking connector.

Another interesting iPod project is to integrate it with your car stereo (no, you need not own a new BMW to do this). The interfaces made by Dension are representative of what you might build (`www.dension.com/main.php?pageid=50&topid=42`); common practice is to interface the iPod through the CD changer port on your car's audio head unit. You'll still likely need a small microprocessor to translate commands from the car unit to ones to the iPod, and to translate iPod responses in return. We'd use the Javelin Stamp for that, too.

Summary

Every project in this book starts with an idea for doing something useful. If you're just stuck for an idea, and this chapter didn't get you rolling, try *halfbakery* (`www.halfbakery.com/ category/Computer`) or *Why Not* (`www.whynot.net`).

Once you have the idea, you have to figure out three elements:

- What information you need, where to get it, and how to process it
- What hardware you need, and either where to get software that does what you need, or how to write it yourself
- What results you want, and how to create those results in the real world

You're likely to find resources to build all three elements of your project on the Internet, far more likely than in stores near you.

Working with Your PC: Software

Important as the ideas in this appendix are — serve you well, they will — nothing we can tell you is as important as this one idea:

If you want to keep a computer up all day, don't play with it.

The number one cause of computer crashes is using the computer, so if you want your computer to stay running, leave it alone. Pick a machine to run the software, and let that be its only job.

That said, on to the rest of what you need to know.

Basics

We based all of the projects in this book on Windows to reach the biggest audience — an enormous number of people know how to work with Windows. Many of the projects operate continuously, however, so your Windows installation needs to be stable and reliable. That's probably a foreign idea to many readers, but in our experience, a stable and reliable installation is achievable. We typically leave some of our Windows computers on all the time and don't reboot them for months on end. This appendix will show you how we do that.

Which version of Windows

The first decision you need to make is which version of Windows you'll run on the computer running your projects. From our point of view, you have only two choices — Windows 2000 or Windows XP. We developed the software we wrote for *Geek House* on Windows 2000 and Windows XP, and some of it may not run on earlier versions.

Our bias is to run Windows 2000. Windows XP is technically superior to Windows 2000, with some very nice added features, including better hyper-threading support, but we choose not to deal with Microsoft's Windows Product Activation (WPA). We properly license each copy of all software we run — intellectual property is what keeps authors fed — but we've seen too many documented cases of WPA failing and shutting down properly licensed machines.

If I have massive computer systems, I will take at least as many precautions as a small business and include things such as virus-scans and firewalls.

Peter Anspach,
The Evil Overlord List

in this appendix

☑ Reliability
☑ Simplicity
☑ Security
☑ Don't get fancy

The choice between Windows XP and Windows 2000 is technically far less significant than between one of them and Windows 9X, which retains a mixture of 16- and 32-bit code, is far less secure, and uses the older and less robust VxD device driver model, causing inherent stability problems. Windows Me is no better, and on some computers, worse. Windows XP and Windows 2000 are pure 32-bit code, are more secure (although they are themselves full of holes), and use Windows Driver Model (WDM) device drivers. They are both much more robust and stable than any version of Windows 9X — 95, 98, or Me — can ever be. Unless you *must* run Windows software that operates only under Windows 98, you should use Windows XP or Windows 2000.

Most software that runs under Windows 98 will run under Windows XP or Windows 2000. The only limitation that would prevent you from using the newer operating systems would be if you needed a device driver that the manufacturer provided only as a VxD. If your only option is a VxD, you're stuck with Windows 98.

Rebuilding from scratch

Your second decision is the path you'll take to set up your PC. You could use an existing, running machine, but we recommend you wipe out the entire disk contents (delete all the existing partitions) and reinstall the operating system from scratch. You'll lose all of the old, accumulated software, files, and registry entries in the process, but that's a good thing, because it leads to a slimmer, more stable installation.

Be sure to make a complete backup of the old disk image before you wipe it out, because you're sure to need something from it you didn't foresee. The simplest way to ensure you have a backup is to replace the existing disk with a new one. You'll gain more disk space and will know for sure that you have all your old files.

Using an Old Machine

You'll want a dedicated PC to run some of the *Geek House* software, such as the security monitor in Chapter 4. If you're like many people we know, you have old, retired computers lying around — there's enough of them that PC recycling has become a growth industry. Only one of the *Geek House* projects — the Home Television Server in Chapter 3, and that only if you plan on burning DVDs — requires more than what an old Pentium III will provide, however, so that old PC can be the dedicated computer you need. You can set up the old warhorse, add network and USB cards or memory if needed, install the application software, start it running, and then leave it alone. Strip it clean first — hardware and software — because with all the junk and detritus removed it will be more stable than you'd expect.

Patches and updates

Patches and updates to Windows are a fact of life. The best source for updates to your running Windows system is Windows Update (`windowsupdate.microsoft.com`). Most of the fixes you'll find here are security fixes categorized as *Critical Updates*. You'll also find corrections to other problems. We install from Windows Update using the following procedure:

1. **Connect to the Internet.** A broadband connection is best because you will be downloading tens or hundreds of megabytes of data.

2. **Connect to Windows Update.** The Windows Update site is `windowsupdate.microsoft.com`. You may have to load some software — a security dialog box pops up if so. Do so, because Windows Update can't work without it.

3. **Scan for updates.** Click the Scan for Updates link to request Windows Update to check your system versions against the servers at Microsoft. The scan progresses in three parts: Critical Updates, OS Updates, and Device Driver Updates.

4. **Deselect Critical Updates as required.** All the Critical Updates are selected in Windows Update by default — you must choose to not load the ones you don't want. Some Critical Updates can only be loaded in isolation, not combined with other updates, and some may be for changes you don't want (for example, we refuse to let Microsoft automatically install updates on our machines, so we won't install any components that require that permission). Click Remove for the Critical Updates you don't want. We typically install most of the Critical Updates and all of the Security Updates.

5. **Select OS Updates.** Review the list of OS updates and select any that are bug fixes or that specifically address capabilities you want. Otherwise, ignore them.

6. **Ignore device driver updates.** Even though (with a few exceptions) we're going to tell you a few paragraphs from now to avoid third-party device drivers if you can in favor of the drivers shipped with Windows, we've found that installing device drivers from Windows Update doesn't always work. When it fails, it can leave inoperable systems in its wake.

7. **Review and install updates.** Once you've finished making your choices, tell Windows Update to install the updates. Once the updates finish, you'll get a list of what worked and what you'll have to retry. You may have to reboot to complete the installation.

8. **Do it again.** You can't assume you're done once you've loaded updates — the fixes you load may themselves need further patching. Cycle through Steps 3 through 7 repeatedly until Windows Update indicates that there are no more useful patches to load.

Third-party device drivers bad! Beer good!

The original joke at Camp Chaos (`www.campchaos.com/show.php?iID=232`) was "Fire Bad! Beer Good!" but our paraphrase applies too. A large fraction of the crashes in Windows systems happen because of defects in device drivers written by companies other than Microsoft. Errors in sample code originally written by Microsoft are the source of some of those defects, but third-party device drivers have a spotty record, which is why Microsoft introduced device driver signing in Windows 2000. Device drivers signed by Microsoft offer some assurance that the code has undergone compatibility and stability testing and therefore that it's reasonably safe to install in your system.

Not that we're saying all third-party drivers are junk. For example, we invariably use the "reference drivers" from the nVidia Web site (`www.nvidia.com/content/drivers/drivers.asp`) for any board using nVidia graphics chips, regardless of the actual board manufacturer. Those drivers are typically significantly faster, more fully featured, and as stable as the drivers included with Windows. If you don't have good, solid experience with a specific vendor's drivers, use the ones packaged with Windows if you can. If that's not possible, search the Internet newsgroups (we use Google at `www.google.com/grphp`) for problems people may have had with the hardware you're trying to install, pour a beer, and think about exchanging the product for something else if your search turns up significant problems.

Anti-virus with automatic updates

You're going to want an Internet connection — preferably an always-on broadband connection — for many of the *Geek House* projects. The Internet is a wonderful source of information and capability, but it's also the hands-down winner in the contest for things likely to attack your computer. Attacks can take the form of viruses, Trojans, spyware, and hacks; you need specific defenses against each. The mean time to compromise of an unpatched, unprotected computer attached to the Internet is now less than the time required to patch that PC through Windows Update, so a layered defense with a hardware firewall as the first line is mandatory.

In the case of viruses, there's no excuse for not running good anti-virus software and keeping it continuously up to date, despite the ugly similarities of anti-virus update to addiction. We run Symantec's Norton Anti-Virus, and let it update itself regularly, but we're not convinced that any of the major vendors are any better than the rest. Worse yet, you pretty much have to take it on faith that the updates won't do anything vile, an implicit contract we've had anti-virus software break when it was apparently time to obsolete the old version and jack up the vendor's revenue stream. Scanning files on access is the minimum functionality you want; be sure you've configured the anti-virus software to scan e-mail if you're ignoring our advice and using the machine to read e-mail.

Don't forget that *every* machine on your network needs to run anti-virus software, because an infected machine can spread the infection to files resident on other machines and bypass the anti-virus protection on the other machine. You'd find out about the infection when you accessed the corrupted files on a protected machine, but by then the damage has already been done. Don't leave gaps in your defense.

Anti-spyware

Viruses aren't the only thing you have to worry about—spyware and the more general malware category is a large and growing threat that can give others full access to your PC, slow it down horribly, and cause a variety of other problems.

We run AdAware (www.lavasoft.de) on our PCs to help deflect spyware, and recommend the Plus version with its real-time scanning. Spybot Search and Destroy is also well regarded (www.spybot.info/en/index.html). What you should not do is install anti-spyware or anti-virus programs (much less "Internet accelerators") without checking them on the Internet. You can run a search, or look on more focused sources such as Spyware Warrior (www.spywarewarrior.com/rogue_anti-spyware.htm). The same periodic update addiction plagues anti-adware software, so make sure you keep it up to date.

Assuming you're using Internet Explorer, you can also improve your defenses against spyware by relegating undesirable Web sites to the restricted zone (in Internet Explorer, look under Tools ⇨ Internet Options ⇨ Security). You can do that manually (for example, restrict Gator by adding *.gator.com to the restricted zone sites list) or automatically with the IE-SPYAD tool (https://netfiles.uiuc.edu/ehowes/www/resource.htm).

Defrag

Once we've configured the basic software load—Windows, the Windows patches, and anti-virus—we run the Windows disk defragmenter. Disk drives give you much better performance reading long stretches of contiguous data from the disk in a single pass, but Windows can't schedule those high-performance reads if the data resides in multiple fragments on the disk. Program loads, covering hundreds of thousands of megabytes of data, are particularly likely to benefit from defragmentation. Your system won't be more stable for having run defrag, but doing the post-install housekeeping should give you the best possible performance.

LANs and the Internet

In case you missed the other 40,000 times we said it, networks make your computers a lot more convenient and useful. You can get at files on other computers from your PC, share printers, and get to the Internet. Follow our suggestions and your network will be easy to use and reasonably secure from outside attack.

Networking and sharing

You make your network easy to use by making everything shared (without access restrictions), by making sure the same network shares are mapped to the same drive letters on every machine, and by keeping your data files on a file server. The file server could double up as your project software host machine, because you want to leave both alone. Let the machine serve files, not run applications for someone at the keyboard. Leave it alone for the same reason you want to leave your project computer alone: You want the file server to be stable.

Here's an example of how we've implemented these ideas:

- Our file server, named orb, sits in the basement. No one uses it, and we literally never reboot it except when the power fails for longer than the uninterruptible power supply can handle. The E drive on orb holds all of the data files we use on any of our computers, and is backed up periodically to an external hard drive on one of our desktop PCs.

- Every other computer on our LAN has \\orb\e mapped to drive letter Q, so no matter where we are, our data files are on Q:\<path>.

- Every drive on every computer is shared, with full read-write access for every user.

LANs built to this design are horrifically vulnerable to attack, so connecting one of them directly to the Internet would be a disaster. Instead, you should connect through a router.

Security and firewalls

You have precisely two objectives in securing your LAN connection to the Internet — keep everyone out, and should something get in (such as a virus, Trojan, or spyware), prevent the rogue program from sending anything out. Beyond the anti-virus software we suggested earlier, you need a combination of two elements to achieve that security:

- **Hardware Router** — A hardware router (or an old PC with two network cards and the right software, such as the Linux Embedded Appliance Firewall at leaf.sourceforge.net) implements Network Address Translation (NAT) and, in the process, prevents external access to your LAN. You can test your network's security at various Web sites, including Speed Guide (www.speedguide.net) and Gibson Research (www.grc.com). Unless you've chosen to open ports on the router to direct specific traffic to one of your computers, the tests on those Web sites should show no response on any of the common Internet ports.

- **Firewall** — The hardware routers available at consumer prices aren't sophisticated enough to trap unauthorized outgoing traffic (which might occur if you've fallen victim to spyware), but firewall software on each PC can. Zone Alarm, which is free and well designed, is a product of Zone Labs. You can download it from www.download.com/3000-2092-10039884.html. Any time a program you haven't already approved tries to open a connection from your PC to the Internet, Zone Alarm pops up and asks if you want to block the connection. It's a little tedious until you get your standard programs set up, but runs reliably after that.

Setting up e-mail and Web servers

We discussed enhancing the automated sprinkler control software in Chapter 9 to add e-mail alerting for unusual conditions. Capabilities like that are a lot easier to use if you create a separate e-mail account specifically for the projects to mail through instead of trying to share your existing e-mail accounts. Using a separate account avoids the problem of multiple e-mail reader programs accessing one account. Many ISPs now provide multiple e-mail accounts with your subscription, so you might not incur any additional monthly costs.

You might want to set up a Web server with more than one of your projects, such as those using HomeSeer. You don't need multiple computers; you just need the servers to run on distinct TCP/IP ports. HomeSeer runs on port 80 by default, which is the standard Web server port. Put an additional server on a different port, such as 8090, and you can run both Web servers on the same PC at once.

Should you need to run other Web servers on that PC, you simply need to keep the port numbers separate. Nearly all Web server software lets you change port numbers, so the only problem you might have is making sure the client Web browsers use the right port number.

Applications

No matter how hard you try, we guarantee that you will have to reboot your project host computer now and then, if for no other reason than long-term power failures. You want to make sure that your software runs when the computer starts up again, so you should create shortcuts in the Windows Startup folder to launch each program that must run continuously. You may also want to protect the PC from short power failures with an uninterruptible power supply (UPS). We use ones from American Power Conversion (www.apc.com); a small UPS capable of handling a 350-watt load can be had for $50 and up.

We keep an archive on our file server of nearly everything we download, which guarantees that we have the files we need should we ever have to reinstall or to rebuild the computer, regardless of any changes companies may have made on their Web sites. We've been doing that for many years, so our archive has grown to over 8 GB. You can argue that that's too much and that the old material ought to be pruned, but none of our installation files ever turn up missing.

We strongly recommend that when you're installing new software you've not used before, you limit installations to one every few days of active use. This way, you can discover whether the new installation causes stability problems. If you install multiple programs you are not familiar with all at once, you'll have no chance of figuring out which program is at fault should the machine become unstable. Of course, even if you install them one at a time, you can't assume that the program that crashes is the one responsible for the problem. For example, we once had the problem of Windows Explorer crashing on a previously stable machine. The only recent change had been to upgrade to version 6 of Internet Explorer, making it a likely candidate. What we found, however, was that the installation of Roxio's EZ-CD Creator on that machine had compatibility problems with both programs, and that uninstalling EZ-CD Creator was required before we could restore both Windows Explorer and Internet Explorer to proper operation.

You're going to need a way to unpack compressed files you download from the Internet. If you're running Windows XP, the ability to open and extract from the ubiquitous ZIP files is built into the operating system. For other operating systems, or if you're looking for stronger features under Windows XP, we recommend WinZip (www.winzip.com).

Summary

The key to managing software on a PC is keeping stability and security foremost. We recommend wiping the computer clean and rebuilding Windows from scratch, and then installing only the software you really need. The more software you install, the better your chances of encountering bugs, so resist the temptation to install a lot of utilities, tools, and other packages. Protect your LAN with a hardware router and software firewall.

Using quality hardware and following the guidelines in this chapter should result in a machine that runs well and never crashes. It's hard to ask for more from a PC.

Working with Your PC: Hardware

More than anything, when you're working with a PC's hardware, or any electronics at all, you don't want any surprises. You want everything to be simple and proceed smoothly, from the point you remove the first screw to when you button it up, power it on, and marvel that everything works. A few solid techniques and guidelines will help you achieve that objective.

Control Static Electricity

Transistors are the tiny devices, made from silicon, that nearly all electronic devices are made from. The first transistor radios marketed in the early 1960s contained only a few transistors. The processor and graphics chips in your computer now contain tens of millions of transistors (see Figure B-1), and Intel has published many articles about its path to chips containing a billion transistors. (Indeed, Intel achieved 1.7 billion transistors in the dual core Itanium) The size of each transistor has shrunk proportionately in the intervening 40 years, which means the transistors in computers today are fantastically small. Most transistors in a computer do nothing more than switch on and off, letting electricity flow when they're on and blocking the flow when they're off. In that sense, switching transistors are much like tiny water valves.

I will not pick up a glowing ancient artifact and shout "Its power is now mine!!!" Instead I will grab some tongs, transfer it to a hazardous materials container, and transport it back to my lab for study.

Peter Anspach,
The Evil Overlord List

in this appendix

☑ Static electricity
☑ Tools
☑ Being organized

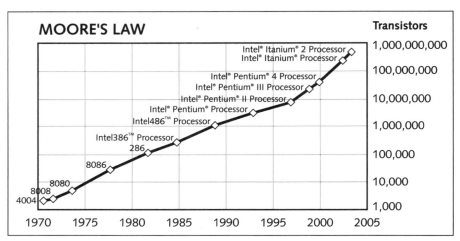

FIGURE B-1: Numbers of transistors in Intel processors (Courtesy Intel Corporation)

A tiny water valve can withstand only a small amount of water pressure before it's destroyed. The analog of water pressure in a computer is voltage, and it's precisely correct that the microscopically small transistors in a computer can withstand only a small voltage before they're destroyed. In the most recent chips packing the most transistors, the absolute maximum voltage they can withstand is less than 3 (or sometimes 2) volts.

You, however, being somewhat bigger than a transistor, can't even feel 2 or 3 volts. If your skin's dry, you can't feel 12 volts from your car battery. You usually notice nothing below 30 volts, ten times what it takes to destroy transistors in your computer. That means voltages you're incapable of sensing can puncture holes in transistors and damage critical chips in your computer beyond repair. Static electricity (also called *electrostatic discharge*, or *ESD*) at the level that sparks as it jumps from you to a metal surface carries thousands of volts, the equivalent of a flash flood to your computer. Your feet scuffing on the floor or clothes rubbing on each other are generating enough power to create major problems. Figure B-2 shows the kind of damage ESD can create inside a chip.

You're not likely to have problems when the box containing your computer or electronic device is closed up, because unless you touch a pin on a connecting cable before you touch a grounded surface, the static charge can't reach anything vulnerable. Most cable connections are somewhat protected (however, see the sidebar "Be Careful How You Handle Ethernet Cables"), but it's good practice to avoid touching the contacts.

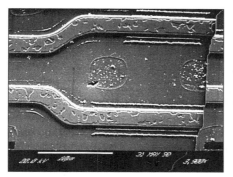 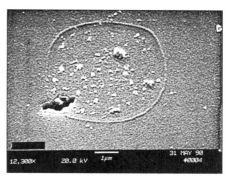

FIGURE B-2: Electrostatic discharge damage to an integrated circuit

It's not that hard to prevent ESD damage — all you really have to do is to make sure to minimize the potential sources and ground the sources you can't eliminate. At a minimum, touch metal before touching your computer when you're working on it, and avoid moving your feet around. Far better is to wear an anti-static wrist strap ($4.99 at RadioShack, see catalog number 276-2397 at www.radioshack.com), connecting the alligator clip at the end either to a cold water pipe or the metal chassis on the computer. However,

UNPLUG THE COMPUTER FROM THE WALL BEFORE CLIPPING ON YOUR GROUND STRAP.

There are some very bad recommendations in books and on the Internet that say you should leave your computer plugged in while you work on it so the ground line in the power cord can help drain off static electricity. It's a good idea only on the surface, because computer power supplies no longer really turn off when you shut down the computer. Instead, a small auxiliary power line remains active to run the circuits that actually turn on the computer when you push the power switch, when a LAN message arrives, or when the modem needs to answer the phone. Therefore, if there's a short in the power supply, you could be electrocuted. Always unplug your computer before you open it up.

You should also be careful about the surfaces on which you work. Wood and metal are good, but plastic and carpet (which build up static charges) are very bad. The anti-static bags that electronic devices are sometimes packaged in (look for the anti-static label on the bag) are good for storing circuit cards, but don't close them with cellophane or adhesive tape. (Peel tape off plastic in absolute dark, after letting your eyes adjust, and watch the light show from the static sparks. Every spark is a death warrant for unprotected electronics.)

Finally, avoid touching other people while you're working on exposed electronics. They likely won't be grounded, and the spark that jumps from them to you won't stop until it passes through you, through the electronics in your computer, and dissipates into ground.

Be Careful How You Handle Ethernet Cables

The RJ-45 modular connectors you find on 10/100Base-T Ethernet cables are potential static electricity problems. If you have one end plugged into a computer or switch, but the other end isn't connected, that open end is a direct path for static electricity to the sensitive electronics at the other end. The cable jacket is always insulated, so it doesn't drain away the static charge. However, if you pick up the cable and even brush against the exposed contacts, any built-up charge goes straight down the cable. We've seen many switch ports fail from just this sort of accident, so pay attention when you're connecting and disconnecting Ethernets.

We're well aware that millions of people have opened their PCs, inserted or removed components, closed them up, and have had nothing untoward happen. (Or, latent damage being what it is, nothing happen right then.) Nevertheless, we're not making this up, and we're not alone in what we say. Consider the following:

- Intel advises its customers about ESD at `www.intel.com/design/packtech/ch_06.pdf` (among others; search the Intel Web site for ESD).

- Gateway Computers warns about ESD and offers guidelines on how to prevent damage at `support.gateway.com/s/Mobile/SHARED/SoloESD.shtml`.

- The United States Marine Corps Aviation Training Branch training on ESD is at `www.tecom.usmc.mil/atb/MATMEP/MS%20Word%20Lesson%20guide%20PDF%20files/Lg13.pdf`.

- NASA provides a general description of their ESD protection requirements at `workmanship.nasa.gov/lib/insp/2%20books/links/sections/11-01%20General%20Requirements.html`.

- `www.esda.org/` is the Web site of the Electrostatic Discharge Association (ESDA).

- Enough people care about ESD to make a magazine devoted to the subject worthwhile; see *ESD Journal* at `www.esdjournal.com`.

Use the Right Tools

Yeah, we know there's nothing you can't do with a vise grip, a hammer, and a screwdriver. Nevertheless, you might want a slightly more comprehensive tool kit for working on your computer. We suggest this list:

- Screwdrivers (both slotted and Phillips) in a range of sizes from small to medium. Magnetic screwdrivers are good because they help keep screws from falling where they're hard to retrieve. The magnetic field isn't strong enough to cause damage to disk drives, although you should keep it away from floppy disks. We used a really tiny watchmaker's screwdriver once to make an adjustment that fixed read errors on the DVD drive in a Sony Playstation 2, but it's rare to need a screwdriver that small.

- Socket (hex head) drivers in $^3/_{16}$, $^7/_{32}$, and $^1/_4$ inch sizes.
- Pliers, including a pair of very long needle-nose pliers.
- Flashlight. We have both a regular flashlight and another with a bright halogen bulb at the end of a stiff but flexible extension.
- Mirror, preferably one on a long handle that can pivot.

A multimeter (even a cheap one) is useful for testing power supply levels. It's been years since we needed a soldering iron to fix a problem in a computer, but if you do need to solder around tiny electronics, make sure you're using a small, low-power iron, not a butane torch, and not the branding iron the family patriarch used to make tin cans with after the Civil War. You can get complete kits (see Figure B-3) including more than the minimum list above with sets of tools sized for what you'll be doing.

FIGURE B-3: Belkin computer repair tool kit

Keep Track of What You Do

Usually, when friends show up at our door with a bucket of computer parts and a sheepish grin, the first thing they say is "Oops." This happens more than you might suspect. The very next thing they say, without fail, is "We couldn't figure out how this goes back together."

Unless you know enough about the insides of your computer to figure out how it goes back together, make drawings or print pictures to refer to later. Be sure to record the location and orientation of connectors (such as from the front panel), and of the striped wire (pin one on the connector) for all the ribbon cables. Power connectors are almost always keyed, but be sure to note which way they're turned. Keep track of screws you remove and put them back where they were — some disk drives have restrictions on screw depth in certain locations, and if you put too long a screw back in the wrong hole, you'll either short out a circuit card or damage the internal mechanism. Egg cartons are good for holding small parts, as is a piece of cardboard you push screws into (and then write on to record where they go).

Summary

Even if you've never done it before, working inside your computer isn't very hard. Follow the manufacturer's instructions for the disk or card you're installing, be careful and methodical, guard against static electricity, and use the right tools, and you shouldn't have any problems.

What's on the Web Site

We thought here about puns involving the end of all things, Samwise, but in proper evil overlord fashion the right thing to do is to wrap it up and exit. That said, all you really need to know about getting the source code is that it's on SourceForge, at

sourceforge.net/projects/geekhouse

Our thanks to SourceForge and the Open Source Technology Group for hosting the software.

SourceForge also provides the e-mail address you can use to contact us:

barrypress@users.sourceforge.net

You can also access the source code on the Wiley companion website at

www.wiley.com/go.extremetech

Table C-1 lists what you'll find on the site. Each set of project software is available as a .ZIP file separate from the others. All the code is under the GNU Public License (GPL), which you can read on the Free Software Foundation (FSF) site (www.fsf.org/licenses/gpl.html). The FAQ for the GPL is also available on the FSF site (www.fsf.org/licenses/gpl-faq.html).

If it becomes necessary to escape, I will never stop to pose dramatically and toss off a one-liner.

Peter Anspach,
The Evil Overlord List

in this appendix

☑ The SourceForge Web site

Table C-1   Geek House Software

Project	Language and Environment	Chapter
Anything Inventory	C++ under Windows	6
Automated BBQ Temperature Control	Java on Javelin Stamp	8
Automated Sprinkler Control	C++ under Windows	9
Kitchen PC database	Microsoft Access	7
Security Monitoring	C++ under Windows	4

We built all the C++ software under Microsoft Visual C++ version 6 with Service Pack 5 installed. We tested the software under Windows XP with Service Pack 2 and the incessant subsequent flood of critical updates.

The Java code is written specifically for the Javelin Stamp. We used version 2.0.3 of the Javelin Stamp IDE.

The Microsoft Access database was developed and tested under Access 2003 with Service Pack 1 installed.

Anything Inventory

All the code you need to compile and run the Anything Inventory is included in the distribution. The UPC Database Web site (www.upcdatabase.com) and the downloadable database files on the site are copyrighted by Rob Fugina and licensed by him under the GPL (www.upcdatabase.com/downloads/README).

Automated BBQ Temperature Control

In addition to the Java code we've provided on SourceForge, you'll need the BPI-216 library available from Parallax (www.parallax.com/javelin/applications.asp#AN009). The .EXE file available there (www.parallax.com/dl/appnt/jav9/appnote9.exe) includes all of the files and documentation for the library, including source code.

Automated Sprinkler Control

The GeekWaterWatcher application source distribution includes all of the files you need to build and run the application, with the exception of the tinyxml source code, which you can find on SourceForge (sourceforge.net/projects/tinyxml). You'll need to add the line

```
#include "stdafx.h"          // Altered to fit MFC project
```

as the first `#include` in the source files `tinystr.cpp`, `tinyxml.cpp`, `tinyxmlerror.cpp`, and `tinyxmlparser.cpp` to make them compile properly with the project workspace we've provided. Place those files and the files `tinystr.h` and `tinyxml.h` in the same directory as the source files we provide.

Kitchen PC Database

The Microsoft Access .MDB file provided on SourceForge is what you need to start using the database. We've included Marcia's recipes for the following:

- Banana Blueberry Muffins
- Barbequed Beef Brisket
- Beef Goulash
- Blueberry Raspberry Muffins
- Brined Turkey
- Chocolate Chip Cookies
- Gravlax
- Pot Roast
- Pulled Pork
- Seared Tuna
- Wicked Shrimp

Security Monitoring

The GeekSecurity application source distribution includes all of the files you need to build and run the application, with the exception of the source code files for the CPJNSMTPConnection class written by PJ Naughter and the library files from Phidgets. The SMTP class files are available on PJ Naughter's Web site (`www.naughter.com/smtp.html`). Add the files `base64coder,h`, `pjnsmtp.h`, `glob-md5.h`, `md5.h`, `base64coder,cpp`, `md5.cpp`, and `pjnsmtp.cpp` from his distribution.

The Phidgets 2.0 library you'll need is on the Phidgets site (`www.phidgets.com/modules.php?op=modload&name=Downloads&file=index&req=viewdownload&cid=1`); download and install phidget.msi (`www.phidgets.com/modules.php?op=modload&name=Downloads&file=index&req=getit&lid=1`).

You may also want to look at the examples Phidgets provides (`www.phidgets.com/modules.php?op=modload&name=Downloads&file=index&req=getit&lid=2`) and at their betas page (`www.phidgets.com/modules.php?op=modload&name=Downloads&file=index&req=viewdownload&cid=2`).

Over to You

Many sources on the Internet can help you with resources that complement this software, such as freshmeat (`freshmeat.net`), thefreecountry (`www.thefreecountry.com/sourcecode/cpp.shtml`), and Code Guru (`www.codeguru.com`). A Google search on *c++ open source* will show you many more.

Index

Continued

Continued